A SCRATCH WITH THE REBELS

A Pennsylvania Roundhead and a South Carolina Cavalier

by
Carolyn Poling Schriber

Chapter title images courtesy of Dover Electronic Clip Art.

ISBN-13: 978-0-9793772-0-4
ISBN-10: 0-9793772-0-X

Library of Congress Number: 2007928766

Layout and Design by Daria Hardisty

Published by

MECHLING BOOKBINDERY
PRINTING & BINDING

1124 Oneida Valley Road - Rte. 38
Chicora, PA 16025-3820
www.mechlingbooks.com

TABLE OF CONTENTS

LIST OF ILLUSTRATIONS AND MAPS

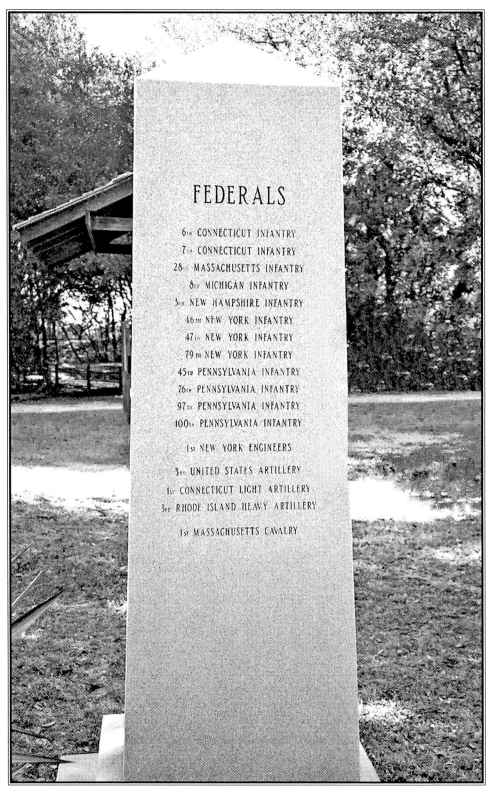

New Monument at Secessionville – Northern Regiments
Photo by Floyd Schriber

THE CAST OF VOICES

These are the voices of the people whose words have helped to tell this story. Some are famous; others, unknown even by name. But it is their words—recorded in official records, printed in local newspapers, published as memoirs or diaries, or simply preserved in a stack of family letters—that allow us to recreate the experience of one small theater of operations in one short period of time during America's Civil War.

THE UNION

Robert Adler	Company F, Roundhead Regiment.
Daniel Ammen	Naval Lieutenant, in command of *The Seneca*, U. S. Navy.
Henry Applegate	Company H, Roundhead Regiment; promoted from corporal to 1st lieutenant by end of war; discharged, 25 November 1864.
Anonymous slave	Left behind when residents of Beaufort fled.
Anonymous soldier	A member of the Jefferson Light Guards, 10th Pennsylvania Regiment.
John S. Barnes	Naval Lieutenant, sometimes in command of the *U.S.S. Wabash*, DuPont's flagship for the South Carolina Expeditionary Force.
Harrison M. Beardsley	Lieutenant, Company K, 50th Pennsylvania.
Samuel J. Book	Company E, Roundhead Regiment; wounded at South Mountain, Maryland, on 14 September 1862; discharged, 2 January 1863.
Arthur Bullus Bradford	Beaver County abolitionist whose home was a major station of the Underground Railroad; founder of the Free Presbyterian Church.
Robert Audley Browne	Minister of the United Presbyterian Church in Lawrence County; early abolitionist; Roundhead Regiment's chaplain from 28 August 1861 to 28 December 1863.
Elias A. Bryant	Private, 4th New Hampshire Infantry.
Simon Cameron	U. S. Senator from Pennsylvania before the Civil War; served as Lincoln's secretary of war until January 1862.
Alexander Campbell	Immigrant from Scotland; 79th New York Regiment; brother of James Campbell, CSA.
Charles Cawley	Lawyer; U. S. Navy.
James H. Cline	Captain, Company F, Roundhead Regiment; promoted to major in March 1863; resigned, 3 May 1864.
Andrew Gregg Curtin	Governor of Pennsylvania, 1860-1868.
Percival Drayton	Naval lieutenant; commander of the gunboat *Pocahontas*.
Hamilton R. Dunlap	Company K, Roundhead Regiment; mustered out with company, 24 July 1865.
E. C. Durbin	Editor of the *New Castle Courant*, the hometown newspaper for many of the Roundheads.
Samuel F. DuPont	Captain, U. S. Navy; commander of the South Carolina Expeditionary Fleet; promoted to rear admiral after the Battle of Fort Pulaski in April 1862.

William Channing Garrett	Young Harvard graduate who joined a group of teachers sent to South Carolina to help with the former slaves.
Alfred G. Gray	Commander of the US transport steamer *McClellan*, operating in Port Royal Sound during 1861 and 1862.
Thomas J. Hamilton	Captain, Company D, Roundhead Regiment; promoted to major in May 1864; served as regimental commander in 1864; died of wounds received at Petersburg, VA, 10 July 1864.
Joseph R. Hawley	Colonel, 7th Connecticut Infantry.
Charles Lafferty	48th Regiment, New York Volunteers, stationed on Hilton Head Island during Christmas 1861.
Elizabeth Blair Lee	The daughter of Francis Blair, presidential advisor to Lincoln; married to Samuel Phillips Lee, a young naval officer who eventually took command of the North Atlantic Blockading Squadron.
Daniel Leasure	Physician in New Castle, PA; founder and commander of the Roundhead Regiment; wounded at Bull Run, VA, 29 August 1862; promoted to brevet brigadier general on 18 April 1865; mustered out with regiment on 24 July 1865.
Samuel George Leasure	Adjutant, Roundhead Regiment; son of Daniel Leasure; died in the Battle of the Crater during the siege of Petersburg, 30 July 1864.
William Lusk	Captain, 79th New York Regiment; served as an adjutant to Gen. Stevens.
John B. Marchand	Captain, U. S. Navy; in command of the *James Adger*; senior officer of blockading squadron at Charleston.
James McCaskey	Sergeant, Company C, Roundhead Regiment; died in Battle of Secessionville, 16 June 1862.
Marius King McDowell	Company F, Roundhead Regiment; wounded at Antietam; leg amputated; discharged 7 April 1863; later re-enlisted in 6th P.V.I. Heavy Artillery.
J. Ferris McMillen	Orderly, Company K, Roundhead Regiment; died of congestive fever at Hilton Head, 28 November 1861.
Robert Moffatt	Company F, Roundhead Regiment; promoted to captain by end of war; wounded at Petersburg; mustered out with company, 24 July 1865; kept a diary until end of 1863.
John Nicklin	Senior columnist for the Roundheads' newspaper, *The Camp Kettle*; organizer of the regimental band.
Bradley Sillick Osbon	Reporter for the *New York Herald*; special to *Harper's Weekly*.
James W. Penney	Private, Company M, Roundhead Regiment; appointed to the color guard.
Edward L. Pierce	Young graduate from Harvard Law School; kept out of military service by his pacifist father; appointed by Samuel P. Chase to oversee the Port Royal missionaries.
Edward S. Philbrick	A Gideonite from Boston, who came as a missionary but became something of an entrepreneur, buying up plantation land, hiring blacks to work it, and making a large profit on his cotton crop.

Winfield Scott	General, U. S. Army; "Old Fuss and Feathers;" resigned as commander of the Union Forces on 1 November 1861.
Thomas William Sherman	Brigadier General; infantry commander of the South Carolina Expeditionary Force.
Hazard Stevens	Captain, 1st Brigade, New York Volunteers; Medal of Honor winner for capture of Fort Huger in 1863.
James C. Stevenson	Company E, Roundhead Regiment; promoted from corporal to captain by end of war; mustered out with company, 24 July 1865.
John H. Stevenson	Company K, Roundhead Regiment; promoted from private to 1st lieutenant by end of war; mustered out with company, 24 July 1865.
Silas Stevenson	Company K, Roundhead Regiment; enlisted February 1864; mustered out with company 24 July 1865.
Susan Walker	Originally from Wilmington, Massachusetts; joined the band of teachers at Port Royal; assigned to Pope's Plantation on St. Helena Island.
Stephen Walkley	Private, Company A, 7th Connecticut Volunteer Infantry.
John P. Wilson	Sergeant, Company C, Roundhead Regiment.
John E. Wool	Major General, USA; Commander, Fortress Monroe, Virginia and Military Department of the East; retired, 1 August 1863.

New Monument at Secessionville – Southern Regiments
Photo by Floyd Schriber

CONFEDERACY

George Bagby	33-year-old recruit from Virginia, trained by a cadet from VMI.
Josiah Bedon	Captain, Company C, 9th Regiment, South Carolina Volunteers.
H. T. Boyd	Civilian, carrying supplies to Confederate camps in the Sea Islands.
John C. Calhoun	Grandson of John C. Calhoun, senator from South Carolina and vice president of the United States under both John Quincy Adams and Andrew Jackson; young Calhoun joined Hampton's Legion and then transferred to the 4th South Carolina Cavalry; mustered out as a captain.
James Campbell	Immigrant from Scotland; 1st South Carolina Infantry, Charleston Battalion; brother of Alexander Campbell, USA.
Mary Boykin Chesnut	Famous diarist; wife of James C. Chesnut, Jr., U. S. senator from South Carolina, 1859-1861; aide to Jefferson Davis.
Ann Drayton	Mother of Thomas and Percival Drayton; died within days of the surrender of Fort Walker.
Thomas Fenwick Drayton	Brigadier General, CSA; commander of Fort Walker; brother of Percival Drayton.
Grace Brown Elmore	22-year-old daughter of a prominent South Carolina family; lived in Columbia throughout the war.
Johnson Hagood	Brigadier General, 1st South Carolina Volunteers Infantry.
John Hart	Private, Irish Jasper Greens, Company A, 1st Regiment, Georgia Infantry, serving at Fort Pulaski in late 1861.
Emma Holmes	23-year-old daughter of prominent Charleston family; moved to Camden after the December 1861 fire destroyed the family home at New and Broad.
Iredell Jones	A member of the South Carolina Cadets; joined Hampton's Legion and was wounded at Manassas; returned to college on crutches and then joined Company D, 1st S. C. Heavy Artillery Regiment.
Robert E. Lee	Commander of the Military Department of South Carolina, CSA in 1861; headquartered at Charleston.
Charles Edward Leverett	Episcopal minister in Beaufort; small plantation owner in the Beaufort region.
Mary Maxcy Leverett	Wife of Charles Leverett; mother of four sons, five daughters, and two adopted sons.
Milton Maxcy Leverett	Youngest son of Mary and Charles Leverett.
Louisa Rebecca McCord	Granddaughter of Langdon Cheves, distinguished lawyer, banker, and builder; married Gus Smythe after the war and eventually became president of the Daughters of the Confederacy.
Frank K. Middleton	Private, Charleston Light Dragoons; son of Henry A. Middleton and nephew of Williams Middleton, signer of the Ordinance of Secession; died of wounds, May, 1864.

Harriott Middleton	Sister of Frank Middleton; unmarried; lived at 44 E. Bay Street, Charleston, until 1863; then moved to High Point, North Carolina.
Susan Middleton	Daughter of Oliver Hering Middleton, niece of Williams Middleton and cousin to Frank and Harriott; lived first on Edisto Island until invasion; then New Street until house burned in fire; moved to Columbia in December 1861.
Francis W. Pickens	Governor of South Carolina, 1860-1862.
Thomas D. Ranson	Private, 52nd Virginia Infantry; mustered out as 2nd lieutenant.
John Schnierle	Major General, CSA; Headquarters 2nd Division, Charleston; responsible for coastal defense of South Carolina before war broke out.
C. H. Simonton	Captain, Eutaw Battalion. Kept logbook during Battle of Secessionville.
John Sheppard	Charleston native serving on James Island.
Robert Smalls	Slave who stole the flagship *Planter* and delivered it to the Union blockade, along with the knowledge of Confederate fortifications that allowed Union troops to move into the Stono River.
Augustine Thomas Smythe	Son of Thomas Smyth; student at South Carolina College; enlisted as private, South Carolina College Cadets on 10 April 1861; service as Corporal, Company A, 25th SCV; became a prominent lawyer in Charleston after the war.
Margaret Adger Smythe	Wife of Thomas Smyth; daughter of one of Charleston's most prosperous merchants, James Adger.
Thomas Smyth	Pastor of the Second Presbyterian Church in Charleston for forty years; known as abolitionist; father of Augustine.
Steinmeyer, John Henry	2nd Lieutenant, Marion Rifles; held the rank of captain at the time of his second capture on 16 October 1864.
John A. Wagener	Colonel, 1st Artillery, South Carolina Militia.
Charles Webb	Sentry on James Island, assigned to Gen. Hagood's command.

PROLOGUE

On a wet and muddy South Carolina battlefield, a sergeant sat propped up against a hedge and tried to focus on the spot where he thought his knee should be. There was nothing—only the tattered remains of his trouser leg and a pool of blood that grew ever larger. The whistle of artillery shells had stopped, and the sudden quiet was as jarring as the previous battle noises had been. Shock had deadened the pain, so that all he felt was exhaustion as he closed his eyes for the last time. Sgt. James McCaskey had bravely fought and lost his only battle. From behind a hedge on that same battlefield, a pale and trembling young private picked his way through the bodies, following orders to gather up the abandoned weapons and tend to the wounded. Pvt. Gus Smythe recoiled from the mayhem that met his eyes, particularly the sight of a soldier who lay with his leg shot entirely away. He whispered a silent prayer, as was fitting for the son of a Presbyterian minister, that he would never again have to witness such horrors.

The Battle of Secessionville, fought in the early hours of 16 June 1862 on James Island, South Carolina, brought these two soldiers together for a single moment. But the events of the Civil War had been drawing the two together for almost a year. James and Gus were approximately the same age. Both were first-generation Americans, the sons of Scotch-Irish immigrants to the United States. Both stood firm in their Presbyterian faith, and both believed passionately in the rightness of the cause for which they fought. Both had wanted to enlist from the day the first shot echoed over Fort Sumter; both had to spend months persuading their parents to allow them to join the army. They set out for their first battle on the same day—7 November 1861—and both missed that action by arriving too late. Both chafed at enforced inactivity and longed to get into a real battle. Each of their Scotch-Irish mothers might have warned her son to be careful for what he wished.

They were just two ordinary soldiers, alike in many ways but different in the one trait that mattered on that battlefield. One was Union; the other, Confederate. Sgt. James McCaskey belonged to the 100th Pennsylvania Regiment, widely known as "The Roundheads." They came from the farms of western Pennsylvania, determined to defend for all men the principles they themselves most valued—self-reliance, industriousness, and liberty. Gus Smythe served in the Washington Light Infantry, part of the 25th South Carolina Volunteers. He was a college student from a well-to-do Charleston family and an ardent supporter of the Confederate right to secede from a political union that did not serve the needs of its people. This is the story of how they came to their opposing positions, and how the Battle of Secessionville altered not only their own lives, but the lives of those who shared their experiences.

America's Civil War has become part of her history and literary heritage. However, for every general whose name has been written into history books, for every Gettysburg memorialized by stirring oration, countless minor skirmishes have faded into oblivion, and unnumbered volunteer soldiers have disappeared into unmarked graves. James McCaskey was one such soldier and the place of his death, ironically enough called James Island, is little known as a Civil War battle site. While Magnolia Cemetery outside of Charleston shelters some 2,200 Civil War veterans from both sides of the conflict, local guidebooks take no notice of the four hundred or more unidentified bodies that were hastily buried in a common pit on James Island in 1862. An effort to restore the battlements at Ft. Lamar began in 1996, and a monument to the Battle of Secessionville, once located at the Presbyterian Church on James Island, has now been moved back to the fort to join a newer memorial. Still, the events that occurred there remain shrouded in obscurity.

New Monument at Secessionville – Dedication
Photo by Floyd Schriber

When I first discovered James's letters stashed away in a yellowed box in my mother's attic, there seemed little hope of reconstructing his Civil War experiences. The most any member of the family could tell me was that James had been my grandfather's older brother. General histories of the war made no mention of a battle fought at a place referred to in the letters as "Sesesha-Ville." Preliminary inquiries to the Military Service Records Division of the National Archives turned up no evidence that such a soldier had ever existed. But James McCaskey did exist. He answered Lincoln's call for volunteers in 1861. His newly formed regiment took part in a joint army and navy expedition to the Sea Islands off the coast of South Carolina. He wrote to his family—letters plaintive with homesickness and revealing his lack of understanding of what factors were driving the war. He died in his first real battle.

The records, too, exist, although they have not caught the attention of many historians writing about the war. The Pennsylvania State Archive in Harrisburg has on file the muster rolls of the 100th Pennsylvania Infantry Regiment. *The War of the Rebellion: A Compilation of the Official Records of the Union and Confederated Armies* contains almost two volumes of reports and correspondence concerning the South Carolina Expeditionary Corps. *The New York Times* gave several days of coverage to the Battle of Secessionville before consigning it to historical obscurity with the editorial comment that enough had been said about the disgraceful affair. Eyewitness accounts of the battle, included in the memoirs of Charles Cawley, Samuel F. Du-Pont, Johnson Hagood, and John P. Marchand, have been published and allowed to languish on library shelves. Only in the 1990s did two more modern studies of these events appear in print. William Gavin's history is a massively detailed account of the Roundhead Regiment's movements; Patrick Brennan focuses on the Battle of Secessionville.

The Engagement at Secessionville—indeed the entire experience of the South Carolina Expeditionary Corps—became a source of embarrassment to the Union Army. It was a common story of inter-service rivalry, governmental red tape, personality conflicts, and strategies gone astray. The Union forces accomplished few military objectives, for the decision-makers could not agree on goals or tactics. Nor was the Confederate Army able to use its victory as grist for its propaganda mill. The original forays of Union troops into Confederate territory met no resistance. Confederate soldiers and civilians alike abandoned the Sea Islands in headlong flight. The result of the Engagement at Secessionville was Confederate victory by default, and, when the Expeditionary Corps was withdrawn, full credit was given only to the mosquito and the flea, whose continuous attacks devastated both armies indiscriminately. The men who died were unknowns—raw recruits without experience or training. The generals who participated, both Confederate and Union, failed to distinguish themselves. Some were reassigned to remote posts where they could be prevented from making further gaffes. Others quietly retired to unassuming civilian employment as gentlemen farmers or high school principals.

This was only one small unfortunate episode in a devastating war. Civil War historians, looking for significant moments and long-range effects, have largely ignored it. What has been lacking in the accounts of the Roundheads and their introduction to battle at Secessionville has been a personal touch—a feeling for what the common soldier experienced. All unaware of what they were doing, James McCaskey and those who shared his experiences, both Union and Confederate, have left us that insight. Perhaps even more important, their comments and reactions provide us a glimpse into the complicated motives that drove young men to risk their lives for a cause they little understood.

During his ten-month military career, James wrote only six letters to his family, and these included little mention of military affairs. James found himself caught up in a cataclysm so widespread that he was unable to perceive more than a very small fragment of the whole. His knowledge of the progress of the war was limited to rumor. His major concerns were with creature comforts—clothes, the weather, the food, prices, and his pay. His overriding desire was for news from home. Yet, his patriotism found its voice in his contempt for those who had not responded to the call to duty and in his inchoate desire to "have a scratch with the rebels."

Two additional letters bundled together with James's letters completed his story. One, written by his commanding lieutenant, contained the official notification that James was missing and presumed dead. The other, written by a neighbor who served in the same company, gave a rather flamboyant account of the battle in which James died. Taken together, these two letters point up a contrast that is also evident in James's letters—between what the official records showed and what the ordinary man felt, between military dispassion and personal emotion, between the reality recognized by army officialdom and the reality experienced by a young farmhand turned soldier.

The present study is an attempt to reconstruct the Civil War experiences of James Mc-Caskey, not because he was important, but because he was an average soldier. It is through such inexperienced eyes that historians can perhaps come just a bit closer to discovering what America's Civil War was really about. Why did a twenty-two-year-old farmer from North Sewickley, Pennsylvania, leap at the chance to leave his family behind and volunteer for a newly forming regiment at the beginning of the Civil War? What anticipation kept him enthusiastic during a jostling ride in a smelly railroad boxcar from Harrisburg, Pennsylvania, to Washington, DC, and later during a treacherous sea passage to South Carolina in the middle of a hurricane? What principles guided his military behavior? What beliefs sustained him through several months of discomfort, illness, and the terrors of the battlefield? Some of the answers may lie in the ethnic identity and the religious background of the family and community from which he came. To find the answers, I have tried to cast the net widely, incorporating not only his impressions, but also those of his fellow Roundheads and those of the men who fought on the other side.

ACKNOWLEDGMENTS

My efforts to trace James's story required much help along the way. Thanks go first to an internet community of descendants of the original Roundheads. Spurred by the efforts of David L. Welch, a great-great-grandson of Col. Norman J. Maxwell, these genealogists and Civil War enthusiasts have combined their efforts to create the "100th Regiment, Pennsylvania Veteran Volunteer Infantry Website." This repository of letters, memoirs, newspaper clippings, pictures, articles, and artifacts that commemorate the Roundheads contains much information available nowhere else. The descendants of the Roundheads have been unfailingly generous when I have turned to them with questions and pleas for help. Although I have never met any of them face to face, I consider them part of an extended family. Similar help came from two local Pennsylvania historians, Dr. William E. Irion at the Research Center for Beaver County and Bob Presnar from the Lawrence County Historical Society. Both responded to my visits by bringing out a wealth of archived material to inform my search. Mr. Presnar once offered coffee and doughnuts while we worked, and Dr. Irion even pointed me in the right direction to locate a cemetery monument and G. A. R. marker dedicated, in absentia, to James McCaskey.

The American Civil War was the first such conflict to be captured on film. Archives overflow with images of proud new soldiers and army encampments. Many of these photos are now available in on-line catalogues, and I found the curators of the images to be incredibly helpful in providing publication-quality prints. I must thank the staffs of the Military History Institute, the Naval Historical Foundation, and the Prints and Photographs Division of the Library of Congress for their quick response to my requests for scans of original images. I am also grateful to Paul McWhorter, who manages the *Harper's Weekly* website, and to Mikel Uriguen, who provides the "Generals of the American Civil War" website, for their co-operation in providing access to other images. Although most civil war photos are now in the public domain, researchers benefit enormously from having access to collections such as these.

In a similar fashion, the experience of civil warfare comes alive in the words of the participants. Their reactions and recollections fill historical collections across America. In Pittsburgh, the staff of the Library and Archives Division of the Historical Society of Western Pennsylvania provided quick access to materials. The Pennsylvania State University Special Collections Library houses the M. Gyla McDowell Collection in its Historical Collections and Labor Archives division. There, seven large file boxes contain unfinished manuscripts, letters, photographs, and other documentation collected by a Roundhead descendant, Dr. M. Gyla McDowell. James P. Quigley and his staff have been most helpful in retrieving these files whenever I needed to see them. The U. S. Army Heritage and Education Center at the Military History Institute in Carlisle, Pennsylvania, possesses a somewhat smaller assortment of documents, but an extensive photographic collection. There, too, the staff was extremely accommodating. My thanks go to all of them for extending assistance beyond the call of their duties.

In South Carolina, I found a similar willingness to help. William J. Hamilton, editor of a website entitled "Civil War @ Charleston," patiently answered my questions about local events and efforts to restore Fort Lamar. Staff members at the South Caroliniana Library in Columbia photocopied and mailed me materials; Roberta Copp retrieved other documents from the Archives, so that they were ready when I arrived for an all too brief visit. The South Carolina Historical Society in Charleston provided almost a home away from home, offering suggestions and facilitating my research in numerous ways. A staff member there first suggested that I should look at the letters of Gus Smythe to see the battle from the Confederate side.

Carpetbagger Tours provided a four-hour guided tour of James Island and the Secessionville site, arranging our stops so that each one illustrated the events of June 1862 in chronological order. My understanding of the battle benefited enormously from their expertise.

Individuals in Charleston provided the colorful details I needed to complete my understanding of what happened at Secessionville. Barbara Doyle, staff historian at Middleton Place, was generous in answering my many questions about the Middletons, offering introductions to other historians, and suggesting further resources for my investigation. Over lunch, Jack Thomson shared his photographs of old Charleston and his knowledge of Gus Smythe, whose letters he had also read to provide the background for his book, *Charleston at War: The Photographic Record*. In Beaufort, David and Carol Painter, new owners of the Leverett House, graciously opened their home to me and shared their knowledge of the house as it existed in 1862. To all of them, thank you for making a Yankee feel welcome in South Carolina.

Finally, no writer manages to produce a book without the help and support of a great many others. My gratitude goes to Rhodes College for research grants to visit the archival resources. Patrick Brennan, author of *Secessionville: Assault on Charleston*, shared his bibliographic knowledge at an early stage in my research. A former research intern, Jessica Paz, spent long hours in libraries, checking footnotes. My friends and colleagues in the History Department at Rhodes College, and particularly Professors Gail Murray and Tim Huebner, offered their knowledge and their personal libraries. At the University of Memphis, Prof. Thad Wasklewicz and his graduate student, Anna Inman, helped by planning and executing the maps. Joe Hawes and Paul Hyams supported my search for funding. I owe a special debt to Kendra Boileau, who encouraged this project from its early stages, and to the editors and staff of Mechling Books, who provided valuable suggestions and assistance throughout the final shaping of the manuscript. Most of all, I am thankful for Floyd Schriber, who is not only my husband, but also my chauffeur, photographer, note-taker, keeper of the home fires, and head cheerleader. Without him, this book would not exist.

CHAPTER 1

Six Houses and a Tavern

The McCaskey family immigrated to western Pennsylvania from Northern Ireland in 1801. John McCaskey had been a flax farmer near the town of Omach, struggling to raise eight children on ever-diminishing returns from his efforts. The economy of Belfast and Derry blossomed with the production of linen, but the tenant farmers who grew the flax itself lived close to the edge of poverty. Adding to the woes of flax growers like John was the tendency of their landlords to engage in something the tenants called "rack-renting." The term, with its underlying connotations of a medieval instrument of torture, described an effort to raise rents on a piece of land because it had become more valuable. Of course, the increased value of the land was usually a direct result of the tenant's efforts to clear the fields, build a substantial house, and add amenities. It seemed unjust to the farmers that the tenant had either to plow his profits back into the landlord's pocket or to watch as someone else bid for the property and reaped the benefits of his own labor. John's neighbors in the small villages of County Tyrone had started to leave as early as the 1730s, no longer able to compete with a profit-driven textile industry centered on Belfast. John had survived by producing a coarse, homespun linen finished by his wife, a strategy that made him less dependent on the Ul-ster linen manufacturers but more vulnerable to the fluctuations of the linen market.[1] By the beginning of the nineteenth century, his efforts could no longer sustain his growing family. He needed a fresh start, somewhere where land was free to those who were willing to work.

The McCaskeys also had religious reasons to justify their departure from Ulster. A major cause of discontent among Ulster Presbyterians was the "Test Act," first introduced in Ireland in 1714. Queen Anne's government, controlled by high-church Anglicans, attempted to enforce religious conformity in Ireland as they had done in England. The act resulted in Presbyterian ministers being turned out of their parishes, the sacraments they had performed being declared invalid, and their schools being closed. A Presbyterian synod, seeking a united response to such challenges, advocated a return to the traditions of Scottish Calvinism. They emphasized their belief in predestination, salvation by grace, and submission to authority by demanding that all church members subscribe to the Westminster Confession of Faith. Opposed to them were those who advocated individual conscience as the only guide to faith. Soon Presbyterians were split between "Old Lights" and "New Lights," subscribers and nonsubscribers, dissenters and nonconformists.[2] Religious turmoil made life in Ireland increasingly unpleasant, and under such conditions the lure of a land known for its support of religious freedom was strong.

The voyage from Ireland to America was long and uncomfortable. The McCaskeys had little money, and their passage was in steerage, where the ship's captain did not even bother to record their names. To pass the hours, Nancy McCaskey used a small collection of books she had brought with her to tell stories of their heritage to her eight children, who ranged in age from thirteen to two. Many of her tales were designed to reinforce the Scottish and Calvinist traditions from which the McCaskeys had sprung. The boys loved the stories of the English Civil War, in which Puritan soldiers overthrew an English king and founded a Commonwealth based on the laws of God. They visualized a Godly army, the likes of which the world had never seen. Cromwell's troops had carried their Calvinist faith into battle, they learned, and an unshakeable trust in predestination had served them well. Puritan soldiers, Nancy McCaskey told them, were always assured of victory and faced more powerful English armies with a confidence bred from the knowledge that God was ever on their side. Never mind that Western Europe's first Commonwealth did not last. For its time, it was a political innovation that could only have been pulled off by Calvinists, whose religious tenets included a firm belief in political liberty and the equality of all men before God. The McCaskey sons remembered such idealized images of religious war and passed them along to their own children.

The older girls particularly enjoyed their mother's story of Jane Geddes. Tradition claimed that a spark of rebellion against Charles I was set off by a woman who, while attending worship services at St. Giles Cathedral in Edinburgh, so objected to the use of the new *Book of Common Prayer* sanctioned by the archbishop of Canterbury, William Laud, that she hurled a small stool at the preacher.

To this day, a plaque in the floor of St. Giles commemorates the act: "Constant oral tradition affirms that near this spot a brave Scotswoman Janet Geddes on 23 July 1637 struck the first blow in the great struggle for freedom of conscience which after a conflict of half a century ended in the establishment of civil and religious liberty." The stool itself remains on display in the Museum of Scotland. It also remained firmly implanted in the memories of McCaskey women for generations to come.

All of the McCaskeys, parents and children, were proud that they were descended from the Covenanters of Scotland. The *National Covenant* had spelled out in unequivocal terms what control over their churches the nobility, clergy, and commons of Presbyterian Scotland would and would not accept. The drafters brought their declaration to Greyfriars Kirk in Edinburgh on the last day of February 1638. There it was read aloud and then spread out so that the assembled noblemen, townsmen, and clergy could sign.[3] In the next few days, copies made their way all through Scotland, so that Presbyterians everywhere could read the declaration and sign their names. Some fervent Lowlander Scots like the McCaskeys did so even in their own blood.[4] In 1643, the more outspoken elements within the Scottish Presbyterian Church united to issue a *Solemn League and Covenant*, which defended the right of Parliament to meet under the authority of the king, but also pledged its signers to a mutual pact that would enforce the removal of all marks of popery, episcopal hierarchies, immoral behaviors, and superstitions.

During the next twenty years or so, the Covenanters, as they were called, found their goals thwarted at every turn. Secret negotiations with Charles II to recognize the *Covenant* after the Restoration also brought disappointment. Fanatical Presbyterians soon found themselves caught up in the horrors of what came to be known as the "killing time." Guerilla bands of dour Scots had little chance against trained English armies, and after a deadly battle at Bothwell Bridge in 1679, there was nothing left of their movement except for their unbroken spirits, their rugged individualism, and their determination not to be dominated by anyone, even if that meant leaving their homeland and finding a more hospitable place to settle. Many of them, therefore emigrated to Ireland, where, at the time, there was less governmental control over religion. Nancy McCaskey used the family's long days at sea to make sure that her sons and daughters understood their Covenanter heritage. She reminded them that they were reprising it as once again they sought a land where they would be free to practice their chosen religion.

Ever true to their clannish instincts, the Scotland-born immigrants from Ireland to America tended not to scatter but to concentrate their settlements among others of their own background and beliefs.[5] In the eighteenth century, many landed first in Maryland and then moved on into Pennsylvania because of its promise of complete religious toleration. As good land was taken up north of Philadelphia and into the Cumberland Valley, later arrivals pushed further west, taking their Calvinist faith with them and preserving their ethnic heritage. Others followed the Appalachian valleys southward into Virginia and the Carolinas. Wherever they settled, they established communities that were homogenous in religious conviction, national origin, and cultural heritage. It was an easy matter for them to transfer their loyalties to a new homeland where good farmland was almost free for the clearing and where religious freedom was taken as a matter of course.

Until the end of the eighteenth century, western Pennsylvania was still very much a wilderness. The way west was blocked at times by various challenges: the uncleared forests, the formidable Tuscarawas mountains, the outbreak of the French and Indian War, the unwillingness of the government to protect its frontier settlements from Indian attack, and the American Revolution itself. During the Revolutionary War, the British had encouraged their Indian allies to take scalps from colonists who moved into the area, and the first settlers in the valley of the Beaver River found the threat to their safety to be very real. The Baker and Dungan families, who may have been the first residents of what would become Beaver County, found no protection in the 1770s from a government that had not even settled the boundary lines of the western states. Nor did the settlers have any sympathy for the "relentless foes that beset them and disputed their right to occupy the land."[6] Stories of atrocities committed by "savages" and acts of revenge by Ulstermen were equally numerous.

Indians in the employ of British soldiers, in fact, carried off the Baker family from western Pennsylvania to Detroit. The family of husband, wife, and five children remained in captivity for several years and gained their release after the war, but only after they agreed to sign a paper saying that they had received no ill treatment.[7] Another early settler was not so lucky. At the end of March 1790, Mary Colvin, wife of Jacob Colvin, died at the hands of local Indians in what was to become Beaver County. She was hit by a rifle shot while she, her husband, and their four-month-old baby were riding to her father's house. Jacob ran for help; the neighbors who responded found her body and that of her child, whose head someone had smashed against a tree.[8] Eventually, the Battle of Fallen Timbers in 1794 put an end to the Indian threat in Ohio, and the new American government straightened out the boundary disputes between Pennsylvania and Virginia. With the creation of seven new counties, one of which was Beaver, along the Ohio border in 1800, the way was open for rapid settlement of the area.

The McCaskey family—John and Nancy, along with their children Jane, Joseph, Andrew, Nancy, William, John, James, and little Sarah—carved a homestead from the hills of Franklin Township in northeastern Beaver County.

The settlement known as North Sewickley, founded in 1801, was appealing for several reasons. Although the land was hilly and full of rocks, the soil was deep and fertile. Small streams provided a more than adequate water supply. Natural resources were plentiful. One historian of Beaver County described it thus: "The scenery on the streams of this region is very wild and picturesque. A good quality of coal is found in several parts of the township, with excellent limestone and sandstone, and the soil is in many portions very rich."[9] The McCaskey land lay in a relatively flat and fertile bend of the Connequenessing Creek, which flowed into the Beaver River.[10] The McCaskey family would flourish there for decades.

The McCaskeys and their neighbors had never used the term "Scotch-Irish" to identify themselves until they settled in America. Although they cherished their Scottish ancestry, they themselves had never lived in Scotland. They had emigrated from Ireland, but they were not Irish in the sense that term was used to describe the Irish of Boston. Their religious beliefs closely resembled those of English Puritans and French Huguenots, although they were neither English nor French. They were Covenanters and dissenters, but those terms had no meaning on the frontier of America. A recent study describes them as "the unsung orphans" of both Scotland, which remained the basis of their traditions, and Ireland, which had somewhat softened their bellicose nature while toughening their ability to endure.[11] Thus they became known as "Scotch-Irish," a term as new as their new American homeland.

Historians have long debated the vices and virtues of the immigrants known as the Scotch-Irish. Contemporary observations by earlier colonists suggest that new arrivals from Ulster were a resilient bunch, inured to hardship although relatively untouched by the finer points of polite society. They were used to fighting for what was theirs and rebelled against any attempt to control their actions. Many of those who first came to western Pennsylvania were, like the Mc-

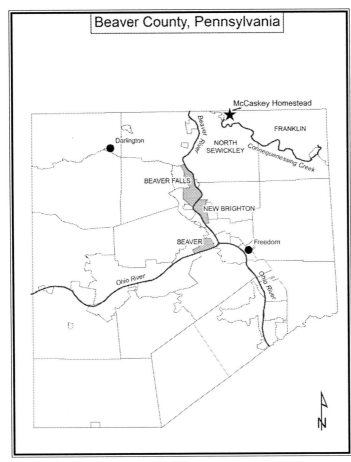

Beaver County, Early Nineteenth Century
Map by Anna Inman

Caskeys, descended from the small group of Covenanters known as "Old Dissenters," who had continued to support the ancient claims of the Stuarts after William and Mary ascended the English throne in 1688. Outlawed, "harried and hunted 'like the partridge upon the mountains',," they had grown used to being persecuted, to hiding in the hills, and to taking up arms against their foes.[12]

New Englanders complained that such immigrants cared little for natural beauty or comfortable surroundings or even the niceties of personal hygiene; they seemed "uncleanly and unwholesome and disgusting."[13] Ethnic slurs—hillbilly, redneck, trailer-park trash, cracker—tend to multiply when modern writers try to describe the Scotch-Irish in America, but the people themselves took pride in those very characteristics that set them apart from the mainstream. The labels also identified them as energetic, independent, and egalitarian. Admirers have praised their love of education, their self-reliance, and their industriousness. They were, some have thought, perfect candidates to become the quintessential American backwoodsmen.

What the Scotch-Irish had in common with each other and with the Cromwellians whom some claimed as their ancestors was their strong Presbyterian faith, their antagonism toward any form of monarchy, and their opposition to anyone who threatened political liberties. From their first arrival in America, the Scotch-Irish had identified with other political protesters, and many of them saw military service during the Revolutionary War. One member of the Roundhead Regiment later described those early revolutionaries and their relationship to Cromwell this way:

> The same devotion to the principles of Liberty of Person and conscience, which caused these ancestors to take up arms against "The House of Stewart," also prompted many of them to seek homes in the wilds of America, where they could "worship God according to the dictates of conscience," also, when foreign oppression became unbearable, impelled them to strike again for more freedom and establish this government "of the people, by the people, and for the people."[14]

It is fairly easy to point to the inherently revolutionary nature of Calvinism and claim that the Scotch-Irish brought the revolutionary spirit with them to America. In his *History of Beaver County*, Bausman puts it this way:

> Thousands of these hardy Ulstermen came to America (as many as twenty-five thousand between 1771 and 1773), most of whom landed in Pennsylvania ... They brought with them a burning sense of hatred to all monarchical and ecclesiastical exactions, and so every settlement of them became a seed-plot of revolutionary sentiments ... And so in all the colonies the men of that blood distinguished themselves in the championship of the Revolutionary cause, whether on the field of debate or on the battlefield.[15]

Even later arrivals were in time to participate in the War of 1812. Records show that three of the McCaskey sons enlisted in local militias as soon as they were old enough to do so. By 1814, both John and William McCaskey were members of the 138th Regiment, Pennsylvania Militia, Capt. David Clark's company.[16] Andrew was in First Battalion, 26th Regiment, Capt. Armstrong Drennan's company.[17] Feeling a further need to declare their allegiance to their new country, John and James became naturalized citizens in August 1823. Andrew followed suit in 1824.[18]

Once the McCaskey farm was cleared and well-cultivated, two of the younger sons chose to seek their fortunes on the western frontier. William found work as a stonecutter in the winter and as a construction worker on the turnpike in Jefferson County, Ohio, during the summer. In a letter written to his mother in November 1826, he urged his brothers to join him, because it was possible to make more money there than from working the land. His brother James became a traveling salesman for a time before poor health urged his return to Pennsylvania. Two of the daughters married and moved into Ohio with their husbands Allen Law and James Dullaghen, but both were drawn homeward to that close-knit community in North Sewickley, Beaver County. Allen Law and his wife Nancy McCaskey Law left Conneaut, Ohio, in 1834, to take up a new farm near Darlington, Pennsylvania. When John Dullaghen died in 1835, his widow, Jane McCaskey Dullaghen, urged her son to leave Wooster, Ohio, and take her home to Beaver County.[19]

Beaver County originally had an area of over 600 square miles, and in 1800 its population total was 5776.[20] The town of Beaver became the county seat for Beaver County. Calling Beaver a town at this stage may be stretching the truth a bit, for a French traveler listed only six houses and a tavern there in 1796.[21] In 1799, the first school opened, and a Presbyterian congregation welcomed its first minister. Ten years later, the town had thirty houses, six taverns, a courthouse, a newspaper and printing office, a stone jail, and a post office. The predominance of taverns in the town—one for every five or six households—reflects the hard-drinking nature of the Scotch-Irish settler. They could, and did, brew alcoholic beverages from almost anything that grew. A favorite potion during the American Revolution was spruce beer, introduced by the early immigrants with this recipe: "Take the young tender sprigs of spruce or pine and boil them in water for three hours. Strain the resulting liquor into a wooden cask and add one quart of molasses to every six gallons of liquor." Notes on the resulting beverage suggest that it was best not to drink it until it was two days old, and that even then, its turpentine smell took some get-

ting used to. It carried with it certain benefits, however; it prevented scurvy, and in a pinch could be used to clean hats.[22]

By 1830, the town of Beaver had 300 households, a cemetery, water lines, a bridge over the Beaver River, a private academy, a law office, and several churches. While still barely a wide place in the road by modern standards, Beaver had experienced a ten-fold growth, which brought with it all the advantages and ills of civilized society. In some ways the area was still a wide-open frontier settlement. The *History of Beaver County Papers* describes the atmosphere this way:

> With a population of about 300, there were seven or eight licensed hotels, with breweries to afford liquid refreshments to all comers. Militia trainings were great features, and "review day" was the day of all days at the county seat, bringing together hundreds of uniformed and non-uniformed people, to be inspected by gaily dressed officers on richly caparisoned steeds. All the feuds of the year had to be settled with fists on that day, and numerous were the scraps going on almost continuously. The vendors of spruce beer, the hotel bars and sellers of quarter sections of gingerbread, would reap a rich harvest by nightfall and would be loaded down with Spanish and Mexican quarters …[23]

In other ways the forces of polite society were working to tame not only the wilderness but also those who had settled it. The Western Pennsylvania Business Directory of 1837 reported that Beaver had "two churches, two Sabbath schools, numerously attended, also a Temperance Society, pretty numerous."[24]

A major boost to the economic health of Beaver County came with the opening of the Erie Canal in 1825. This artificial waterway, extending across New York from Albany and the Hudson River to Buffalo and Lake Erie, lowered shipping costs, opened western markets, and eased the passage of immigrants seeking land and independence. Private companies leaped to join the transportation boom by extending the canal system in all directions. The Ohio and Erie Canal, begun in 1825, ran from Cleveland to Portsmouth, connecting Lake Erie to the Ohio River. Canals crisscrossed Pennsylvania, too. In the west, the Beaver Division Canal, built between 1832 and 1834, followed the valley of the Beaver River and extended from Rochester to New Castle, just to the north of Beaver County. The Erie Extension Canal from New Castle to the Port of Erie was completed in 1844. Two east-west canals connected the Pennsylvania system to the Ohio and Erie. The Crosscut Canal ran from Akron through Youngstown to New Castle. The parallel Sandy and Beaver Canal started in Bolivar, Ohio, and came into Beaver County at Glasgow, just west of Industry, on the Ohio River.

The canal system, for all the labor that went into it, did not long survive. The Sandy and Beaver Canal, for example, was completed in 1848 and closed only three years later. But while the canals operated, they made it possible for western farmers to send their corn and wheat back to eastern markets and to bring out to their homesteads the iron stoves, glass windows, and china dishes that transformed primitive log cabins into comfortable urban dwellings. It is easy to see the economic benefits of improved transportation in Beaver County. The population of the county in 1840 had grown to over 29,000, a five-fold increase. It had four iron furnaces and some ninety-one persons engaged in coal mining. Farmers had an annual harvest of over a million bushels of cereal grains and their livestock amounted to over 144,000 animals. The county also had eighty-six retail stores, eight manufacturers of woolen goods, thirty tanneries, sixty-four saddle makers, thirteen distilleries, nine breweries, two paper mills, seventy-one flour mills, and seventy-three saw mills. A total of $1,083, 268 was invested in manufacturing companies.[25]

Beaver's population in 1837 was 1,100, and the Bridgewater area alone had 110 homes, four stores, and a tavern. The town council was busy improving the water supply, replacing log pipes with iron ones, and planting shade trees in public parks. They passed laws that prohibited horses, pigs, sheep, and geese from roaming the streets of the town. In 1837 there were some protests against that ordinance, but the councilmen remained resolved to keep their town clean. They provided a fire department, created a public school district, and opened the schools to girls. More congregations built fine churches, and upstanding citizens erected homes that reflected their economic well-being.

Businesses also boomed. Brickyards and potting sheds turned the local clay into bricks and stoneware pottery. Lumberyards and woodworking shops had as much business as they could handle. According to *Gordon's Gazetteer* of Pittsburgh in 1832, the Bridgewater community contained "a lime kiln, salt works, brewery, boat yards, patent tub and bucket makers, and several iron foundries. These foundries, the Darragh, L. M. Porter, Anderson, and the Iron Queen, made stoves, iron grate bars, sash weights, and tin, copper, and sheet iron."[26] But of all of these industries, none was more profitable than the boatyards. The invention of the steamboat in 1807 had made water transportation easier and safer, and although the yards at the mouth of the Beaver River produced boats of all kinds, the steamboat took pride of place. Six major steamboat builders in Beaver County accounted for the production of at least forty-nine large steamboats, with an average tonnage of 12,000 tons, and a cost of nearly $70.00 per ton.[27] A distant branch of the McCaskey clan established an early boatyard at

Freedom, east of the mouth of the Beaver River; the company of McCaskey and Kerr shared in the economic boom fostered by the advent of steamboats.

In the northern part of the county, however, the family of John and Nancy Mc-

McCaskey House, North Sewickley, PA
Photo from Author's Collection

Caskey preferred to live from the land. John Junior took over the homestead established by his parents and proved to be a successful farmer. By 1832 he had married and begun to raise a family. In the 1840s, he was sufficiently prominent in the community to begin acting as a deputy marshal.[28] The 1850 census shows him holding land valued at $4000 and supporting his mother Nancy, his older brother Andrew, his wife Jane, and four children—Sarah Jane, born in 1833; James in 1839; Eunice in 1841; and John in 1846.[29] The McCaskeys had found a permanent and prosperous home among their fellow Scotch-Irish Covenanters in western Pennsylvania.

The coming of the railroads brought further changes to Beaver County and its residents. River valleys provided natural rights-of-way for the railroads, and the Beaver River provided a path to the Ohio River. The town of New Castle attracted construction because it was the natural connecting point between the Ohio border and the Beaver River. As early as 1836, the Conneaut & Beaver Railroad

began construction. On the Pennsylvania end, the track followed the Shenango River to New Castle, crossed to meet the Beaver River just north of the Beaver County line at Wampum, and then followed the western banks of the Beaver, through Brighton and Fallston, all the way to the Ohio. If the canals had fostered the original economic boom of the county, the rails brought even greater prosperity. By 1850, a large portion of Beaver County had been sheared off to form the separate entity of Lawrence County, with its county seat at New Castle. As a result, Beaver County's population dropped temporarily, but the railroads brought new settlers and new business. By 1860, Beaver County had more than recovered its original population figures. On the eastern bank of the Beaver River, the Cleveland & Pittsburgh Rail Road began service through Beaver County in 1852, and numerous branch lines sprang up to connect outlying farmlands. One such branch line followed the Connoquenessing Creek, bordering the McCaskey lands and offering to the McCaskey children, now including Theodore, born in 1851, and Joseph, born in 1856, a daily vision of visits to far-off places.[30] Personal travel by rail, however, was still out of the reach of most of the inhabitants of Beaver County. Only one station offered passenger travel, and that was located in the Enon Valley in southwestern Lawrence County near the Ohio border.

On the eve of the Civil War, the town of Beaver, and indeed all of Beaver County, was flourishing, thanks to the railroad and the telegraph. Ease of communication and reliable commercial transportation brought western Pennsylvania into the mainstream of American life. New buildings were springing up everywhere, and there was both the time and the money to encourage architectural elegance rather than stark utilitarian structures. Private homes built of solid oak and stone boasted two or three stories, high ceilings, sweeping staircases, and fireplaces in every room. Some imitated the architecture of tidewater Virginia, while others took the basic farmhouse and updated it with the latest conveniences.[31] Schools, a female academy, a musical institute, and numerous churches served the cultural needs of the citizens, while foundries, mills, and factories contributed to the economic health of the area. Civic pride encouraged improvements to the water supply, including a stone reservoir and an updated system of distribution pipes. City fathers saw to it that public spaces were kept clean and planted with trees; farm animals were confined to their pastures, and miscreants were swiftly treated to a stay in the new county jail.

But for all their newfound prosperity, the Scotch-Irish had not altered the fundamental nature of their character. They were still devout Presbyterians. The majority of them were still farmers who adhered to the Calvinist values of hard work and the importance of family. Most of all, they valued personal liberty and stood ready to do battle against anyone who challenged their rights, whether from a religious or political view. They cherished their freedom even as they became a more integral part of American society. The great social movements of the nineteenth century found a welcome in Beaver County—women's suffrage, the temperance movement, education and prison reform, improved labor conditions, and cooperative associations—all found supporters among the Scotch-Irish. But most of all, the Scotch-Irish were early and natural opponents of slavery.

As early as 1780, a Pennsylvania law had declared that all children born to slaves in the state would become free at the age of twenty-one. The original settlers of Beaver County had held a few slaves, but as a result of this legislation, the number of slaves in the county had dropped to three and then

to none.[32] The Abolition Movement found strong support in Beaver County, not only from the Scotch-Irish Presbyterians, but also from the Quakers who had settled in New Brighton and particularly from Arthur Bullus Bradford, whose home near Darlington was a noted station on the Underground Railroad. Three major routes through Beaver County led escaping slaves to safety.[33] Those who managed to cross the Ohio River could follow its banks to the Beaver River and from there move by water to Canada via Lake Erie or Niagara Falls. Others moved from Washington County to Beaver County and along Raccoon Creek and from there through Black Hawk to Achor in Columbiana County, Ohio. But the most important route passed from Wellsville, Ohio, and Wellsburg, Virginia, to the New Brighton station. The Quakers at New Brighton had a variety of hiding places to offer—a trap door to a cellar, a cave with a hidden entrance, even an island in the middle of the Beaver River. They fed and clothed the escapees before passing them along to *Buttonwood*, the home of Arthur Bullus Bradford between Enon and Darlington, Pennsylvania. Bradford's son and a hired man transported them at night to Salem, Ohio, using the familiar ploy of a wagon apparently filled with vegetables but harboring a very different cargo beneath the top layer of turnips.

Rev. Paul Weyand of Pittsburgh once stated, "The Reformed Presbyterians (Covenanters) were probably the original Abolitionists of the county."[34] He may well have been correct. The North Sewickley Presbyterian Church had been founded in 1846. Its small Scotch-Irish congregation strictly observed the tenets of their Calvinist faith. One local historian has noted, "The meetings appear to more closely resemble the legendary Salem witchcraft trials than modern Session meetings. At that time persons were subpoenaed to appear before them to answer charges such as failure to attend church, swearing, or making defamatory remarks about other members."[35] But for some of its members, the standard Presbyterian line was not strict enough.

One of the more dramatic moves in the local battle against slavery came on 22 June 1847 in Beaver County. Under the urging of Rev. Bradford, the North Sewickley Presbytery, home church of the McCaskey family, separated itself from the jurisdiction of the General Assembly of the Presbyterian Church because of the assembly's decision that holding slaves did not bar the holder from Christian Communion. Bradford's statement declared that "in the course they [the General Assembly] have pursued, and the misrepresentations they have made … they have greatly erred and greatly sinned."[36] The signers of this declaration thus removed their names from the rolls of the Presbyterian Church and formed their own religious movement, known as the Free Presbyterian Church. Eventually, they formed some twenty congregations, held their own synods, and published their views in newspapers and anti-slavery pamphlets. Their purpose was to stand on one clear principle: "The Fugitive Slave Law, of 1850, is not entitled to the sacred name of law."[37] The Free Presbyterian Church at North Sewickley maintained its separate status until after the Civil War, rejoining the Presbyterian Church only when the cause for which it stood had become the law of the land. Thus, as the United States teetered on the brink of civil war, many of the citizens of Beaver County had already taken their stance.

CHAPTER 2

We Know Only Our Country

By the late 1850s a unique ideological struggle was taking shape in America—one in which the same rhetoric could be employed to explain two opposing sides. Supporters of the Union argued for their right to defend themselves against those who would destroy their state. Those who wanted to secede from the Union defended their right to rebel against injustice. Abolitionists spoke out against slavery because it denied the slaves their individual liberties; slave-owners opposed any governmental interference in their affairs because it denied that same individual liberty to the slave owner. Northern Abolitionists called slave owning a form of tyranny and wanted it abolished; Southern planters called attempts to control their affairs a form of tyranny. Both sides sought political freedom, and both believed passionately in the righteousness of their causes. When civil war finally broke out, it would see men of Scotch-Irish ancestry fighting in both the Union and Confederate ranks—men who quoted identical scriptures to defend their opposing positions.[1]

As many historians of the period have recognized, neither side in the struggle over slavery and states' rights was ready for war when it broke out.[2] The United States Army in 1860 comprised slightly over 16,000 men, most of whom were assigned to the western frontiers, and a third of those resigned to side with the South when the attack on Fort Sumter precipitated a war. The navy had less than twelve ships at its disposal in American waters. No plan of war existed; maps were unavailable, and weaponry was largely obsolete. The Confederacy was even less prepared for war. It had no navy, no standing army, and no industrial base to provide the necessities of war. Both sides relied upon the enthusiasm of their volunteers to supply not only the needed men, but also their own equipment. Young men flocked to answer the call to military service on both sides, but they were raw recruits, lacking in everything from uniforms to an understanding of what war was all about. Both sides seemed to assume the question would settle itself in a matter of weeks, and few expected all-out warfare. For the young, joining the military effort must have seemed like a great adventure, not to be missed by dilly-dallying.

One notable sign of this enthusiasm, and its accompanying naiveté, was the proliferation of troops of Zouaves. The original Zouaves had come from Algeria and Morocco in the 1830s, to form a part of the French army noted for its flamboyance and bravery in combat. They distinguished themselves in the Crimean War, where they were known for their rigorous physical training and morally upright character. Pictures of them in their colorful and distinctive outfits—baggy trousers, collarless jacket trimmed in braid, flowing sash, and tasseled fez—caught the imagination of young men around the world. As talk of war punctuated the news stories of the late 1850s, local militias in both the North and the South adopted the sobriquet "Zouaves" and created their own versions of the flamboyant uniform of their heroes. During the Civil War such troops formed parts of infantries from New York, Pennsylvania, Ohio, Louisiana, Indiana, New Jersey, and Virginia. But perhaps nowhere were they more popular than in Charleston, South Carolina, where by November 1860 some forty Zouave Cadets answered the roll on the drilling field. Their recruiting broadside addressed "any person of MORAL CHARACTER AND GENTLEMANLY DEPORTMENT, and who is 17 years old and measures 5 feet 4 inches in height." They followed a rule that demanded, "No drinking in uniform. No patronage of saloons. Don't enter a house of ill-fame. No gambling." In return, recruits were to have a uniform of a blue jacket, scarlet trousers and "the jauntiest little headgear ever worn by a practical fighting man."[4]

The Zouaves were not alone in their eagerness to get into the fight. Charleston produced forty-two companies of part-time soldiers, each with its own identity. Firemen armed themselves and drilled while waiting for a fire to break out. Students at the Citadel and Charleston College formed their own companies, while local politicians campaigned to be elected officers of various militias. Some observers complained with good cause that these "city companies frittered into social clubs and rural militia musters into picnics."[5] Without training or organizational structure, about all the militias could do was get together and try to imagine what the future might bring. Unskilled and weaponless though they may have been in 1860, the next year saw many of the militia members in uniform, fighting for a cause in which they truly believed.

In Columbia, South Carolina, Augustine Thomas Smythe, an 18-year-old college student from Charleston, missed the chance to be a Zouave, but compromised by joining the South Carolina College Cadets. Young Gus provides an informative counterpoint to James McCaskey and his Pennsylvania neighbors. He was the son of Thomas Smyth, who had served as pastor for the Second Presbyterian Church in Charleston for forty years.[6] Rev. Smyth was Scotch-Irish, born in Belfast but an immigrant from Ireland in 1830. He trained for the ministry at Princeton Theological Seminary in 1831 and was awarded a Doctor of Divinity by the same institution in 1843. Called to serve the church in Charleston, he soon married Margaret Milligan Adger, daughter of James Adger, one of Charleston's wealthiest citizens. That advantageous alliance meant that the Smyth family would move in Charleston's highest social circles, and that their nine children, of whom Gus was the second son, would profit from every advantage that old family money could provide.[7]

Rev. Thomas Smyth had conflicted views of the coming war. In his church and in his writings, he had defended the slave as a full human being and had urged reforms in the institution of slavery. When he helped to organize the Zion Presbyterian Church for slaves, local slave-owners vilified him as an abolitionist. But his moderate take on slavery and his refusal to condemn the whole idea of slaveholding earned him a similar condemnation in Britain as a supporter of slavery.[8] Rev. Smyth had long planned to enroll his second son in his own Princeton *alma mater*, but he changed his mind in the face of the coming conflict. On 7 February 1860, Rev. Smyth wrote to Rev. Jos. H. Thornwell in Columbia, South Carolina. He had decided not to send Gus to Princeton as planned, he explained, but to South Carolina College "by a deference to present public feeling and to the just claims of the south."[9]

For young Gus, his father's moderate position must have been somewhat embarrassing in the face of the growing support for war among his fellow students. He welcomed the chance to demonstrate his own Southern sympathies by signing on with the College Cadets. The Cadet Corps had been established in 1825 to help welcome Gen. Lafayette to Columbia. It had flourished for years as the primary social milieu for the college's students. Cadets sported fancy uniforms, drilled occasionally, and held regular dinners that skirted the rules of the college. Their preeminence ended in 1856 when what the papers called "The Guard House Riot" erupted over the stuffiness of the college's faculty and their strict regulations. The fight was originally between Edward Niles, an intoxicated student, and the chief marshal, John Burdell. The student was injured and then locked in the guardhouse; more unrest among students who demanded his release led the mayor of Columbia to call out the militia. Several students were expelled and the college cadets disbanded. The *Columbia Examiner*, 1 March 1856, called it "an unfortunate state of affairs."[10]

Efforts to reorganize the corps were unsuccessful until the Ordinance of Secession was signed on 20 December 1860. Faced with the reality that the state might need to go to war, the Board of Trustees passed the following: "RESOLVED, that the students of the South Carolina College be permitted to organize a military company under the direction and control of the faculty."[11] By the time students returned from their holidays, they found an official organization, but it was to be held tightly in check by the faculty. Their new rules said that the cadets could not be called to military services except by order of the President. Their weapons were to be kept in a storeroom under the library and released only upon proven need. They were to "observe strict economy" and were not allowed to hold company suppers or other festivities.[12]

As tensions mounted around Fort Sumter in the early months of 1861, a flurry of letters home announced a major change in the disposition of the South Carolina College Cadets. John C. Calhoun, grandson of the John C. Calhoun who served as vice-president of the United States under both John Quincy Adams and Andrew Jackson, wrote to his parents on 9 April 1861, telling them that 250 students had left for Charleston; others were planning to follow in hopes that Gov. Pickens would find a place for them.[13] Gus Smythe quickly joined the effort; he enrolled as a private on 10 April 1861, just two days before Confederate artillery opened fire on Fort Sumter. The Rev. Robert W. Barnwell, who served as company chaplain at South Carolina College, loaned the cadets $100 so that they could hurry back to Charleston.[14] Iredell Jones, writing to his parents on 11 April, reported that he and the other cadets donned their fancy dress uniforms, which closely resembled the long gray coats worn at West Point, complete with tails, sashes, three rows of brass buttons, and chevrons of braided trim. They reported to Hibernian Hall in Charleston for rooms and then traveled to Sullivan's Island because Gen. G. T. Beauregard wanted to keep them far from combat. Obviously, the general did not want these young, untrained teenagers underfoot; he did, however, give them guns and ammunition.[15] Most of the other students joined their fellows as soon as the firing on Fort Sumter began on the morning of 12 April 1861. Jones's letter dated 15 April says they got to watch the South Carolina flag fly over Sumter and do some drill. In a letter dated 16 April, John Calhoun bragged, "We drill five hours a day & are now regular soldiers; we live on raw beef & water & stand guard all night."[16] Although they did not get to fire a single shot in combat, they were having a grand and glorious time of it. They stayed in the Charleston area for about three weeks, living in comfortable residences around town. But when no further military action occurred, they returned to the college and resumed their studies.

Mary Boykin Chesnut reported in her diary that every boy at the college had volunteered for the company of soldiers being raised by one of the professors. It was, she said, "… a grand frolic, no more—for the students at least!"[17] Mary Chesnut's awareness that this was just the beginning of a terrible conflict did not reflect the opinions of those around her. In Columbia, the fifteen-year-old daughter of a prominent family remained blithely oblivious to anything more momentous than the comings and goings of the young men at the local college. Louisa McCord's memoirs recorded little of the period when secession was declared: "Strange to say I remember very little about the next few months except a quiet, and to us younger people, happy life … And so the year went round and in the fall another set of students came, among them a rather short, stoutish one with beautiful hair, named Smythe, from Charleston." She did observe in April, however, that these fascinating college boys in the fancy-dress uniforms "offered themselves to Gov Pickens and came down to Sullivan's Island all ready to do wonders; but their time had not come yet, and they were told to go back to their books. They obeyed, but I doubt if much studying went on."[18]

At almost exactly the same time, the ethnic unity, patriotic spirit, and abolitionist sensibilities of the young men of western Pennsylvania led them to answer when the call went out for volunteers for the Union Army in 1861. Fort Sumter came under attack on 12 April 1861—the twenty-second birthday of James McCaskey. By 15 April, Lincoln issued his famous proclamation, raising a militia and calling upon all citizens " … to favor, facilitate and aid this effort to maintain the honor, the integrity, and the existence of our National Union, and the perpetuity of popular government; and to redress wrongs already long enough endured."[19] One of the first to respond was Dr. Daniel Leisure, a physician from New Castle, in Lawrence County, Pennsylvania. In a memoir of his early military experience, Dr. Leasure recalled, "I was about to mount for a long, hard day's drive [to visit patients] … when the President's call came … Instantly my duty seemed clear, and as instantly without a moment's consultation with wife, family or friends, my resolution was formed. I had more military training in the state militia than any other man in my section and therefore somewhat better prepared to assume military direction of affairs in my own locality, and to take command of the young men, whom I knew would call for a leader to take them to the front."[20] He immediately shut down the offices of his newspaper, the *New Castle Chronicle*, and sent his printer, Johnny Nicklin, out with a drum to beat for recruits. He turned his medical practice and his medical students over to a colleague, Dr. M. Baker, said a quick goodbye to his wife, and set off to catch the train to Pittsburgh with a small group of local volunteers, all recruited from Lawrence County.[21] There his recruits organized themselves into two companies, F and H, within the Twelfth Pennsylvania Infantry Regiment. Daniel Leasure commented on their assignment: "Our post is really a post of honor and our regiment is in the most active duty of any of the Pennsylvania line. We are *detached* from Negley's Brigade, and are not attached to any other, but are what our facetious Major Hays calls an 'Orphan Regiment' with-

Col. Daniel Leasure, USA
Photo courtesy of Roger D. Hunt Collection, USAMHI

out any relations except stepfather Curtin."[22] As members of this unit, they traveled first to Harrisburg and then to York, where they received some basic training, but not much in the way of uniforms or equipment. Leasure described their early exposure to military life:

> Here we were drilled in squads (and pretty awkward squads at that), company, and battalion drill every day, and did our best to learn to live on our rations, and do our own cooking and washing …

> Think of it! We had no outfit at all. No blankets, no uniforms, no camp kettles, no pots or pans, no haversacks, till the 19th of May, almost a month after our arrival … I went twice to Harrisburg, to urge the Legislature to buy us at least something to cook our food in. The members were very complaisant, and promised everything, but the truth was, there were no cooking utensils in the market, and the Legislature had no constitutional authority to make them; and so we did not get them until somebody made them.

> However, we had bought, begged, and borrowed utensils from the good people of York, and managed to get along, if not comfortably, at least jollily. The cooking was very primitive, and fortunately so were our appetites; and on the whole, in the light of the experience some of us gained in the "after years" (with the Roundheads), it was not so bad.[23]

Their assignment was to guard the Baltimore and Harrisburg Railway from the Pennsylvania state line to Baltimore. Near York, the men scattered out to build rough shanties and to get to know their civilian neighbors. Occasionally they saw troops moving off to battle, but they themselves saw no official action. In a letter written to E. C. Durban, editor of the *Beaver County Courant*, on 15 June 1861, Daniel Leasure described one of their "non-events":

> We have just enough suspicious surroundings to keep us on alert, and last night during my absence at York, to see Miller, my line had an alarm but it did not amount to anything. It was merely some night prowlers who got a little too close to J. H. Gilliland who was on sentinel duty, and failing to come to time when challenged, he sent a Minie ball at them by way of hint that we were not all asleep. In my absence Orderly Book had charge, and the fellows pitched into the bushes to feel for the enemy with their bayonets, but whoever had been there kept shady, and the guards lay on their arms till morning. These little affairs keep us sharpened up, but I shall not absent myself from the line again after night. The alarm last night satisfied our fellows, that they can come out in double quick, and rally into line of battle the entire length of our line in a few minutes, and gave them to understand that they can depend on each other. I had carefully prepared and instructed them for all night attacks, and they now see the advantage of instructions against all possible emergencies.[24]

Nevertheless, Leasure was sure of the importance of their task:

> We perhaps, just now, do not realize the exact relative importance of our present duties, but the delay of a single train on this great army thorofare, for a single day, might change the results of a whole campaign, and derange the best laid plans of the Commander-in-Chief. All these weeks soldiers have gone whirling and cheering past us to Harper's Ferry via Chambersburg—now they go back to make a similar demonstration on some other stronghold, and we here are with watchful eyes and willing hands keeping open the channel of communications, for if this road were left unguarded for a single day or night, every bridge would go down.[25]

The volunteers from western Pennsylvania suffered a number of casualties, not from battle but from the general hazards of military life. Illness, of course, was rampant wherever they went. Despite Dr. Leasure's best efforts to enforce standards of sanitation, several men ended up in hospitals where local women tried to care for them. On 20 June, Leasure sorrowfully reported that R. S. Gibson had died and that J. R. Miller, whom he had visited several days earlier, was not expected to recover. Private Childs lost an arm when he fell asleep on the railroad tracks and a train of cars passed over him. Another private was severely cut on the face and head when he was run over by a handcar. "Loafer Bell" and three others from Capt. Stewart's company went to town, became intoxicated, and resisted arrest when the guards arrived to bring them back to camp. In the fight that ensued, one man was killed and the other three were sent to Fort McHenry to be hung for insubordination.[26]

Despite these casualties and the lack of real action, the men were anxious to continue to serve their country when their first three-month period of enlistment expired. No officer came to sign the paperwork, however, and the volunteers were mustered out on 5 August 1861. The homecoming of the "Lawrence Guards" was an occasion for great rejoicing. The local paper in New Castle commented, "Our citizens had decorated the town in beautiful style. Arches were built on nearly all the streets, and the town seemed a forest of flags and evergreen."[27] Some of the men settled back into civilian life, but Captain Leasure immediately began to plan for a new regiment.

On Monday, 12 August, Dr. Leasure traveled to Washington, DC, where he met with General Winfield Scott and Secretary of War Simon Cameron, a fellow Pennsylvanian. There he received his appointment as a colonel and asked permission to organize a volunteer regiment recruited primarily from Lawrence, Mercer, Butler, and Beaver Counties. According to one of Leasure's biographers, he told Cameron that "any group of young men from that region would of necessity be men of Scotch-Irish stock." The biographer went

on, "It is well to explain that the Western part of Pennsylvania was at an early date settled by a large number of descendants of the old Cromwellians and the Scotch-Irish. The children of these groups inherited traits of the fathers and the traditional devotion of their fathers to the principals of liberty of persons and of conscience."[28] Another account of this meeting described the granting of that permission:

When Captain Leasure applied to the Secretary of War for authority to raise an independent regiment among the yeomanry of central Pennsylvania, Cameron said, "Yes, Captain, if they will be men that will hold slavery to be a sin against God and a crime against humanity and will carry their bibles into battle." "I have no other kind to bring," responded the Captain. "All right," exclaimed General Scott who chanced to be present. "We will call them 'Roundheads'."[29]

The suggestion that such a regiment be called "The Roundheads" was apparently in honor of Cameron's own Scotch-Irish ancestry. The original Roundheads had been members of Oliver Cromwell's army during the English Civil War of 1641-1661. Most were supporters of parliamentary government and staunch believers in Calvinist reforms. After the war Cromwell rewarded their service with grants of land in Ireland, and the descendants of those soldiers had so intermingled with other immigrants to Northern Ireland that their original English background had become blurred. Many of the men Col. Leasure recruited were not actually Cromwellians but descendants of the supporters of the Scottish National Covenant of 1638, "Covenanters" who had emigrated from Scotland to Ulster during the English Civil War and from there to America. Leasure's wife was of Covenanter stock, but he himself was descended from French Huguenots who had migrated to America via Switzerland and Ireland. Nevertheless, the Roundhead label stuck, even though most of the recruits would have no direct ancestral connection to Oliver Cromwell and the original English Roundheads.

The Pennsylvania Roundheads had, however, something more important than a bloodline that tied them to their older counterparts; they had psychological and ideological ties. Their Scotch-Irish heritage provided them with the personal characteristics of born soldiers. They were, first, almost entirely self-sufficient. They were descended from pioneers who had broken through a mountain barrier and carved new settlements out of the wilderness. Left to themselves they would not starve because they knew how to hunt, and scavenge, and turn a furrow. At the same time, they were intensely clannish, clinging to the community that shared their values and gave them an identity. They were indifferent to wealth, believing, as Calvin had taught, that success came more from good reputation than from the accumulation of money. They were disciplined and obedient because these qualities were essential if they were to survive in a hostile environment. They were bold leaders because they understood that the world would never cater to those who hesitated or lagged behind. They displayed remarkable physical courage, engendered by a lifetime of tackling tough and dangerous tasks. And perhaps most important, they did not fear death. Their Calvinist faith taught them that two classes of people—the elect and the reprobates—inhabited the world. Their pastors assured them that, as diligent practitioners of the Calvinist faith, their signs of election were evident. Thus they had nothing to fear. They would not die until their appointed time, and their salvation was assured. Such men carried themselves as soldiers, whether or not they wore the trapping of military uniforms or conformed to standards of military training.

And so the precedents were set. Col. Daniel Leasure received permission from the Secretary of War to begin recruiting a regiment among the Scotch-Irish who lived in southwestern Pennsylvania.[30] The New Castle newspaper reported:

We understand that some twenty-seven military companies have been tendered to Col. Leasure within a few days past, to fill up his regiment now being formed. Five companies have been accepted, and three conditionally. Companies from Lawrence, or the immediate vicinity, preferred. The Colonel received marching orders on Friday (yesterday) and in fifteen days intends to be able to report his regiment as ready for duty.... . The Dr. is an energetic and efficient officer and if an opportunity is afforded he, with his men, will make a good report of themselves at home, and be a terror in the ranks of the enemy.[31]

In some ways, Leasure's enthusiasm outran the usual process by which units became a part of the state's military organization. His early recruits immediately adopted the suggestion of Gen. Scott; from the beginning they would be known as the "Roundhead Regiment." But they had not yet been assigned a regimental number.[32] Their lack of official status would later cause them some administrative difficulties. For a time, their assignments came directly from the secretary of war, Simon Cameron, and the usual distribution of uniforms and equipment was hampered by their lack of numerical designation. Eventually rumors began to circulate that the men would not be paid or that they would not be eligible for state benefits because they were independent. It took the intervention of Col. Leasure himself to gain official recognition from the State of Pennsylvania. Not until 2 October 1861 did Gov. A. G. Curtin send a letter to Leasure, officially recognizing the Roundheads and granting them the designation of "One Hundredth Regiment, Pennsylvania."[33]

But technicalities of designation had not hampered Col. Leasure's recruitment efforts.

By 27 August twelve companies of volunteers had assembled. Among the recruits was James McCaskey. He was the second child and oldest son of John and Jane McCaskey, born on 12 April 1839, and named after his Uncle James, who had died earlier that spring. He had attended the local school and then gone to work for his father as a farmhand.[34] Some recruits faced stern opposition from their families, who expected their sons to put the welfare of the family ahead of their duty to country. James, however, had eventually won his parents' approval and support when he and several of his neighbors responded to the recruitment efforts. Colonel Leasure's plan was to enroll one company from each county; however, it was easier for James and his neighbors to make the six-mile trip to Portersville than to travel to their own county seat of Beaver, a journey of over ten miles. Therefore, on 27 August 1861, James McCaskey enrolled in Company C from Butler County.

On the morning of Wednesday, 28 August 1861, the recruits traveled by wagon or on foot to Enon Valley to catch a train to Pittsburgh. Robert Moffatt, a young soldier from New Castle, kept a diary during those early days.[35] He described a four-hour ride from New Castle to Enon Station, followed by a two-hour train ride to Pittsburgh—a total distance of about thirty miles. The train ride itself was a grand adventure for most of these young men, who might have seen trains but had never ridden on one. James C. Stevenson reported:

> We arrived at Enon station where we exchanged our hundreds of horses of flesh for two of the iron, the snort of which many of us had never heard. It was very amusing to one accustomed to such things to hear the remarks, suggestions and exclamations of those who never heard anything but "pigs crowing and roosters squealing." Some thought the "locomotion" as they called it would be a good thing to call hogs.[36]

There were no complaints about the rough ride; to those used to bumping along in a wagon, the rails were amazingly smooth. Nor did any of them complain about the fine layer of soot that settled on every surface as the train chugged along. Stevenson noted, however, that some of the men looked very serious, "as if they were afraid the lines might break, the horses run off, or some other awful strange thing happen to the big wagon with little wheels."[37]

In Pittsburgh, officials had appropriated the Allegheny County Fairgrounds to wartime needs and rather haphazardly retrofitted the grounds as a military camp and drill field. During the early months of the war, "Camp Wilkins" housed some 2000 men at any one time, although there were few refinements. When the Roundheads marched to Camp Wilkins, their quarters turned out to be cattle barns and pigpens. Stevenson described their settling in, "where, in a few minutes, with good straw for bedding, we might be found in our stalls, kicking at fleas, bed bugs, and many other awful creeping things which existed only in imagination."[38] When the regiment assembled at Camp Wilkins in Pittsburgh on Saturday, 31 August, for their official mustering, they numbered some 985 men and officers organized into twelve companies.[39] Six of those companies came from New Castle and the rest of Lawrence County; the others from the surrounding counties—Washington, Butler, Beaver, Mercer, and Westmoreland.

Col. Leasure had an advantage in picking his field officers. As one member of Company K reported, "A large number of Capt. Leasure's three months' company [Company H] … also members of Capt. Edward O'Brien's company [Company F] of the "Old Twelfth," joined these … New Castle companies, and the commissioned and noncommissioned officers of the same had seen service therein. In this way we had skilled officers for squad and company drills."[40] But at the staff level, the recruits elected their own officers—a system that seems designed to ensure that the enlisted men would willingly follow the orders of those they had chosen themselves. In practice, however, this meant that the staff officers were not chosen for their experience or their military training. James McCaskey, age twenty-two, became a sergeant, while his nearest neighbor, George W. Fisher, a year or two older, was named the first sergeant.[41] Both were fresh off the farm, with only the rudiments of an education and no military experience at all.

Food service at Camp Wilkins was hit or miss. A welcoming committee of local citizens had fed the Roundheads at the train station upon their arrival, but no arrangements had been made for the next day. The soldiers reported being dismissed to go into town to get meals at their own expense, while mess arrangements were in the works. Eventually, of course, things fell into place, but there must have been some hungry young men for a while. Few of the Roundheads registered complaints, although one soldier remarked in his diary on 30 August, "It is an old saying that 'That fingers were made before forks,' but for my part, I think it would be a decided improvement when eating rice and beans to have spoons."[42] Records from the Ninth Pennsylvania, who arrived just ahead of the Roundheads, tell of a diet based primarily on hard tack, salt pork, beans, coffee, and sugar.[43] A member of the Jefferson Light Guards, writing about

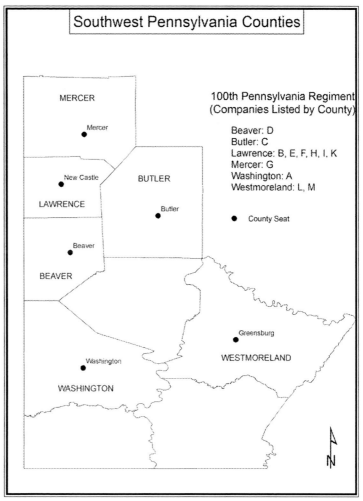

Home Counties of the 100th Pennsylvania Regiment
Map by Anna Inman

the Camp Wilkins food in May, had admitted that the soldiers adopted the "appropriating system." His fellows, he said, "make free use of all the milk cows, ducks, chickens, etc. that come into camp; and whatever of onions, lettuce, and other vegetables they may meet with in their strolls through the neighborhood."[44] The Roundheads, for all the reports of their exemplary behavior, were not above using the same system to supplement the camp mess. It was, in fact, a skill they would exercise frequently in the coming months.

Col. Leasure had many details to take care of during these few days in Pittsburgh. Among his responsibilities was the need to fill positions on his staff. Some choices were easy. His son, Samuel G. Leasure, became his Adjutant, along with William H. Powers. A popular local minister had immediately signed up as regimental chaplain, although he had to delay his departure until he received an official leave of absence from his congregation. Alva H. Leslie, prominent businessman and politician from New Castle, brought his business acumen to bear on the Quartermaster's office. Ferdinand H. Gross, with whose medical talents Leasure was very familiar, initially signed on as Surgeon, bringing with him his assistant, Dr. Joseph P. Rossiter. Dr. Gross, however, was so well respected that he was almost immediately promoted to the general staff, U. S. Volunteers. Within six weeks, Dr. Horace Ludington replaced him on the Roundheads staff. Several young men from the printing office of the *New Castle Chronicle* followed John Nicklin to enlist as regimental musicians, but Col. Leasure sent home the little drummer boy, William Mehard, when he discovered that he was only twelve.[45]

One volunteer arrived uninvited. Mrs. Nellie Leath presented herself to Col. Leasure without credentials, offering her services as regimental nurse.

Surgeon Horace Ludington, USA
Photo courtesy of USAMHI

Dorothea Dix had just begun her work as Superintendent of Women Nurses, but Nellie would not have met her criteria for commissioning. Dix demanded that her nurses be above reproach: " ... sober, earnest, self-sacrificing, and self-sustained; who can bear the presence of suffering and exercise entire self-control of speech and manner; who can be calm, gentle, quiet, active, and steadfast in duty ... plain looking women ... with no bows, no curls, no jewelry, and no hoop-skirts."[46] Nellie was too young, too attractive, and too experienced to win official approval as an army nurse. She could only

offer herself as an unpaid volunteer, bringing with her a kindness and gentleness that suffering young soldiers far from home might find comforting. She declared that she had chosen to join the Roundheads because she had been told that they were God-fearing and morally upright; it was a plea Col. Leasure could not refuse.

Nellie Leath had come to Pittsburgh a year or so earlier from Elyria, Ohio, with her husband, an alcoholic and felonious musician who treated her badly. Saving her pennies, she had finally managed to buy a sewing machine, so that she could leave her husband and support herself. She had overestimated the demand for seamstresses, however, and could only find work as costume mistress for a somewhat disreputable theater company. The neighborhood was a brutal one, and although she was not herself an actress, her employment labeled her a loose woman. She shared room and board with Miss Bell Morgan, an actress with the same theater, an arrangement that provided some protection to both of them. But when the theater closed, throwing them both out of work, Bell proved unstable. After she tried to commit suicide with an overdose of opium, Bell left Pittsburgh, and Nellie found that she was too vulnerable as a single woman to remain where she was. Enlisting in the war effort seemed a good way to escape Pittsburgh and to escape her past.[47] Thus Nellie Leath, who later reverted to her maiden name, Nellie M. Chase, became an essential, although unofficial, member of the Roundhead Regiment.

The enlisted soldiers themselves had relatively little to do at Camp Wilkins. They held a dress parade on Friday morning, and H Company received some lessons on marching from an unidentified Zouave. Most of their time seems to have been spent going into downtown Pittsburgh to purchase supplies or to see the sights. Robert Moffatt's diary reveals that he had time to make two visits with family friends in town, to entertain the daughter of those friends at his campsite, to purchase oil cloth and blankets, have his picture taken, and attend Sunday services with the rest of the regiment at the nearby Presbyterian Church.[48] Little else transpired at Camp Wilkins, for it was only a layover for the Roundheads on their way to Washington, DC. By Monday evening they were again on the move. Robert Moffatt's father and others had come to see them off; they even brought a trunk full of apples to share with the ranks.

The train left Pittsburgh at 4:00 in the afternoon; they traveled all night and arrived in Harrisburg at 11:00 AM. After a visit to the State House, they boarded cattle cars for the next leg of the journey—from Harrisburg to Baltimore. It was not a pleasant trip; Gavin reports that these cars had recently been used to transport hogs and had not been cleaned.[49] Perhaps more disturbing were the rumors that a hostile mob awaited them in Baltimore.

Maryland was one of four "border states" during the war. Although the state did not secede, its large cadre of slave owners guaranteed that the state would feel a sense of loyalty to the Confederacy. President Lincoln recognized the state as a threat to Washington, DC, since Maryland surrounded Washington on three sides, and Baltimore controlled the railhead of the line that carried troops into the nation's capital. Maryland for its part remained in the Union but supported the right of states to leave the Union if they so desired. But because Marylanders supported the right of secession, they could not support the northern war effort. Feelings were exacerbated when Lincoln ordered troops into Baltimore itself to safeguard the rail lines being used for troop movements. Baltimore's "Plug-Uglies," one of the firefighter gangs that had turned the process of election into something of a blood sport in Baltimore, had transformed that city into a center of violence during the 1850s, and their predilection for taking the law into their own hands spilled over again when Union troops began moving through their city. There was not much help for it; no rail line ran completely through the city, so troops had to disembark from a train at one end of the city and march across town to pick up a new line at the far end. As early as 19 April 1861, the volatile atmosphere of the city burst into flames. The 6th Michigan Regiment was confronted by a mob as they marched toward the train station. The fight started with rock throwing and escalated into gunfire. Before it was over, twelve citizens of Baltimore lay dead next to four members of Michigan's regimental band, and many more were injured.[50]

The following weeks were marked by fear on both sides. As early as May 1861, Maryland's General Assembly issued a proclamation protesting the war and calling upon the president "to cease this unholy and most wretched and unprofitable strife" and to recognize the independence of the Confederate States. Maryland's legislature also called upon the citizens of Baltimore to "abstain from all violent and unlawful interference of every sort with the troops in transit through our territory, or quartered among us, and patiently leave to time and reason the ultimate and certain reestablishment and vindication of the right." They feared that the presence of the Union Army might result in further angry confrontations drawing Maryland into the war.[51] Such a call for restraint, however, may only suggest that the crowds were already out of control; Union troops could expect something less than a warm welcome when they changed trains in Baltimore. Apparently, however, the angry crowd waiting for the Roundheads' train from Harrisburg dwindled as the hours passed. By the time the men arrived in the early morning, the protesters had traded the damp of the night for the warmth of their beds. The Roundheads marched through the city to board a new train without incident. Captain Cline described the scene as "the streets lit up by the uncertain glare of the streetlamps, with double police at every corner. It looked more like a funeral cortege of some departed spirits than the march of a regiment of soldiers."[52]

On 4 September, the regiment arrived in Washington, DC, where they encamped on Kalorama Heights, a wooded hill overlooking the capital city from the north.[53] The Greek name of the site, which means "beautiful view," was given to the area by Joel Barlow, the poet of "Columbiad" fame, who built his estate there in 1805. After these troops had moved out, the army established Kalorama Hospital on the site and used it as a pest house to isolate victims of a smallpox epidemic.[54] The mansion was torn down at the end of the war out of fear that it still contained smallpox. For the young soldiers from Pennsylvania, their first days were filled with sights and sounds to amaze them. One Roundhead described the scene this way:

> Quartered as we are on the Kalorama Heights, we have an opportunity to look about us, and from our camp we can see in all directions, the white tents gleaming in the sunshine, on the hills, and in the valleys, in the fields and half hidden in the forest, but everywhere camps, camps, and the sun goes down amid the continuous roll of drums, at "retreat," to rise again welcomed by the "reveille" from a hundred camps in sight of the Federal city.[55]

The nation's capital had become the hub of the Union effort. Troops assembled and drilled on every open ground. Weapons and supplies were stockpiled in government buildings. Cannons rolled down the streets while cattle destined for army stewpots grazed on the National Mall. Soldiers with day passes gawked at the sights, and Union generals formulated plans in the public rooms of the Willard Hotel near the White House. Lincoln held audiences in the afternoons, allowing all petitioners open access to the presidential ear.

For a newly formed regiment, a period of training was an absolute necessity. Although some of their officers had a few months of military experience behind them, the Roundheads were, in the best sense of the word, amateur soldiers. Not even Col. Leasure had formal military instruction, although he had served with the state militia since 1832.[56] It is to his credit, however, that he possessed a good understanding of human psychology. He well knew that his men would need more than a drill field to turn them into a crack fighting unit, and he immediately set underway a series of morale-boosting measures.

One such morale boost came from creating a regimental newspaper.[57] These small broadsheets gave the common soldier a voice. They provided a place where soldiers could complain about the quality of the mess or the depth of the mud without fear of reprisal. Staff officers could also offer instruction in the management of camp life, serve up mild rebukes when necessary, and quell the rumors that seemed to plague every military encampment. To a surprising degree, they also provided a forum to discuss the issues of the war, the institutions of government, and the morality that governed the lives of the soldiers. Almost immediately upon their arrival in Washington, Col. Leasure spent $10.00 of his own money to purchase a second-hand printing press. He had with him a ready-made staff, for among his earliest recruits were the men who had worked as writers and printers of the *New Castle Chronicle*, which Leasure owned. The first issue of *The Camp Kettle*, bearing the regimental motto, "We Know Only Our Country," on its masthead, appeared on 21 September 1861:

> We have little room to spare, and none to waste in the "Camp Kettle," and shall briefly state that it is our intention to publish it as a daily, or weekly, or occasional paper, just as the exigencies of the service will permit. It is our intention to cook in it a "mess" of short paragraphs replete with

useful information on a great many subjects, about which new recruits are supposed to be ignorant. We shall endeavor to make it a welcome visitor beside the campfire and in the quarters, a sort of familiar little friend that whispers kind words and friendly advice to inexperienced men concerning the new position they have assumed, and the new duties that follow. Everything relating to a soldier's duty, and camp life, from mounting guard, to cleaning a musket, will be fit ingredient for the "Kettle." Rules for preserving health and cooking rations will be in place, and all sorts of questions relating to a soldier's duty, and his wants, when respectfully asked in writing, over a responsible name, will find an answer in the next mess that is poured out of the "Kettle."[58]

James McCaskey wrote his first letter to his family on 22 September 1861 and demonstrated another use for *The Camp Kettle*. The small paper was designed to inform those who waited at home as well as those who served in the regiment.

Dear friends,

I take my pencil in hand to inform you that I am well at presant, and I hope that these few lines may still finde you engoying the same. I have not much to write to you, but here I send you a little paper that will give you some information. Tell the children that I think of them one and ol. And I would like to hear from them ol, and dear father in petickular I would like to hear from you.[59]

The "little paper" became quite popular at home because it contained the kind of information that soldiers' families were looking for. One copy of the first issue made its way to the editor of a local paper, *The Lawrence Journal,* who in turn reported on its contents:

We learn from its columns that the Regiment is fully armed, equipped and clothed, "except coats, pantaloons and overcoats." Rather an important exception; but it is said they will have all these in a few days.

The health of the men is generally good, and the character of the Regiment for the sobriety and good morals is becoming a subject of remark. There has been no case of discipline or drunkenness, since Regiment left home, no soldier in the Guard house, and the officers and men keep up the observances of the religion of their fathers in the camp, as they did at home. We hope the Kettle may always sing as pleasant a tune.[60]

The newspaper also printed the following "Orders" to show how the soldiers occupied their time:

Reveille at sunrise. Company roll call—breakfast—Put the company quarters in good order. Squad drill till 9 o'clock. Company drill from ten till twelve. Roll call. Dinner. Squad and company drill from two o'clock P. M., till half past three. Regimental drill from half past four till six to conclude with dress parade. Roll call. Supper. Roll call at half past eight. Tattoo at ten when all lights except in officer's head quarters must be put out, and all the men not on guard must retire to bed. Guards will be detailed by the First Sergeants at the morning roll call, for duty at ten o'clock, the hour for guard mounting.—The Surgeon's call will be beaten at eight in the morning, when all the sick must be mustered to the hospital by the first Sergeant for medical attendance. Commandants of companies will see that these orders are strictly carried out.[61]

The Camp Kettle grew rapidly in popularity, so much so that the printers decided to reduce the size of the type so that they could include all the news:

We are going to enlarge the "Camp Kettle" without making it any bigger by printing in smaller type. Now if that aint a pretty good Irish "animule" of cow kind we are no judge of beef. We meant to say, but dident, that we have sent for minion type, which will enable us to put more thickening in our "plate of hasty soup" if even that can be of use; for, we must acknowledge, that some of the fellows in "our mess" have a most unconscionable appetite for the contents of our "kettle" and we feel like gratifying them if possible.[62]

Two months later, the circulation figures had exploded. The staff "printed five hundred more than we expected to sell—ran out—Colonel ordered a thousand extra—first side was distributed—set it up again—printed the thousand extra—exhausted the supply… ."[63]

The bulging tent of a sutler made camp life seem more like home. These civilian venders were appointed to supply the troops with little extras such as candy, books, tobacco, tin cups, razors, writing materials, and special food items. *The Camp Kettle* welcomed the arrival of sutler James T. Sample because he had been a soldier himself until he lost a leg at Chapultepec during the Mexican War. The editor expressed the hope that "he will have a soft side to his heart, for the frailties of men tempted to spend their money for that which is not bread, and give the honest fellows the worth of their penny."[64] This optimistic hope was short-lived; by the next week, the same writer was chiding the "boyish tastes" of men who stood around the door of the sutler's tent chewing on sticks of mint candy.

Staff officers had spent considerable time making sure that the soldiers were well fed. The second issue of *The Camp Kettle* devoted an entire page to instructions on cooking beans, vegetables, and meat so as to preserve flavor and tenderness. Company cooks were routinely admonished against waste and slovenly cooking practices. And periodically, *The Camp Kettle* published a list of the rations consumed during the preceding month: 25 barrels of pork, 11,000 pounds of fresh beef, 7 barrels of preserved beef, 41 pounds of bacon, 172 loaves of hard bread, 162 barrels of flour, 58 bushels of beans, 1600 pounds of rice, 2000 pounds of coffee, 45 pounds of tea, 3500 pounds of sugar, 300 gallons of vinegar,

742 pounds of potatoes, 28 gallons of molasses, 14 bushels of salt, and 740 pounds of hominy fed the men in September. Such fare, the editor reassured his candy-munching readers, was "the best furnished to any army in the world." [65]

Music was yet another way to pull a group of men together. To a far greater degree than today, when music has become part of the background noise of our daily existence, nineteenth-century life relied upon music to tell stories, arouse emotions, and create community bonds. Families sang together, children improvised musical instruments to amuse themselves, and every social occasion was an opportunity to express feelings through song. The regimental band, so much a feature of the early Civil War, served many purposes. On 22 July 1861, a Congressional act, "An Act to Authorize the Employment of Volunteers to aid in Enforcing Laws and Protecting Public Property, Section 2," authorized the creation of a band in each regiment.[66] The musicians were meant to perform on all occasions—from sentimental ditties around the campfire to the drumbeat that regulated marching drills, from the dirges that accompanied a military funeral to the rousing numbers played to spur men into battle. Everyone and every occasion demanded music, and the Roundhead Regiment was no exception.

Col. Leasure had enlisted eleven musicians, most of them printers by trade, and one of the greatest expenditures in those early days at Kalorama was to purchase instruments for the band. The Camp Kettle's first issue reported, "We expect the instruments for our band in a few days, and then we will be able to vary our amusements on parade. We are getting up a splendid drum corps under the direction of Drum Major Nicklin."[67] A couple of weeks later, the paper announced, "At last the instruments for our band have arrived, with the exception of one large horn, which is yet in the hands of the manufacturer. They are the best we have ever seen, are made of

German Silver, and for tone and power have no superior."[68]

Pvt. John B. Nicklin, Musician, USA
Photo courtesy of Roger D. Hunt Collection,
USAMHI

Perhaps the most important decision Col. Leasure made in regard to the welfare of the regiment had to do with the religious convictions of his men. Col. Leasure had recruited Rev. Robert Audley Browne, a hometown minister known to many of the men and one who knew exactly what those young men had been taught in their homes and churches. According to one biographer, the Rev. Robert Audley Browne was " ... born, baptized, reared, licensed and ordained in the Associate Reformed Presbyterian, now the United Presbyterian, Church. He [was] descended by blood and church connection from the Covenanters of the West of Scotland."[69] Rev. Browne had arrived in New Castle in 1846 to serve a widely scattered parish. At the beginning of his ministry, he had only twelve church members in the town itself; the rest were located in East Brook, Shenango, "the Harbor" and New Wilmington. He spent his time traveling, preaching in whatever structures were avail-

able, and visiting with the people of Lawrence County. He was an early abolitionist, speaking

Rev. Robert Audley Browne, USA
Photo courtesy of Civil War Library and Museum,
MOLLUS

out against the institution of slavery, praying for the slaves, and supporting the political party that best represented his views. He had denounced the Fugitive Slave bill and supported those who wanted to see Kansas remain a free state. In fact, he first met Dr. Daniel Leasure at a meeting called to provide Sharp's rifles for the Free State settlers in Kansas. Thus he was well known throughout Lawrence County and in the neighboring counties and a natural choice as the chaplain of the newly formed Roundhead Regiment.

Rev. Browne asked the congregation of the United Presbyterian Church of New Castle for a leave of absence to join the military effort. He arrived at Camp Kalorama on Saturday, 14 September, just in time to prepare his first sermon, based on the story of Jacob's vow: "If God will be with me, and will keep me in this way that I go, and will give me bread to eat, and raiment to put on, so that I come again to my father's house in peace; then shall the Lord be my God."[70] The text, of course, was carefully chosen, not just to describe the new experiences of recruits receiving their first uniforms and organizing their messes, but to offer them reassurance that they would be returning home again. The next Sunday, his text was taken from the Psalms: "The Lord is on my side; I will not fear."[71] On Thursday, 26 September, Browne wrote to his father:

> I preached on Heb. 12, 5, 6…Taking occasion to show that God's design in imposing adversity and suffering was to develop a gracious and noble character in man. So the stern discipline we are now experiencing here deprived of home and its comforts, should be accepted as proof of love and used to secure higher developments of character. At the evening service at 4 1/2 P.M., I intend to apply the principle to our national affairs and show that God would make a greater and better nation, by putting us anew in the furnace of national trials.[72]

Rev. Browne was to fulfill many roles in the months to come. When things were quiet, he traveled back and forth from camp to the hills of western Pennsylvania, carrying messages, delivering goods from home, and recruiting new soldiers to bolster the ranks. When the regiment was on the move, he was with them. He held the hands of the sick, prayed over the dying, and offered comfort and reassurance to the homesick. But always he was the voice of the Calvinist tradition that tied this regiment together. Within days of his arrival, *The Camp Kettle* commented on the growing devotion of the regiment:

> The descendants of England's "Roundheads" and Scotland's "Cameronians" take to the "art of war", as their fathers did of old, with trusty sword and firelock, in strong faith that, "the God of Jacob is their refuge" and their shield in battle, as well as their God at home, and they observe their religious exercises with the

same regularity, as their drill, and their morning and evening devotions, alternate with their lessons in the "school of the soldier."[73]

So the crisp fall days of September and early October passed. The band played, the chaplain preached, and the journalists continued to pass on valuable instructions concerning military life. The men spend hours each day on the drill field, and munched their mint sticks during their breaks. The cooks grew more skilled at putting together meals from the rations, and day by day, the men accumulated their soldiers' gear. But beneath this pleasant picture, a certain restlessness prevailed. Soldiers had to be cautioned against excessive passes to leave camp, and even Rev. Browne succumbed to the temptation to take an hour away and visit the White House.[74] Like Camp Wilkins, the camp at Kalorama saw a constant flow of troops. The Roundheads began to feel that they had been forgotten as the other units came and passed. *The Camp Kettle* mused:

> Over the river—over the Long Bridge— over into Dixie—over the Chain Bridge— so they go, one steady stream of staunch men in serried columns, bristling with bayonets, rumbling with heavy or light batteries, clanking with sabers; and still they come—the morning sun finds but the debris of the camp of the evening before, and the same sun sets upon the same spot, a busy camp of fresh troops hurrying up and down the streets of their canvas city, like the shadowy figures in some shifting panorama. The Roundhead Regiment has lain four weeks on the heights of the Kalorama, and it is by three weeks the oldest settler to day. Its turn must come, we know not at what hour, but the hour will find us ready to "strike our tents and march away," leaving our "beautiful view" to be enjoyed by some younger brothers of the bayonet and sabre.[75]

CHAPTER 3

A Wonderful Sheet of Water

Organizing a band of raw recruits into an effective fighting force takes more time than was allotted the Union Army at the beginning of the war. As early as July, plans had been brewing for a joint Army-Navy expedition into southern waters, but there had not been enough soldiers available to make the venture feasible. Now new recruits were arriving in Washington daily, the defenses around the capital were adequately, if not expertly, manned, and the organization of the South Carolina Expeditionary Corps could begin.

On 2 August 1861 Brigadier General Thomas William Sherman received his orders: "You will proceed to New York immediately and organize, in connection with Captain DuPont of the Navy, an expedition of 12,000 men. Its destination you and the naval commander will determine after you have sailed. You should sail at the earliest possible moment."[1] Under his command would be three brigades of infantry and several unattached artillery units. The First Brigade, commanded by Brigadier General E. L. Viele, consisted of the 8th Maine Infantry; the 3rd New Hampshire; the 46th, 47th, and 48th New York; and the 55th Pennsylvania. The Second Brigade, led by Brigadier General Isaac Ingalls Stevens, comprised the 8th Michigan; the 79th New York; the 50th Pennsylvania; and the 100th Pennsylvania, the "Roundhead Regiment." The Third Brigade, under the command of Brigadier

General H. G. Wright, contained the 89th Maine; the 4th New Hampshire; the 6th and 7th Connecticut; and the 76th and 97th Pennsylvania. Attached to the corps and under the temporary direction of General Wright were the 1st New York Engineers; the 3rd Rhode Island Artillery; Battery E, 3rd U. S. Artillery; 1st Connecticut Battery; 1st Massachusetts Cavalry; and the 38th Massachusetts Infantry.[2]

At the same time, Captain Samuel F. DuPont was organizing the naval contingent. In mid-October, the fleet consisted of some ten ships, including the flagship *Wabash*, the *Augusta*, the *Unadilla*, the *Curlew*, the *Alabama*, the *James Adger*, the *Mercury* and the *Pettit*.[3] Fighting ships and troop transports, however, were arriving daily in the harbor at Hampton Roads. By the time the fleet was ready to sail, it would comprise some seventy to eighty vessels.[4] Dupont was confident that his naval forces were the best that could be assembled, but he had serious doubts about the untested army troops who were to accompany him. In a letter to his wife he commented, "But the truth is soldiers and marines are the most helpless people I ever saw … [Sherman] has whole regiments who do not know how to shoulder a musket let alone fire one."[5]

The criticism did not apply to every regiment. The Scotch-Irish volunteers in the Roundhead Regiment had grown up with guns in their hands and stories of warfare in their ears. Their ancestors had fought the

English Cavaliers, the Redcoats in the Revolutionary war, and the Indians on the frontier. Even as children, the Roundheads had helped to defend their mountain settlements and had hunted the plentiful wild game in the forests of Pennsylvania. If there was indeed a critical flaw in their preparation, it was not so much a lack of experience with firearms as a lack of formal combat training. Battery E, 3rd U. S. Artillery, had served under General Porter, and the 79th New York, organized since May, had received a baptism of fire at Manassas and the First Battle of Bull Run.[6] The rest of the troops were new organizations like the 100th Pennsylvania—fresh off the farm, eager, and unaware of their own inadequa-

Brig. Gen. Thomas W. Sherman, USA
Photo courtesy of Library of Congress

Gen. Isaac I. Stevens, USA
Photo courtesy of Mikel Uriguen

Adm. Samuel F. DuPont, USN
Photo by Frederick Gutekunst

Maj. Gen. Horatio G. Wright, USA
Photo courtesy of Library of Congress

cies. But they brought with them two cultural trademarks—the bonds of a faith based on democratic principles and a long-standing warrior tradition. James Webb described the results of such a background: "As the ministers reinforced the notions of individual freedom, the leaders of the backcountry militias inculcated the reality that every able-bodied male had an obligation to risk his life for the common good."[7] So while generals struggled with the logistics of creating a military force from these raw materials, the Roundheads and the other units destined for Sherman's army waited impatiently for their orders.

James McCaskey wrote another letter home on 4 October 1861:

Most dear and affectionate father,

I take my pencil in hand to inform you that I am well and harty, and that I received your vary affectionate letter of the 20th on the 2d, and it gave me a gradeal of pleasure to learn that you ware ol well. I received a vary pleasant anseer to the first letter that I rote that was riten by Eunice, Sarahjane, and Simon, which gave me a gradeal of pleasure And I rote one rite away and poot ol three of thare names on it, and I received no anseer. And then I rote a gain and sent a smal paper in it coled the Camp Ketel. And in a day or to after I sent a newspaper coled the National Republic and still received no anseer til now, and I was beginning to think thare was up some whare or other.

You wanted to know how things was with me. Thay ar ol rite, and it is vary pleasant weather here and has been so ever since we came here. We hafto sleep on the ground, but we have plenty of blankets to sleep on. We ar vary turnover comfortable. We have plenty of evrything to eat and plenty of clothes, to. I have got since I came here 1 pare of shoes and 2 pares of firstrate stockings and 2 shirts and a cap and a splendid pare of pants. We will get our coats soon. Thare is part of them here now but not a nuff for ol, and the cornel sade that he would not distribute them til he got a nuff for ol. And as for a blanket you need not send one, for I donte

nead it. And if I did, it would bee of no youse for you to send one for I would never get it.

You need not fret about us, for we have a cornel that will not see us want for any thing that is in his power to get for us. And we have one of the best captains in the regiment that will not see us want for any thing that is in his power to get for us. He has gon home to recruit, and I expect he will bee round that way. And if he dos, I want you to give him my watch for me. I gave him a few lines to give you if he was down that way. This is ol at presant, but I reman your affectionate sone,

James

Unlike his first short note to let his family know that he had arrived in Washington, this letter provides real insight into the nature and attitudes of the raw Union recruits. James's emphasis on the uniform he had received, for instance, reveals the enthusiasm of the farmer, who was used to homespun, for real "city-made" clothes. The uniforms distributed to Union soldiers were probably neither stylish nor well made; certainly they were not designed for the southern climates into which the soldiers would be going. The shoes were mudscows, made with the rough side of the leather out, with broad soles, low heels, and rawhide laces. Issue stockings were of wool and shirts of flannel. The trousers were made of sky-blue kersey, cut loose and without pleats or cuffs. The forage cap was of dark blue cloth with a welt around the crown and yellow metal numbers in front to designate the regiment.[8] Nevertheless, to the young men of the 100th Pennsylvania, they were both "splendid" and "first-rate." Their needs were simple; they felt themselves fortunate because they had "plenty" of blankets, clothing, and food.

James's letter gives no indication that he was aware of what was going on in the war nor that he had any idea at this point of his ultimate assignment. The men of the 100th Pennsylvania knew that they were preparing to depart, but their destination was a closely guarded secret. Private James Stevenson recorded in his diary that "Some think we are going to Missouri, some to Kentucky, some to North Carolina—but it is all guesswork. No one, not even the officers, know 'where' or 'when'."[9]

Perhaps the most notable aspect of this letter is the degree of trust and loyalty James expressed for his officers. The Roundhead Regiment was a tightly knit group, and part of their unity derived from the fact that their immediate officers were also their neighbors and friends. The "cornel," of course, was Colonel Daniel Leasure. The captain of Company C was James E. Cornelius from Butler County. He was moderately successful on the recruitment trip mentioned in the letter. On 18 October 1861, nine additional men from Butler County mustered into Company C.[10] Cornelius seems to have found time to visit the McCaskey family, for James was wearing his watch at the time of his death.[11] The Roundhead and Covenanter heritage of this regiment provided a tradition of "devotion to the principles of liberty of person and of conscience."[12] In defense of that tradition, the men were willing to follow their officers wherever their military duty called them.

Just four days after this letter was written, the troops were on the move. The Roundheads marched out of their Kalorama camp on 10 October, headed for the train station and transport for Annapolis. It was not a particularly pleasant trip. The train did not depart until midnight, and daylight found them "only twenty-two miles from where [they] started." All day long the train stopped and started. Stevenson reported that, "Several times we got out a mile or so, but would meet another train and have to back out."[13] Men tired of trying to rest on hard wooden planks climbed to the tops of the cars to get a look at the countryside. Others jumped off the stalled train and once more exercised their "appropriating system" to gather fresh produce in the nearby fields. The two-day trip ended on

the morning of 12 October at Annapolis: in a letter to his wife, Rev. Browne reported that they "could have marched through sooner and been in better condition had they come afoot."[14]

The Roundheads resided on the Naval Academy grounds overlooking Chesapeake Bay. The superintendent of the Naval School had feared for the safety of his young charges and had moved the entire corps of 300 cadets to Newport, Rhode Island, leaving the beautiful grounds and buildings to the use of the growing Union forces. Joining the Roundheads when they arrived at Annapolis were several women who had volunteered to go along as nurses. They included Mrs. Mary Pollock, daughter of Captain Bentley; Mrs. Sample, the sutler's wife; and Mrs. White, who had some connection to Dr. Leasure's medical practice.[15] These women seemed to have met the strict criteria for army nurses, but the men themselves mentioned none of them when they needed nursing. Somehow it was always Nellie who was there to offer comfort and gentle care.

There followed a week of light drill, with plenty of time to eat oysters and enjoy the sights. Most of the soldiers found that Annapolis was an agreeable place to linger. Robert Moffatt called it "a good time in general" and recorded only one incident that "raised quite an excitement in the grounds."[16] The Roundheads experienced their first encounter with the South's "peculiar institution" when a runaway slave came into their camp looking for protection. An officer from Company K took him on as a "servant," but the slave's master was not far behind. When the owner demanded the return of his "property," Col. Leasure stalled to protect the man. A member of Company K later recalled the scheme that the colonel had devised to protect runaway slaves:

> The plan was to have the soldiers gather around the slave holder, a big pompous fellow, and hold him in the human pen

until the slave could be taken to the gates and given a good start for his freedom. This we did, and in a few minutes about two hundred enthusiastic soldiers got around the Southerner and made [life] very interesting to him for ten minutes or more. He swore and threatened all of us with a zest and said Governor [Thomas H.] Hicks [of Maryland] would see that we got the full penalty of the law. This did not scare us very much, and our back talk made him furious. At last we released him and allowed him to depart after his slave.[17]

Two other incidents marred the pleasant respite of the Roundheads at Annapolis. First came the death of Corp. William S. Sample, Company B, from an unidentified fever. He had become ill on the train ride from Washington, DC, and despite the efforts of Nurse Nellie, who tended him all the way to Annapolis, he lingered only three days. His passing served as a grim reminder that not all would survive this war. The second incident involved Col. Leasure himself and the new brigade commander, Gen. I. I. Stevens. On 18 October, Gen. Stevens sought lodging for his newly arrived brigade quartermaster, Captain William Lilly. The two made a distasteful pair; Stevens was often drunk and profane, while Lilly was arrogant and demanding. Together they descended on the Roundheads' quarters and ordered all of Col. Leasure's belongings transferred to another room, so that Lilly could move in. Rev. Browne was shocked when the general declared that "he had to blow somebody up and he would do it, sending our Col's effects to 'hell' and swearing 'by God' and by 'Jesus Christ' in a style to make the blood of every Roundhead tingle."[18] Col. Leasure returned to find the move in full swing, but he managed to cool tempers and find a solution that satisfied all. Still, it was an unwelcome reminder that in this new army, righteousness would not always prevail over power and rank.

Rev. Browne had a keen appreciation for his surroundings. He addressed a letter to the editor of the New Castle newspaper on 18 October, describing what he saw from the heights of Annapolis:

Since I wrote to you a number of steamers have glided into the harbor, and silently tied by the shore or anchored out in deeper water. The latter are ocean Steamers. Four of them have not come in at all, but lie at anchored outside in the deeper waters of the Chesapeake Bay.

There is something suggestive of mystery, combined with the conception of wisdom and power in the appearance of these vessels in these waters, and their riding at anchor there so quietly day by day. When I arrived here there were none at all. Now I count seventeen of them from the cupola of the State House. They are beautiful objects, with their clean cut keels, their single chimney stacks, and two masts each; and there they sit like birds upon the water; they resemble to my eye, eagles upon their perch, that seem to be oblivious to every surrounding thing, but whose eyes sweep the horizon, while we know not what moment they may swoop down, and fall like thunderbolts upon their prey.[19]

On 17 October, General Sherman had issued orders assigning the 100th Pennsylvania to the steamer *Ocean Queen,* along with five companies of the 50th Regiment Pennsylvania Volunteers.[20] They embarked at Annapolis on 21 October and arrived at Hampton Roads, Virginia, the next day. For many Union soldiers, just being aboard such a ship was a wonder almost too great to be absorbed. James Penney kept a tiny leather-bound notebook in his pocket, and on this day he recorded: "We embarked on the steamship Ocean Queen today from Annapolis, Md. It is the first day that I ever was outside of land."[21]

At Hampton Roads, they remained on board their ship awaiting the final assembly of the fleet. The *Ocean Queen* herself was undoubtedly the largest ship the Roundheads had ever encountered. Rev. Browne estimated that it was "330 feet long, 65 feet wide, three stories above water, 2 below;" James C. Stevenson thought it even larger at "380 feet long, 80 feet wide, and 60 feet high."[22] Despite its size, conditions were not particularly comfortable. The ship housed some 1800 men, sleeping between decks in four-layer bunk beds that were less than two feet high and two feet wide. They shared space with horses and their huge quantities of oats and hay, building tools, carts, sandbags, grindstones, and gun carriages. Meals, for those who were not busy "trying to throw up their socks," were served twice a day to ease the logistics of getting everyone to table.[23] Seasickness plagued many of the Roundheads, but they took it with at least a grain of humor. James C. Stevenson remarked, "I wouldn't care for throwing up the rice and beans, but I hate to lose the crackers after so much hard chewing to get them down."[24]

Even Rev. Browne was tempted to complain to his wife about the short rations available to the officers' table and to gloat over the capture of one of the sailors who was plundering the mess supplies:

Pies, bread, cakes and pickles, the ship's alcohol (which was always being replaced by water) and perhaps other things, have been sold to the soldiers at exorbitant prices—the Captain's suspicions were aroused and a watch kept, which resulted last night in the discovery of a man issuing from the cook's room with a plate of pickles. He was closely pursued along the slippery deck of the careening vessel. He ran in great alarm, as the guard ahead of him, at the cry, "Stop that man," tried to obey the orders. The soldier threw his plate, pickles and all at his head, which not being the best way to keep the pickles on the plate, they flew round the deck. At the same time, the man fell and his pur-

suer, Nichols, second mate, fell over him, receiving a punch in his vest by mistake from the bayonet of the guard.[25]

The appropriating system, it seems, was acceptable when it involved feeding hungry young recruits from the land. It was quite something else when sailors appropriated soldiers' stores.

Despite such inconveniences and discomforts, the purpose and destination of the South Carolina Expeditionary Corps were now becoming clear. They were headed to the southern Atlantic coast to strengthen the effort to bring the Confederacy to its knees by blockading its access to shipping. Shortly after Fort Sumter fell, Lincoln had officially declared a blockade of all states that had seceded and dispatched the *Niagara* to hold Charleston Harbor. Her arrival, to be sure, had caused some initial consternation; on 9 May 1861, Miss Emma Holmes, a Charleston resident, worried:

Old Abe has at last fulfilled his threats of blockading us by sending the *Niagara* here … The *Niagara* is a splendid steam propeller, so contrived that she can withdraw the wheel from the water & thus use either steam or her sails at pleasure, and is probably the fastest ship in the U. S. navy. It carries 12 guns, is manned by 600 men, and fully supplied with provisions, implements & munitions of war. She has already warned off two or three vessels …"[26]

Concern soon gave way to nonchalance, however; within days the *Niagara* was gone. The same resident wrote in her diary for 18 May, "Since last Tuesday, the *Niagara* has not been seen anywheres [sic] along our coast … So, the much talked of blockade is at an end, not having done us any harm, but plenty to Old Abe …"[27]

Blockading the South Carolina coast was no easy task. If the North planned to maintain an effective blockade against the Confederate States, their overriding need was for a safe southern harbor from which to operate. The international understanding was that other countries would respect a blockade only so long as it operated effectively. The English, in particular, had questioned the validity of the Northern blockade, and understandably so, since they were in large part dependent on southern cotton to keep their textile mills in operation. English lawyers probed the clauses of the Union's Blockade Act, pointing out that an absolute blockade had to be effective before it could be legal. If some ships could penetrate the blockade, no foreign government was bound to observe it.[28] The withdrawal of blockading vessels for repairs or supplies would be interpreted as abandonment of the effort; it was therefore essential that Union ships have quick and easy access to a supply depot.[29] In late October, *Harper's Weekly* speculated that there were only three southern harbors deep enough to let large ships enter. Beaufort, South Carolina; Brunswick, Georgia; and Pensacola, Florida were all possible destinations for the Expedition.[30]

Naval intelligence had already focused on Port Royal, South Carolina, as one of the more important southern harbors.[31] From Port Royal, blockading vessels would be less than a day's sail from such important Confederate ports as Charleston and Savannah. It was further hoped that from a naval base at Port Royal, it would be possible to take and hold these vital harbors. As Lieutenant Daniel Ammen, commander of the *Seneca*, explained in his memoirs, a blockade from within a harbor could be effective with only one ship. If the blockade had to be maintained outside the range of coastal guns, it could take up to thirty ships to achieve the same degree of effectiveness.[32]

The role of the Army would be to take out the coastal guns and to prevent the Confederate forces from driving the Union naval vessels from the harbors. Although the men had not been told their specific destination for fear of security leaks, General Sherman sent the following rousing message to his troops waiting aboard their transports:

> The general commanding announces to the expeditionary corps that it is intended to make a descent on the enemy's coast, and probably under circumstances which will demand the utmost vigilance, coolness, and intrepidity on the part of every officer and man of his command. In consideration of the justness and holiness of our cause, of the ardent patriotism which has prompted the virtuous and industrious citizens of our land to fly to their country's standard in the moment of her peril, he most confidently believes that he will be effectually and efficiently supported in his efforts to overthrow a zealous, active, and wily foe, whose cause is unholy and principles untenable.[33]

Captain DuPont, however, remained unconvinced of the usefulness of the Army. As one of the very few who knew the ultimate destination of the fleet, he could see little purpose in taking the soldiers along and feared that they would actually hinder his plans. He wrote of his doubts to his wife, "At Port Royal the soldiers will have nothing to do—they are obliterated—though we did work out a distant landing for them when we investigated the subject; whether Sherman will agree to be a looker-on is another element."[34]

Tension between the leaders of the expedition came to a head before the ships ever left port. Although his men were loaded on the transports, General Sherman felt them woefully undersupplied and refused to embark until he could obtain more ammunition. Major General John E. Wool of the Department of Virginia provided them with supplies in hopes of hastening their departure, but intermittent bad weather delayed the sailing and caused the men to use up supplies of water and food at an alarming rate. On 28 October, General Wool articulated his opinion in a letter to Simon Cameron, the secretary of war: "It is now nearly seven days since the general received the ammunition, and the fleet is still in port, and when it will sail is more than I can tell … I will venture to assert that a worse-managed expedition could not well be contrived. Every opportunity has been given the rebels to be prepared to meet them at any point on the coast."[35]

The delay was obviously irritating to the 1800 men crammed on board the *Ocean Queen*, but once again, most of the Roundheads tried to preserve their reputation for good behavior. Captain Cline reported to his wife, "Our regiment is quartered on this vessel with 5 companies of the 50th Penna. I have seen more card playing among the officers of the 50th since on board than I have seen among the Roundheads in two months." He also noted that Rev. Browne used his Sunday sermons to denounce those who were guilty of "profanity, gambling, and drunkenness. The officers of the 50th play cards in the cabin and some of our men are guilty also. Many did not like it, but that makes no difference to Mr. Brown."[36]

Meanwhile, DuPont was having his own problems. He commanded the largest fleet ever assembled under American leadership—over eighty vessels, counting the tugs and other small boats that had been pressed into service—and each ship's captain had his own opinion concerning weather forecasts and the proper time for departure. The fleet left Hampton Roads at last on 29 October in what promised to be fine sailing weather. Aboard the flagship *Wabash* was a reporter for the *New York Herald*, Bradley Sillick Osbon, an experienced sailor, pirate-hunter, sketch-artist, and storyteller. It is thanks to his daily dispatches that *Harper's Weekly* was able to carry colorful illustrated accounts of The Great Naval Expedition.[37] Osbon reported on 31 October that "the sea was as smooth as a millpond, only a gentle swell disturbing its bosom." The weather was balmy, the temperature at 70 degrees, and not a cloud to be seen in the sky. The sea-sick had recovered,

and "not one vacant place was to be seen at the dinner-table."[38]

Such halcyon conditions, of course, could not last. On 1 November the fleet ran full-tilt into a late-season hurricane. DuPont's ship's log recorded a southeast gale, a rapidly lowering barometer, torrential rains, and gusting winds shifting to the west. Looking back on the experience, the *Camp Kettle* attempted to describe the soldiers' feelings:

> If any body wants to get to the very depth of deepest misery, let him just go to sea, and encounter a small gale the first day out. At first it is all very nice, and consummately funny. The ship rises and sinks, and rolls and pitches, and settles away and comes right up again to go through the same gyrations over and over again, and your gait becomes unsteady, and rocky, and your companions laugh at you, and then you laugh at them, and it is all very delightful, but by and bye, you begin to experience a sort of goneness all over, some thing not exactly desirable, until at last the vessel rears up at the bow and again goes down and you feel as if the bottom of the briny deep was rushing up through your epigastrium. And you make a rush for any convenient place, and aah! It's disgusting.[39]

For most of the Roundheads on board the ships, the hurricane was simply another new experience to be observed and endured—evidence of God's power, perhaps, but also proof that their faith could carry them through. Robert Moffatt called the raging storm "terribly grand." Rev. Browne went up to the afterdeck, which he called "a magnificent see-saw … sick as I was, I enjoyed the grandeur of ocean in one of its most fearful moods."[40] Major T. J. Hamilton shrugged it off: "I considered that Providence could take care of us on the sea as well as on the land. I thought if he intended to bury us in the bottom of the Atlantic we could not help ourselves much and if not he would deliver us in his own good time and way …"[41] James McCaskey never even mentioned the storm.

Naval officers, however, were more aware of how narrowly they had escaped disaster. On 2 November, DuPont wrote in his journal, *"L'homme propose, Dieu dispose.* The fine ordered fleet, the result of so much thought, labor, and expense, has been scattered by the winds of heaven; at this moment only five or six of the fifty are in sight."[42] Fortunately, most of the fleet was able to reassemble off Port Royal Harbor by 4 November. Several transport steamers, including the *Governor,* the *Belvedere,* and the *Peerless,* did not survive the battering they had taken, but no land forces were lost. The *Winfield Scott* almost foundered when its engines flooded; after pitching everything that moved overboard, and off-loading much of the crew, soldiers from the 50th Pennsylvania bailed water for eight hours until the ship reached calmer waters.[43] Aboard

the *Ocean Queen,* Rev. Browne tried to keep an eye on their tow, the little whaler *Zenos Coffin,* which was pitching and foundering in their wake. On Saturday morning, he learned that the whaler had broken its hawser during the night, but he speculated that she "would do better without us than with us."[44] The most serious problem was the loss of the Army's landing vessels, which would render the soldiers useless in the effort to take the harbor. The transports would have to lay offshore and watch while DuPont's naval forces fired upon the Confederate fortifications on Hilton Head Island on 7 November.[45]

The citizens of South Carolina were not oblivious to the inviting target offered by the waters around Port Royal Sound. As early as 28 December 1860, Major General John Schnierle had warned that the coastline lacked defenses. He ordered the establishment of a "coast watch to provide rapid communica-

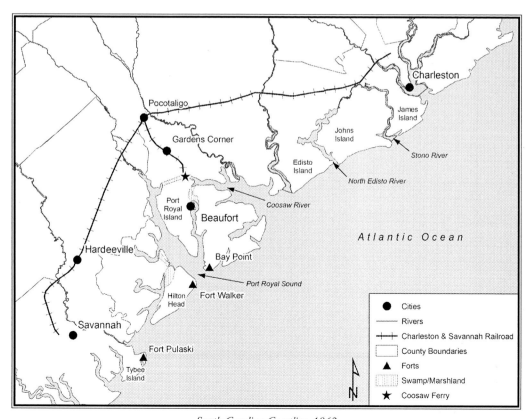

South Carolina Coastline, 1862
Map by Anna Inman

tion to the governor's HQ in Charleston of any attempt made by the United States vessels to land troops or of any predatory or marauding excursion or suspicious craft shewing themselves off shore or inlets of that Battalion coast line."[46] In May, Governor Pickens began construction of two forts to guard the harbor. Fort Walker, on Hilton Head Island, faced Fort Beauregard on Bay Point across an expanse of water over two and a half miles wide. With heavy-duty guns, they might have been able to mount an adequate defense of Port Royal Sound, but those guns never arrived. As the Union fleet headed toward Port Royal, the forts relied on what one author has described as "a motley collection of re-bored and small guns."[47] A Charleston newspaper reported that Fort Walker had four small Columbiad guns, three 42-pounders and six 32-pounders, plus a water battery of three Howitzers, one lacking a carriage, and five smaller guns. Fort Beauregard had only fifteen guns of all sizes.[48] The harbor itself lay under the protection of Commodore Josiah Tatnall's "'mosquito fleet,' consisting of three small river steamers and a tug, each armed with two 32-pound guns (smooth-bore)."[49] Twice before the Union attacked, Tatnall ventured out to take potshots at the fleet anchored at the mouth of the harbor, but without inflicting any real damage. When the Union fleet weighed anchor, Tatnall's only hope was to flee to the safety of the shallow waters of Skull Creek.

At South Carolina College in Columbia, the academic year had barely begun. Less than half the students had returned, and only six professors were on hand. All the rest had already gone to war. Among the returnees was Gus Smythe, still attracting the attention of Miss Louisa McCord, who noted that after a summer bout of typhoid fever he had slimmed down and grown taller. Gus's mother, Margaret Adger Smyth, kept up a steady barrage of letters to her favorite son, urging him to take care of his health, to concentrate on his studies, and not to live too lavishly in the face of the coming shortages threatened by the war. Gus, however, was more preoccupied with "Miss Lou," as he called her. Louisa's memoirs recorded that he frequently sent her "notes and flowers, kittens, dogs, squirrels, anything that could amuse and make a little joke in these days fast becoming more and more dreary."[50]

This brief but pleasant interlude was interrupted when the approach of the Union fleet signaled a need to call up more recruits for the Confederate army, and the College Cadets, who had received only a bit of drill in April, were called back to active duty. In a letter to his mother written on 7 November, Gus Smythe reported that all cadets were traveling to the coast the next morning, provided that they had permission of their parents to join up. Gus did not have that permission; his Presbyterian minister father had long been against the idea of Secession, and his mother was adamantly opposed to his signing up. But there were ways around the need for parental approval. As Gus explained, the requirement was "to have permission from our parents, or assent of one of the Faculty or one of the Trustees; it would be sufficient if we sign a paper to the effect that we think that our parents or guardians would, under the circumstances, give their permission." This was the path Gus took, presenting his peace-favoring father with a *fait accompli*. He reported that his company would be headed for Port Royal and then Beaufort, under the command of Gen. Thomas F. Drayton. He asked that his parents supply him with "some sort of weapon with a bayonet, two blue shirts, one or two pairs of thick (not too thick) knitted socks, and one pair of thick gloves with gauntlets."[51]

Manipulation of parents has long been an art practiced by the young, and Gus was no exception. He played one card he knew would appeal to his father: "I would prefer to keep with the Cadets, for I do not intend to give up my College Course; if I stay with the company I am still, in a measure a member of college, & will be sent back—if I live—with the rest of them, & thus lose no time." And for his mother, he offered this reassurance: "If, however, Father & yourself determine that you would prefer me to stay at home, then I would feel it my duty to acquiesce & and would do so willingly, tho' much preferring to stay with my companions."[52]

His letter left a clear impression that the college faculty and trustees were firmly behind this move; in fact; they were strongly opposed to it. The departure of "every man in college who is not lame, except for two or three," as Gus had described the call-up, would mean the closing of the college and the loss of employment for the remaining faculty. Faculty and trustees immediately petitioned Gov. Pickens to rescind his call, declaring that the state government had no authority to close the school, but it was too late. The governor had already arranged transport and issued weapons to the eager young men.[53] Thus the College Cadets set off for their first real encounter with the enemy, but by the time they arrived in Charleston, the battle was nearly over. As it turned out, they would only observe the results of the battle for Port Royal from behind the lines, just as Gus's Union counterpart, James McCaskey, would watch from the safety of the deck of the *Ocean Queen*.

Another "matched pair" was not so fortunate. Civil wars frequently pit members of families against one another, and the battle for Port Royal was no exception. The commander at Fort Walker was

Gen. Thomas F. Drayton, CSA
Photo Curtesy of Mikel Uriguen

Comm. Percival Drayton, USN
Photo courtesy of Naval
Historical Foundation

Brigadier General Thomas Fenwick Drayton. He struggled to prepare his men for the approaching battle, knowing that they would be massively out-gunned. Their only hope would be to use their small cannons against the Union ships and sink them in the harbor. But the commander of the Union gunboat *Pocahontas* was Percival Drayton, Thomas's brother.

The Drayton brothers were natives of South Carolina, but their views on slavery were markedly different. "My brother ... thinks I am not quite sound on the constitutional rights of slave owners," wrote Percy, "and thinks that they [the slaves] cannot be looked upon as humans. My answer to him was that when a poor [fugitive slave] woman comes crying to me of the loss of her children whom she could rejoin [only] by returning to a state of slavery, she has at least two of the distinctive attributes of the rest of the human race, love of liberty and offspring."[54] Percival was particularly concerned that any failure on the part of his ship would be construed as the commander's reluctance to shoot at his countrymen. Similarly, Thomas did not want his lack of firepower to be seen as an excuse for not firing upon his brother's ship. Thus the Drayton brothers set out that fine November morning knowing that they must make every effort to kill one another. For their mother, Ann Drayton, the reports of the battle for Port Royal Sound struck a death knell. Already lying mortally ill at the Drayton house on the outskirts of Charleston, her dying words were "Percy fired at Tom; Tom fired at Percy."[55]

DuPont's plan of battle was deceptively simple. He led his steamer fleet of fifteen ships into Port Royal Sound to sail a roughly elliptical course. Staying on the starboard side of the channel, each ship would fire upon Fort Beauregard as it passed Bay Point. Then the ships executed a wide turn to port that brought them to an eastern heading in front of Fort Walker. Again each ship fired as it passed and continued toward the mouth of the harbor and another sweeping turn to port that brought it back onto the course, ready for a second pass at each fort. A separate column of six gunboats blocked Tatnall's "mosquito fleet" from attacking the ships not actively engaged in the fight. A tremendous and unanswerable bombardment ensued. The gunners in Fort Walker had little hope of hitting the moving targets of the Union navy, even if their cannons had been mounted on carriages that allowed rapid swings. The Union guns, however, could remain almost stationary; when one gunship sailed out of range of the fort, the next ship took over. The reporter from the *New York Herald*, Bradley Sillick Osbon, observed the battle from his privileged position on the flagship *Wabash*: "The noise was terrific, while the bursting of the shells was as terrible as it was destructive. I counted no less than forty shells bursting at one time, and that right in the battery and in the woods where about eight hundred rebels lay… A moment or two elapsed—just time enough to load the guns—and again the scene was enacted afresh."[56] The Wabash alone fired over 800 shots at Fort Walker; against so much firepower, the Confederate guns were practically useless.

Bombardment of Port Royal Sound, 7 November 1861
Sketch courtesy of Naval Historical Foundation

Such an uneven battle could not, and did not, last long. Capt. Josiah Bedon, Company C, 9th Regiment, South Carolina Volunteers, reported that the engagement began at 9:00 A.M. By 2:30 that afternoon, all Confederate guns were out of commission and the men were out of ammunition.[57] General Drayton ordered a retreat, and the defenders of Fort Walker began a long and slow six-mile trek to the safety of the main coast. They left behind all of their equipment and their dead. Most of their guns and equipment were so buried in the sand after the battle that nothing could be found. The final tally showed that there were eleven killed and fifteen wounded among the German Battalion of Artillery alone, and one hundred killed and wounded within the fort out of a defending force of 220 men.[58]

Much to Sherman's chagrin and DuPont's evident relief, the soldiers did not land until Fort Walker had been smashed into submission and the Confederate forces had fled the island. When the guns of Fort Walker ceased to respond to shots fired from the invading ships, DuPont ordered a landing party, led by Commander John Rodgers, who planted the Union flag over the fort by 3:00 P. M. Not far behind him was the intrepid *New York Herald* reporter, Bradley Osbon, who exulted in his report, "A glorious and brilliant naval victory has been won. All honor to the gallant seamen of the United States Navy." Osbon included in his description of the abandoned fort a mass of detail intended to impress and shock his readers—the pools of blood under smashed gun carriages, the dinner left sitting on tables, piles of abandoned swords, the shattered glass, scarred trees, and worst, "fragments of skull, and pieces of flesh, evidently from the face, as portions of whiskers still clung to it … Everything, indeed bore the marks of ruin. No wonder, then, that the rebels beat a hasty retreat."[59] But Osbon was not exaggerating. Lieutenant Barnes, who commanded the enlisted men in the landing party, was also shocked by the extent of the damage: "Near each [gun], one or two dead,

horribly mangled, were lying, crushed out of all semblance to the human form divine, a mere miserable dusty heap of gory clothes and flesh."[60]

The Army's Expeditionary Forces took possession of Hilton Head Island the next day. Sherman's report, written on 8 November, recorded the sight that met the disembarking soldiers: "The island for many miles was found strewn with arms and accouterments and baggage of the rebels, which they

Rear of Fort Walker, Hilton Head Island, after Battle of Port Royal
Photo courtesy of Library of Congress

threw away in their hasty retreat."[61] As later became evident, the Confederate forces had not expected to win such a battle; they were, in fact, under orders to abandon the Sea Islands if challenged.[62] The on-going policy of the Confederate generals was to continue pulling back from the shore, in hopes of separating the Union army from its naval support. General Lee thought that he could meet the enemy on a more equal footing in the interior.[63]

As it turned out, the Union forces took a very long time to settle into the Sea Islands, not even venturing far enough inland to attack the Charleston and Savannah Railroad, which served as a Confederate lifeline in the area.[64] Instead, they made repairs to the enemy camps, so that they could house their own men. General Sherman moved into the headquarters of Gen. Drayton—an old plantation house surrounded by outbuildings and former slave-quarters. The Roundheads told of wandering around all day, gathering up whatever useful items the Rebels had left behind. Once more, they put into operation their "appropriating system," claiming pigs, chickens and turkeys as spoils of war, collecting oysters from the shore, and digging pounds of sweet potatoes out of the fields.[65]

If the Union forces were somewhat surprised by the relative ease of their victory, the plantation owners in the Sea Islands were positively terrified. Just a couple of days earlier, the Charleston *Daily Courier* had offered this reassurance: "There is not the slightest danger of our being subjugated by the North … They are vastly defective in all those qualities necessary for effective military organization, particularly for purposes of invasion, while the institutions of the South train our people to individual self-reliance, and to police regulations with disciplined order." And on Friday morning, they had been told that Georgia was prepared to send a thousand troops to help garrison the threatened batteries along the coast.[66] They had relied on the assurances of their government that Forts Walker and Beauregard would protect them; when they saw the Confederate troops in full retreat, panic reigned.

Mr. H. T. Boyd, a civilian who delivered supplies to the Port Royal fortifications, was in a unique position to observe the reactions of the low country planters. On the morning of 6 November, he was aboard the Confederate steamer *Gen. Clinch*, on his way with supplies for Hilton Head and Bay Point. The delivery to Hilton Head went ahead with no problems, but the next morning, in the middle of unloading goods for Fort Beauregard, the invasion began. The *Gen. Clinch* immediately raised anchor and fled for the safety of the city of Beaufort, where the crew found the people of the city preparing to abandon their

homes for the safety of the mainland. Catching some of their fever, Boyd decided that it might be safer to move all of his Beaufort supplies onto his ship, but while he was making arrangements to do so, the panicked citizens stormed the boat and loaded it with their own goods. The ship's captain, fearing that he was already dangerously overloaded, only offered to take the paper records belonging to the Quartermaster's Corps. Instead, Boyd and the Quartermaster attempted to carry the papers to safety in Pocotaligo in two mule carts. Hearing more rumors there, they thought about returning to Beaufort to rescue more public documents, but the mules were unfit for more travel, no horses were available, and the plan had to be abandoned.[67]

This was the first real defeat for the South, and, for South Carolina, the first time that the war had closely touched their own daily lives. The women left behind and the families of the men doing the fighting were frighteningly close to the battle this time. And as often happens in times of war, those who wait must suffer as much from lack of knowledge as their men do from the actual experience of war. In Charleston and beyond, reports of the disaster spread rapidly. Waiting for news from her husband, Mary Chesnut, wife of James C. Chesnut, an aide to Jefferson Davis, was in Camden during the invasion. The first messages indicated Confederate success: "At night came the papers. The fleet beaten back from Hilton Head—Commodore Tattnall doing valiantly." By the next day, the truth was filtering in: "Mrs. Reynolds came with the horrible news that the enemy was getting in at Port Royal." When the full story reached Camden on 9 November, Mary could only mourn and pray:

> … read our defeat at Port Royal & Beaufort. DeSaussure's & Dunovant's regiments cut to pieces & 100 men killed. Telegraphing for help.
> Oh my heart—

… Gen. Drayton wounded! One of his aides shot from his horse. Then ammunition gave out—*shame* some where.

Oh my country—

… Yankee invaders have succeeded in establishing themselves on our soil—

… Oh God help us![68]

Grace Brown Elmore, daughter of a prominent Columbia family, plunged into despair at the news: "What times are coming—what blood must be shed—where will this cease. Are our homes to be taken, ourselves maltreated. God be with us. People are flying from the sea board, even Charleston is threatened, the city t'is found can be shelled from the islands, one by one are the islands being taken, not yet has the burning commenced, but who knows when the things will come upon us."[69]

One notable feature of the Battle for Port Royal was the bravery of the losing forces. Among the Confederate records is this report from Col. John A. Wagener, 1st Artillery, South Carolina Militia:

The enemy had chosen a day which was entirely propitious to him. The water was as smooth as glass. The air was just sufficient to blow the smoke from his guns into our faces, where it would meet the column of our own smoke and prevent our sight, excepting by glimpses … the deep water permitted him to choose his own position, and fire shot after shot and shell after shell with the precision of target practice … The battle of Port Royal, it is true, has been lost, but the enemy, I sincerely believe, have paid very dear for their success, and we may console ourselves with the conviction that we have not only done our duty manfully under the most terrific circumstances, but that we have for five hours defended a position against the most scientific and bravest seamen which one of our best generals and engineers had pronounced untenable.[70]

For his part, DuPont was exultant: "This is a wonderful sheet of water—the navies of the world could ride here … this is a gloomy night in Charleston. I shall soon stop all communication between it and Savannah by the island sounds—and it is a far better harbor than either and will enable us to command both in the blockade, etc."[71] After the expedition's narrow escape from disaster at sea, the Union forces had gained a propaganda and moral victory, one that gave them a firm foothold on the South Carolina coast.

CHAPTER 4

The Sinking of a Stone Fleet

Port Royal Harbor was in Union hands. Fort Walker, now renamed Fort Welles in honor of Gideon Welles, Lincoln's secretary of the Navy, had been refortified to protect the newly won harbor. General Sherman and Captain DuPont had found luxurious abandoned summer homes on Hilton Head Island in which to house their headquarters. The Union blockade of Charleston was functioning well. The primary goal of the South Carolina Expeditionary Corps—obtaining a safe southern harbor for the use of the Union naval forces—had been accomplished.

Now, however, it was becoming evident that not enough forethought had gone into the planning of the expedition. The forces had embarked prepared for all contingencies except those that they actually encountered. Sherman had refused to depart without sufficient supplies of ammunition; there was no one at whom to shoot. DuPont had worried that Sherman's military objectives would interfere with his naval operations; the Army had nothing to do. An abolitionist plan to rescue the slaves from their cruel overlords proved unnecessary; the slave owners had already abandoned them. The expedition had been planned for the winter because it was recognized that the South Carolina coast was unhealthy during the summer; the cool months slipped past in enforced inactivity.[1] The overriding question during the first few

months after the landing became, "Now that we're here, what do we do?"

On 21 November, James McCaskey wrote to his family from Hilton Head Island, South Carolina. Although it was less than two weeks after the victory, he made no mention of his first sea voyage, his first hurricane, or his first exposure to battle:

Dear friends,

It is with the gratest of pleasure that I take my pen in hand to inform you that I am well at presant, and I hope that these few lines may finde you ol engoying the same blessing. It is just noon, and I have just came in off dril, and my ies is full of sand as it is vary windy here to day and the sand is flying in every drection. This is ol that I donte like here. As for anything else, we get along vary well.

We ware payed off on Monday or Tuesday, and I donte recollect which, but it donte make any difference which. We got our money any how, and I sold my revolver, too. And I"ll tell you the reason why I dun so, and that is this. I could neither get powder nor caps for love nor money and it was a goodeal of bother to take care of it and keep it in order, olthough I would not have cared for that if I could have got ammunition. And I gist though that it would not pay to carry it, and I got a good chance to sel it, and so I let her rip. I got eighteen dollars for it, and I drawed thirty-six dollars and seventy-nine cents from Uncle Sam. And I sent forty-five dollars of it to Mister George Henderson of Newcastle by Ad-

amses Express, and I want you, Father, to lift it for me. Thare will bee some litle frate or postage to pay on it, and I supose that Mister Henderson will haf to have something for his troubel, too. However, you can ficks that, and then gist take anuff out of the pile to pay ol expenses and you for your trouble, to. And then take care of the balence for me til I come home, or if you need it, gist make use of it, and if I should never get back again, it will ol bee rite. And if I ever get home again, I will exspet to get it again. It is ol in United States tresury notes, and that is sade to fetch the golde any whare in the union states. And if you donte need to lay it out, you can go to some bank and draw the golde for it and lay it away or dispose of it as you think best.

We are caveing in to the work prety strong at presant, makeing intrenchments. We ar going to make regular fortress here—one that ol the rebles in the United States or in any other state and part of Butler County can [not] drive us out of. And then when we get this dun, we exspect to have easy times and plenty of fun.

We ol get along together just like brothers and would fite to our neas in blud for one another. Our regiment is noted for its behaveure and good conduct whare ever it goes. And thare is yet room for any who wish to show them selvs to bee men to goin our regiment. And our company is not yet qwite full, and it would please me vary much if some of the boys around home thare would once in thare lives show selves to bee a man or a mouse or a longtaled rat and come and goin our company. But I am afraid that they will ol turn out longtaled rats and stay at home as usual. Preacher Brown is gowing to start home this eve-ning to recrute for our regiment. And if thare is any one that feeles inclined to come, [he] will bee fetched thrue with out it costing them a sent and without beeing in danger of foled off into any other regiment. And any young fellow that can come and is to big a cowerd surely showes his as without takeing down his trouser. This is ol the consolation that the cowerds can get from me.

This is ol at presant on this subject, and I am geting tired writing, and my time is about to come to a close, so good by for the presant, but remain your afectionate friend til death. Give my best respects to ol inqwiring neighbors and friends, and tel Con Fisher that I would like to hear from him and give him the adres.

Just as he had at Camp Kalorama, James seems to have accepted whatever circum-stances were attached to his location without major complaint. The sand irritated his eyes when the wind blew, but he made no men-tion of the other conditions that must have made life difficult on the island. Rattlesnakes, frogs, alligators, sharp palmetto stalks, pluff mud, and primitive living arrangements were simply facts of existence—ones which any good Calvinist would have recognized as part of God's plan. Money matters, however, were vital. An enlisted man's salary was $13.00 a month.[2] Assuming that James's statement was correct, the regiment had not received any pay for their first three months" service until this date, perhaps because of the delay in getting their regimental number. A letter from Rev. Browne to his wife, written on 12 November, confirmed the delayed payday; he blamed it on the "newness and greenness of all hands and consequent unpreparedness in the rolls."[3] But in his next letter of 19 November, he re-ported that the paymaster had arrived and the soldiers "are all rich tonight."[4] Since there had been little opportunity or need for the soldiers to spend their pay, however, James was more concerned with its safekeeping. His decision to sell his revolver is somewhat curious, but easily explained. New recruits frequently received a Colt revolver as a go-ing-away present from family or friends; the Army did not issue this type of weapon. But some commanders had forbidden their men to carry the revolvers because of their inef-fectiveness in battle and because of the many different types of ammunition they required. Many men simply threw them away, so James seems to have driven a good bargain.[5]

One new element in this letter is an overt attitude of military bravado. Despite some new realization that he might never get home again, James did not yet have any real idea of what it meant to be a soldier. He had witnessed the only battle of the engagement so far from a safe and sterile distance. He visualized the entrenchments he was building as an impenetrable barrier behind which the men would relax and have fun. The same general military naiveté led James to scorn those who had not volunteered to serve their country. Despite James's pessimistic opinion of the "boys around home," the recruitment drive of the regiment's chaplain, Robert Audley Browne, was a success. By the end of December, twenty-one additional men from Butler County had mustered into Company C alone.[6] And James was right; the new Roundhead recruits would join one of the few regiments with a reputation for camaraderie and good behavior.

In general, however, the volunteer soldiers of the South Carolina Expeditionary Corps lacked training and often displayed conduct unbecoming to the military. DuPont was particularly outspoken in his criticism of their behavior. In a letter written to his wife on 1 December 1861, he described the soldiers as "simply a rabble in regiments."[7] Writing to William Whetten on 28 December 1861, he commented: "These volunteers are really a study—they require excitement, [are] brave and reckless as pickets, growl because they are not led into battle, rush in with the spirit of a French Zouave, and when under hot fire turn round and run."[8]

The criticism was in some ways well justified, for in those early weeks the lack of preparation and training had taken its toll. The inexperienced soldiers who were among the first to set foot in the Sea Islands found shocking scenes of abandonment and destruction. The Confederate defenders of Forts Walker and Beauregard had fled in some disarray, and for days after the battle, the Union soldiers were likely to come across bodies and abandoned equipment left behind in their headlong flight.

One Roundhead from Company F reported that on the first night ashore, "No dead were seen but we found fingers, arms, and legs of the rebels that had been shot off."[9] All along the paths taken by the retreating Confederate troops, knapsacks and weapons littered the muddy ground.

The white residents on Hilton Head Island had similarly abandoned their plantations, fleeing in despair when they heard that the forts had fallen. Many of their slaves stayed behind, despite their masters' warnings that the Yankees meant to sell them in Cuba. Gen. Sherman announced that he did not intend to interfere with the lives of the planters, but his words fell on deaf ears—or, rather, on no ears at all. Within a few days, he admitted that "St. Helena, Ladies [Island], and most of Port Royal are abandoned by the whites, and the bountiful estates of the planters, with all their immense property, left to the pillage of hordes of apparently disaffected blacks."[10] Unfortunately, many of the young soldiers, when presented with such scenes of destruction, could not resist joining in the plunder. Captain John S. Barnes, of the U. S. S. Wabash, later reported: "I could have got any quantity of trophies. My men brought me things continually. I took a sword and sash of some high officer, a very pretty fan, and several little things that were strewed about. Everything betokened the greatest haste: swords, pistols, sashes, watches, money, ladies paraphernalia, jewels, etc.… ."[11]

As the Union forces took over Hilton Head Island, order was gradually re-established. Buildings were repaired, and efforts were made to preserve what the island planters had left behind. Private Elias A. Bryant, of the 4th New Hampshire Infantry reported:

Whenever we found houses or plantations deserted we were permitted to take freely of provisions, whatever might be wanted, but were ordered not to molest dwellings … We killed beef cattle and sheep, and ducks and chickens, and had sweet potatoes in plenty. We had trouble in getting our poultry, the negroes considering that it belonged to them, and showed such determined fight for their rights that we were obliged to give it up for that day.[12]

The young Pennsylvania Roundheads were reportedly better behaved than many of their compatriots, but they had much growing up to do in those first weeks ashore, and the lessons they learned were not pleasant ones. The work was hard and unrelenting. Samuel J. Book of Company E wrote of their duties:

> After landing at Hilton Head Island and our baggage being brought to shore, we had to fix up our camp, dig wells and stand picket guard, and make out reports, and then our Pay Rolls were to make out, which was no small job, and our brigade had to build a fortification about a mile long 40 feet through at the bottom 15 or 20 feet at the top and 15 feet high, then in front of it, we dug a mighty ditch pretty near equal to the Ohio River … [13]

Rev. Browne complained to someone back home that the men were forced to do guard and picket duty and to work on the entrenchments on Sundays: "General Sherman seems to think the case requires Sabbath work; and, of course he it is whose judgment must determine what are works of necessity for his army; and, ours is to obey. The obedience has been bravely rendered; but I can assure you it has not elevated our General commanding in the estimation of our noble boys; reared amid the institutions of Western Pennsylvania."[14]

The landscape seemed barren and not at all like the countryside they had known. The Roundheads missed the hills and crisp fresh air of home: "If I walk outside to see the beauties of nature, there are none to see," complained one soldier. "The Palmettoes are interesting; the live oaks with their silvery moss are beautiful, but all else is a flat waste of dreary, dirty sand … the matted vines trail down into the dank edges of the swamps and the hot sun by day decays them enough to exhale malarious gases by night. Aside from the fort I have not seen a hill a foot high nor a rock big enough to throw at a robin."[15]

Adding to the minor miseries that plagued the Roundheads was the shock of disease and sudden death among their ranks. They must have thought, of course, about the possibility of dying in battle, but these fatalities among their friends and neighbors were unexpected and inglorious deaths. Rev. Browne reported:

> It has been a week to try our faith, bravery and patience. Death has been busy in our ranks. The process of acclimation goes hard with our Northern constitution; and many are sick. We brought the measles ashore with us, and it has spread till there are many cases, but in general they are progressing favorably. There are some cases of dysentery, pneumonia, and remittent fever. The latter is of a severer type than is common in our climate … Since we landed as many as nine more have died, two of whom were last week and seven this week; and these sudden strokes of death among us have filled the Colonel, physicians, nurses and others including myself who feel care and responsibility, with sadness."[16]

Particularly devastating to Browne was the death of Benjamin Scott Stuart, a young man from Washington County. Stuart had found an unexploded shell fired from the Union fleet and was trying to disarm it when it exploded in his hands. Browne held him while he was dying, and offered to his parched lips cups of cold water, although he could see that the man's mid-section had a hole blown clear through the place where his stomach should have been. And he prayed with him although the hands the young man tried to clasp in prayer were only dangling shreds of flesh. "Inscrutable indeed are God's Providences," he mourned.[17]

On 6 December 1861, the 50th and the 100th Pennsylvania regiments moved to help occupy Beaufort, a beautiful rural town that, before the war, had supported a population of approximately 10,000 whites and 30,000 slaves. According to Charles Cawley, the town was "named for the beautiful Gabrielle d''Estrees, mistress of Henri IV of France, who made her Duchess of Beaufort."[18] The district surrounding it had produced abundant crops of rice and cotton on some 1500 square miles of arable land. Now, however, the region stood virtually deserted; the white inhabitants of the town had abandoned it when the first Union gunboats appeared in Port Royal Harbor. The editor of the *Camp Kettle* saw clear evidence of divine intervention in Beaufort's fall:

> Heaven's ways are just, and retribution for wrong is sure, though apparently tardy. It was meet that, this, the "sanctum sanctorum" of the traitors should be the first to fall into the hands of an insulted government, and that the "Nemesis" of free labor, so heartily despised and insulted by these proud people, should send hither a Brigade of "small listed farmers, and greasy mechanics" to look upon the handy work of the "contented and happy slaves."[19]

As had happened on the Hilton Head plantations, only a few of the white families of Beaufort had convinced their slaves to accompany them. One soldier in the occupying force later described the scene as the slaves celebrated the departure of their masters:

> These ignorant and benighted creatures flocked into Beaufort on the hegira of the whites and held high carnival in the deserted mansions, smashing doors, mirrors and furniture, and appropriating all that took their fancy. After this loot, a common sight was a black wench dressed in silks or white lace curtains, or a stalwart black field hand resplendent in a complete suit of gaudy carpeting just torn from the floor. After this sack, they remained at home on the plantations and

reveled in unwonted idleness and luxury, feasting upon the corn, cattle and turkeys of their fugitive masters.[20]

Despite the dire predictions of their masters that the Yankees would sell them off to Cuba, the abandoned slaves greeted the Union forces with evident delight. DuPont recalled, "One called out in a broad grin to [Captain] Ammen, 'Massa, they thought you could not do it'."[21]

No opposition met the young Pennsylvania backwoodsmen when they moved into Beaufort. The *Camp Kettle* reflected on the changes that had occurred at Beaufort:

> One year ago, this aristocratic and excruciatingly select little city, would have been a hot place for the publication of the "Camp Kettle," and the citizens dwelt secure from the inroads of "vile Yankees" with their steam engines and printing presses, disturbing the "patriarchel order" of things in general, but the "Yankees" are here, the steam engine and the printing press are here and the Camp Kettle is here along with its editors and publishers, the ubiquitous "Roundheads" but where are the citizens that dwelt so securely a year ago? Echo would have answered, but "Cuffy" takes the word out of her mouth and answered "a runnin like the debble ober to de main land."[22]

Despite the solid month of plundering that had preceded their arrival, there were still souvenirs to be taken. Samuel Book apologized for his failure to write letters from Hilton Head by saying, "I did not have a sheet of white paper for two weeks previous to our coming up to Beaufort and then only succeeded in getting this, on which to write you by breaking into a Lawyers office."[23] Robert Moffatt's diary recorded that because there was nothing else to do on 10 December, he and some of his friends "rummaged several houses in town." When he tried to send the box of "old secesh things" such as crockery and books back to Pennsylvania two days

*John Mark Verdier House, 801 Bay St., Beaufort,
SC. Used as Gen. Wright's Headquarters
Photo by Floyd Schriber*

*Leverett House, 1301 Bay St., Beaufort, SC,
used as Roundheads' Headquarters
Photo by Floyd Schriber*

*Gen. Stevens and Staff on
Porch of J.J. Smith House, Beaufort, SC
Photo courtesy of Library of Congress*

*Fuller House, "Tabby Manse," Used as Roundheads'
Hospital in Beaufort
Photo by Floyd Schriber*

later, the Provost Marshall at Hilton Head confiscated the lot.[24] In effect, everything left behind by the citizens of Beaufort, including the houses, the furnishings, and often even the slaves, became the property of the newly encamped Union army. General Wright established his post headquarters in the Verdier House on Beaufort's main street. General Stevens moved his staff into the J. J. Smith residence at the corner of Bay and Wilmington. Across the street, the Roundheads' regimental staff took over the house of Charles E. Leverett, former pastor of the Episcopal Church of Beaufort. Rev. Browne moved into the residence of Dr. Thomas Fuller, where he employed the services of a former slave boy named Tony. In a letter to his wife, Browne

commented that because the boy knew a "smattering" of Christianity, he hoped to be able to teach him to read the Bible.[25] When they were assigned to guard duties outside of town, Company F moved into the Barnwell Plantation mansion, where they reported having beds, couches, pianos, and the services of an "old negro mammy who had stayed to be our cook."[26] More than one of the Roundheads remembered their five-month stay at Beaufort fondly, as "the nicest soldiering I ever did."[27]

Comfortable though they were, the Scotch-Irish soldiers from western Pennsylvania were not likely to forget the cause they had come to defend, nor were they unmindful of the grand tradition they represented. The *Camp Kettle* ran a long article on the religious activities of the Roundheads—designed, one might suspect, to reassure those back home that their young men had not forgotten their origins. The article ended with this historical comparison:

> Had any of the fugitive citizens of this forsaken city been present on either of the past Sabbaths, they might have found food for reflection, in witnessing the devotion of the "Roundheads" in the forsaken sanctuaries of the "Cavaliers." It is the old fight over again—the men only are changed. The proud old Cavaliers fought for the "Divine right of Kings," while the equally proud Cavaliers of these days fight for the "Divine right of the 'Peculiar Institution.'" The principle is the same—so will the result be.—Meantime, Beaufort is not a bad sort of a place to go to church in, and one of the soldiers remarked that "it did not seem to be so far from Heaven, though it was in South Carolina."[28]

In Charleston, the first shocked reactions to the landing of Union troops on South Carolina shores slowly gave way to blithe denial, muted anger, or resigned acceptance. Mary Chesnut's husband was a would-be senator, hopeful of election to the new Confederate Congress. While he waited, he served as an aide to President Jefferson Davis, and because of his position, Mary herself was sometimes privy to discussions over military matters. No one seemed to notice the small woman who paid unladylike attention to such debates, and few of her casual acquaintances credited her with having the keen intellect to evaluate what she heard. Because she had neither anyone with whom to discuss her understanding of the war effort, nor anyone to listen to her version when the opinions of civilian society were far off the mark, Mary vented her feelings of anger and frustration in her diary.

In the days immediately following the Port Royal debacle, she shook her head in disgust at the criticism being levied against Gen. Drayton's handling of the battle. She was not nearly as surprised as were her acquaintances, who were "horror stricken by the evident exultation they perceive in their servants at the approach of the Yankees." Gossip, too, irritated her. On 12 November, she recorded a rumor that " ... at Beaufort our people were burning their cotton & killing *their negroes* to keep the Yankees from getting them! If they think *that*—alas for us."[29] But her anger extended to government officials as well as uninformed civilians, and she vented her rage against the man who had failed to provide the South Carolina coast with adequate defenses: "Poor Confederate States—if that booby Mallory had only given us a Navy—had he even taken old *Morrow's* offer of the Iron Steamers for the coast."[30] The reference was to Stephen Russell Mallory, a former U. S. senator from Florida who was Secretary of the Navy, CSA, and who was at least partially responsible for such underwhelming defenses as Tatnall's mosquito fleet.

Grace Brown Elmore's anger was more pointed and childlike. At the age of twenty-two, she still clung to the idealized notions of her adolescence. Her old nurse meant more to her than her own mother, and she wanted to believe that black "servants" felt intense loyalty to their masters—even when they were sold—and that they trusted their masters to protect them, often returning "home" when they were ill because they needed to be with their "families." Moreover, because she believed that, she could not understand why northerners would fight against the institution of slavery. "Who but devils," she asked, "would seek to destroy the pleasant relations existing—between Master & servant."[31] As for the dashing young men of the Confederacy, Grace was hugely disillusioned that not one of them was riding in to save her and her beloved land from harm. On 7 December, she observed rather caustically that it had been " ... one month since the battle of Port Royal, one month since the Yankees gained foot hold on our soil and still are they there—

not yet are they spurned from the land that boasted rivers of blood should flow before their homes and firesides should be invaded …" She went on to mourn that she used to believe in "Carolina courage." Now she was so disgusted with the defeat and the men who would not volunteer that she wished women could take over and "shoulder the musket which they refuse."[32]

Miss Emma Holmes, at age twenty-three, handled the problem by denying its existence. She faced the week after the invasion with characteristic equanimity. In her diary, she consoled her "dreadfully mortified" brother Edward when he was judged too "delicate" to serve on active duty. She poked gentle fun at her 85-year-old aunt and her cousins for "running from the Yankees & dreadfully scared." She visited the Race Course, where many soldiers were encamped, and found her first view of an encampment "interesting." On 14 November, she wrote in her diary:

> The weather for the past week has been like the most delicious spring days. The sky of the deepest azure with here & there a fleecy cloud floating lazily along the horizon, & the air as balmy as if direct from Paradise. I sit in my chamber busily sewing on homespun drawers, with both windows open, & occasionally glancing up the Cut, which is [a] scene of great interest now—the floating battery lying on one side, a guard boat with several heavy guns on the other, & steamers, schooners, sloops & numerous smaller craft continually plying its placid waters.[33]

She handled the war by the simple expedient of refusing to acknowledge it.

It was not only the women left behind who deluded themselves about what was going on. Frank K. Middleton came from a prominent Charleston family. His great-grandfather, Arthur Middleton, signed the Declaration of Independence; his grandfather, Henry Middleton, served as governor of South Carolina and as minister to Rus-

sia; his uncle, Williams Middleton, signed the Ordinance of Secession. Frank, grandson of Arthur's younger brother, Thomas, and son of Henry A. Middleton, enlisted as a private in the Charleston Light Dragoons, where he should have been in a position to have a realistic view of the Port Royal situation, but his letters to the women in his family offered only reassurances that all would be well. On 16 November, he sent to his mother some news gained from a certain Capt. Ives, an engineer in General Lee's staff.

> He does not think that Charleston is now in any danger, although he thinks that the Yankees might have taken it immediately after capturing Port Royal if they had had sufficient courage to have pushed their gunboats though the inland passage, but now that passage is completely blocked to their vessels. [34]

A week or so later, he wrote to his sister Harriott:

> It is impossible down here to gain any insight into the plans of the Yankees, but beyond fortifying the entrance to Port Royal and holding Beaufort, people do not appear to think that they intend to advance. Several of our men have gone at different times over the Island of Beaufort, and they represent the Negroes as being perfectly orderly and as having returned to their work, although all the planters have left the island, so much for a servile insurrection which the Yankees predicted.[35]

The tone in both letters was identical: "Don't worry, everything's going to be fine."

As for Gus Smythe and the rest of the South Carolina College Cadets, they were safely camped on the Washington Race Course, north of the city. Governor Pickens had dealt with their disposition this time by assigning them to act as his personal bodyguard, should he need them. In fact, they were once again without a role to play. Gus described their situation in a letter to his Aunt Janey Adger:

"We are very comfortably situated here for soldiers, only our tents are too small & poor. As far as eating is concerned, what we get from the commissary is very poor, but we are so near Charleston that we can buy anything that we wish."[36] The governor mustered them out of service on 1 January 1862, after allowing many of the cadets to spend Christmas with their families in Charleston before their return to school.

In this stage of the war, Gus and his friends were in no way truly representative of the average Confederate soldier, but they do reveal some of the differences between Union and Confederate forces. Certainly the contrast between James McCaskey and Gus Smythe could not have been more vivid, even though they were both Scotch-Irish, both Presbyterian, both dedicated to a cause they believed to be just. If James and the Roundheads represented that element of backwoods Calvinism that prided itself on frugality, hard work, and good reputation, then Gus and the College Cadets were their polar opposites—a Calvinist aristocracy of the elect, their election demonstrated by privilege and wealth, and required by their family position to behave honorably and charitably toward the less fortunate. The Roundheads had little idea of what the war was about, but they were willing to suffer all discomforts, ready to fight when challenged, and prepared to make do with whatever they had. The College Cadets could talk at length of the causes of the conflict, but they were unprepared to deal with the small crises of day-to-day living under wartime conditions. The Roundheads had little theoretical understanding but great practical experience. The Cadets had a solid understanding of their social and military heritage but little idea of how to translate that heritage into action.

It would take more of a blow than a fleet of Yankees landing on Carolina soil to upset the complacency of Confederate Charleston, but when that blow came, it was delivered not by northern soldiers but by a more serious enemy—fire. On the evening of 11 December 1861, H. P. Russell closed his machine shop at the foot of Hasell Street and went home to dinner. A short time later, flames burst out of the building, leaped across the street to Cameron's foundry, and then spread rapidly to the southwest. Hand-pumpers and volunteer firefighters were no match for the flames driven by winds blowing off the Cooper River and fueled by the wooden buildings of downtown Charleston. When the fire finally burned itself out on the banks of the Ashley River across the peninsula, it had consumed some 540 acres, destroyed most of the businesses and 575 homes in the downtown area along Meeting, King, Market, and Broad Streets. Five churches, including the Congregationalist Circular Church and the Cathedral of St. John and St. Finbar on Broad, collapsed, as did St. Andrews Hall, the Art Association building, and Institute Hall, which had witnessed the signing of the Ordinance of Secession. The Mills House, where General Lee was staying, survived the fire, thanks to the efforts of the staff who used water buckets and wet blankets to ward off the flames. So, too, did St. Michael's Church and St. Philip's Church, both just on the northern edge of the fire.

Louisa McCord, her mother, and her sisters were in Charleston at the time of the fire, having moved there to be nearer her brother and the other boys from the college. They were staying in the Charleston Hotel at the corner of Hayne St. and Meeting St., just north of the market area, which appeared to be in the path of the fire. The proprietor demanded they remove themselves from danger, so a rather bedraggled group of women gathered what they could carry in the middle of the night and walked to safety. Later they were able to return and rescue their other belongings, which, after all, had escaped the flames. The next day, the McCords moved to the Mills House at Meeting and Queen, much to the displeasure of the young girls who found it stodgy and dull. Louisa noted that it was full of "humdrum women and children, with the occasional old gentleman" instead of the exciting soldiers and their glamorous wives they had known at the Charleston. Louisa was more excited over the adventures of Gus Smythe during the fire. According to her memoirs, Gus was helping fight the fire with the Pioneer Fire Engine Company. He was so exhausted by his efforts that he fell asleep on a pew in St. Peter's Church on Logan Street and barely escaped with his life when the roof caved in and awakened him.[37]

Frank Middleton's family home at 44 South Bay Street lay two blocks beyond the fire's devastation, but the home of his uncle, Oliver Hering Middleton, at Number 3, New Street, burned. As a friend of Mrs. Oliver Middleton later told her story:

> … all their Edisto furniture & even a bale of cotton bagging (*which cost $700.*) had been taken to Charleston to save from the Yankees, & all was burnt, family pic-

tures & every thing except the silver. She says she [was] walking out of their burning house at 4 o'clock in the morning with literally nothing but her spectacles in her hand and added smiling, "and even that was without its case."[38]

Gus Smythe's family home, a fine three-story brick structure at the foot of Meeting Street, was spared, along with his father's church, well to the north of the fire. General Lee escaped from his hotel unharmed and took shelter at the home of Charles Alston at 21 East Battery.[39] Emma Holmes, however, was not so fortunate. The Holmes residence at Number 2, Council Street, burned to the ground, although late enough in the spread of the fire to allow the family to rescue many of their most treasured possessions. Emma's diary entry, when she finally was able to set down a description of the fire, is eloquent and much removed from the carefree attitude she had displayed only days earlier:

> The past week will never be erased from the memory of Charlestonians. The ter-

Rev. Thomas Smyth Residence, Lower Meeting Street, Charleston, SC
Photo by Floyd Schriber

ror! The misery & desolation which has swept like a hurricane over our once fair city will never be forgotten as long as it stands … A light rain was then falling, & we earnestly prayed for more … But God had decreed that we should be purified through fire as well as blood & and still the flames swept on with inconceivable rapidity & fierceness … Throughout that awful night, we watched the weary hours at the window and still the flames leaped madly on with demoniac [sic] fury … The Cathedral & Circular Church are beautiful, though melancholy, ruins. But the shock has been so great in extent, so sudden & so awful, that private feeling seemed merged into public feeling, and each one seems to forget their own losses to regret that of their friends.[40]

Still, Emma remained confident in the future as she noted that the fire had done much to unite the Confederate States. As donations poured in from throughout South Carolina and Georgia, she saw hope in the middle of disaster: "I look beyond to brighter times & firmly believe that God has permitted this to unite us still more closely than before & to prepare and purify us through suffering for the great position he means us to occupy."[41]

The truth was less cheerful. Looking back upon the fire, one writer has summed up its effect on the city: "With the great fire, the old life of Charleston ceased to be. Staggered by uncountable losses, the people settled down to endure the war with grim determination. Reconstruction was beyond their means in the midst of siege. The swath of the fire remained like a dreadful scar across the city until the end of the war."[42]

Meanwhile, for DuPont's naval forces, now firmly encamped between Charleston and Savannah, the expedition had been both busy and successful. Their highly satisfying bombardment of Forts Walker and Beauregard in Port Royal Harbor had resulted in the loss of only eight men.[43] Now that a safe

harbor had been captured, DuPont threw himself into efforts to strengthen the southern blockade. Secretary of the Navy Gideon Welles constantly urged DuPont to tighten his control of the entire southern coast.[44] Such a task was difficult, if not impossible. Dark nights, foggy weather, and numerous ship channels protected by strong fortifications at Charleston and Savannah encouraged repeated attempts by blockade-runners.[45]

One effort to control these forays occurred in late December 1861. The plan, conceived by Assistant Secretary of the Navy Gustavus Vasa Fox, was to block Savannah Harbor by sinking old ships into the shipping channels. A fleet of twenty-five old whalers, near the end of their usefulness, assembled in New Bedford, Connecticut. The ships' crews drilled five-inch holes into their hulls; they then plugged the holes before they filled the holds with blocks of New England granite. Each carried a skeleton crew whose only task was to keep the ship afloat until it reached the southern coast. This "Stone Fleet" sailed on 2 November 1861 and blundered its way down the coast. The first ship that arrived at Savannah on 5 December caught the senior Union naval officer there entirely by surprise, since no one had explained to him what the ships were supposed to do. A couple of the whalers ran aground while others were already leaking. In desperation, he informed Captain DuPont that he was having the remaining sixteen ships towed out into Port Royal Sound. From there they sailed to Charleston, where on 20 December, they finally sank into the main shipping channel just off Morris Island on the south side of the harbor. Five staggered lines of three or four ships each settled into the sand, some with masts still showing above the waves.[46]

An observer for *Harper's Weekly* reported:
But with a fleet of ships sunk across and blockading an important channel, leading to what was once a thrifty city, but what is now the seat of rebellion, and an object

of just revenge, the dismasting of the hulks, within sight of the rebel flags and rebel guns, is really an unalloyed pleasure. One feels that at least one cursed rat-hole has been closed, and one avenue of supplies cut off by the hulks, and any thing that adds to the efficiency of the work affords additional pleasure.[47]

It was, in fact, a wasted effort, for there was more than one channel into the harbor. Blockade runners simple shifted their efforts to the north side of the harbor and came into Charleston through Moffitt's Channel between Rattlesnake Shoals and the shore of Sullivan's Island. A second "Stone Fleet" of twenty vessels arrived on 20 January 1862, and, within the week, these had similarly settled into Moffitt's Channel. Still, illegal ships made their way into Charleston down the center of the harbor through the Swash Channel. Charles Cawley described the scene as the whalers "disappeared like phantom ships" and chided the citizens of Charleston for "complaining of this imaginary peril."[48] Marchand also analyzed the attempt: "Though an imaginative innovation, it was to prove a disastrous failure. Underwater currents disturbed the sunken rockpiles, and the strategic fallout to the endeavor was the elimination of 27 ships."[49] This move, on the first anniversary of South Carolina's secession, elicited only scorn from Robert E. Lee. In a letter to J. P. Benjamin, the Confederate Secretary of War, he wrote:

The enemy brought his stone fleet to the entrance of Charleston Harbor to-day, and sunk between thirteen and seventeen vessels in the main ship channel … This achievement, so unworthy any nation, is the abortive expression of the malice and revenge of a people which it wishes to perpetuate by rendering more memorable a day hateful in their calendar. It is also indicative of their despair of ever captur-

Charleston Fire Damage, Taken from Porch of Circular Church, 150 Meeting Street
Photo courtesy of Library of Congress

ing a city they design to ruin, for they can never expect to possess what they labor so hard to reduce to a condition not to be enjoyed.[50]

At Savannah, the Union Navy faced a different sort of problem—the need to unblock a channel. The city lay twenty miles up the Savannah River. The mouth of the river was protected by Fort Pulaski on tiny Cockspur Island off the coast of Tybee Island, a fortification believed safe from both land and sea bombardment. The channels were staked and mined to prevent enemy penetration. At Sherman's urging, DuPont sought a way to by-pass the main channel and open a path for a military attack. In late January and early February he sent expeditions both north and south of the harbor to determine whether it was possible to reach Savannah by way of the smaller rivers, thereby avoiding the guns of Fort Pulaski. Because of low tides, these attempts failed. Late in February DuPont declared that a military attack on Savannah was impossible and turned his attention to a plan to take Fernandina, Florida, thus interrupting communications along the intracoastal waterway. On 4 March 1862, the fleet took the town without opposition.[51] The naval forces, therefore, had good reason to take pride in their accomplishments.

For the Army the situation was quite different. DuPont had predicted that at Port Royal the soldiers would be irrelevant, and so they proved to be. The Confederate Army would not fight to hold the coastal islands. Reiterating a policy that had been in effect since the previous fall, Lee wrote to General James M. Trapier, commander of the District of Florida, on 19 February 1862: "The force that the enemy can bring against any position where he can concentrate his floating batteries renders it prudent and proper to withdraw from the islands to the mainland and be prepared to contest his advance into the interior."[52] Thus, the Union Army had little to occupy its attention.

CHAPTER 5

Grinding the Seed Corn

A J-curve is a tool used by economists, educators, sociologists, and other researchers to predict future outcomes. Some historians adopted the figure in the 1960s to explain the causes of revolution.[1] Roughly speaking, the J-curve theory of history says that revolutions do not arise among the dregs of society, who are so inured to hardship, deprivation, and hopelessness that they cannot foresee anything bringing about a brighter future. Nor are revolutions likely to crop up among the upper crusts of society, where the wealthiest segment of the population have no unmet desires, are protected from unforeseen disasters, and see no need for personal betterment. Instead, revolutions occur under very specific conditions of the middle class, at a time when optimism reigns, conditions are seen to be improving, and the expectations of citizens in this group are steadily rising. At some point, the gap between the expectations for the future and the reality of present experience begins to widen, and at that point, frustration and discontent creep in. When the reality of present circumstances drops off dramatically from expected levels, riots, rebellions, and even revolutions on a massive scale can be anticipated. Such a disjuncture, or rather a series of them, occurred in the early months of 1862 in South Carolina, and the result was an emotional upheaval strong enough to affect the region's contributions to the Civil War effort.

Much of the dissatisfaction that emerged during the first three months of 1862 resulted from inactivity. The Confederate decision not to defend the marshy coastline of South Carolina but to wait for the Union troops to move inland may have been strategically sound, but it took away the ability of the Southern soldiers to seize the initiative in battle. The Northern troops, however, were not ready or equipped to make any incursions away from the coastline. Thus, as the winter months set in, the troops on both sides settled into a period of watchful waiting. For the Confederate soldiers, it was a time to relax a bit, for the minor deprivations of camp life were easily alleviated by their proximity to home. The Georgia troops at Fort Pulaski near Savannah celebrated Christmas 1861 with food sent in by friends and eggnog parties all over the camp. One young Georgia private made a diary notation: "Fine day here. Plenty of fighting and whisky drinking."[2] But Christmas had passed without much fanfare for the Union troops. Harrison Beardsley, stationed at Beaufort with the 50th Pennsylvania, wrote to his parents: "I guess I shall not hang up my stocking for Old Santaclaus don't come down here in Dixies land."[3] The 48th New York Regiment "bought sassiges of the nigers and hoe cake and built a fir and cooked our sassiages."[4] The Roundheads played ball all day and tried not to think about how far from home they were.

One bit of action gave the Roundheads a more exciting way to spend New Year's Day. General Isaac I. Stevens ordered Col. Leasure to take his men ten miles across the island from Beaufort to a spot where a rope ferry across the Coosaw River connected Port Royal Island to Pocotaligo, a station on the Charleston and Savannah Railroad. There they were to help storm the enemy fort on the mainland and then build a "bridge on boats" across the channel. The companies were split up. Companies E and H remained behind to protect Beaufort; B and C were sent ahead to Seabrook on the west side of across the channel to seize the works and capture the munitions.[5]

Lieutenant Bankhead, one of the gunboat commanders, had a special incentive to fire on the fort. Some time a bit earlier he had received a taunt from a Mrs. Chisholm, a former Beaufort resident, in the form of a gift delivered by one of her slaves. Neatly wrapped in a box were "half a dozen pairs of silver plated coffin handles." *The Camp Kettle* reported, "The insulted officer had vowed in his wrath that he would furnish a 'line market' in Secessia for that kind of 'post mortem' furniture, and verily he did!"[6] Lieutenant

Coosaw Ferry, Port Royal Island
Photo courtesy of Library of Congress

the island to join the 79th New York; A, G, I, and M formed the storming party; F went ahead to relieve the 50th Pennsylvania at the crossroads; and D and K were charged with constructing the bridge. Several gunboats were on hand to fire on the batteries across from Seabrook and then transport the troops William St. G. Elliott of the 79th New York commanded the troops who challenged the fort. His report indicated that he began to take his men across the marsh on flatboats at 8:00 A.M.; by 10:30 the rebels had abandoned the works. James's company participated in the embarkation but missed the action because Lt. Elliott determined that the Roundheads' presence was unnecessary and ordered them not to disembark. Although one Union soldier died and ten others were wounded in the first assault, the fighting was over before Company C could get off the boat.[7] The battle of Port Royal Ferry did not last long; the enemy retreated without firing a shot. The next day there was only a small exchange of gunfire. Col. Leasure was happy to report, "The Roundheads were first into the fort, and our flag first floated over the ramparts of the first stronghold *on the mainland* of South Carolina captured from the enemy … We are all safe … My men behaved nobly … When we returned to the fort to cross the Ferry, one of the marines who was standing there, remarked we were the coolest set of men he ever saw."[8] In fact, this had been only a minor skirmish, with few, if any, long-range results. *The Camp Kettle* dismissed it thus:

> Some may ask why, when we had made a lodgement on the mainland we did not go on? We did not understand that any advance was intended. The enemy had become insolent and taunted us in many ways, besides erecting batteries and fortifications along the shore at various points, and it became necessary to give them a slight rebuke, and besides our fellows up here in front were "spilin' for a fite" and it was thought best to give them a "New Years frolic" and an opportunity of getting accustomed to stand fire at the same time. We had the frolic, and we stood fire, which is more than can be said by some other people we saw that day.[9]

For the College Cadets from South Carolina, the new year had brought yet another rebuff. The Confederate army's use of cadets, many of them merely boys aged fourteen to eighteen, was an ongoing problem. Looked at from one point of view, the students from southern military academies were often the best-trained soldiers to be had. They were perfectly capable of taking a ragged bunch of civilian recruits and turning them into a fighting unit. They were not always popular, however; one thirty-three-year-old recruit had strong words to say about his drill instructor:

> To get up at dawn to the sound of fife and drum, to wash my face in a hurry in a tin basin, wipe on a wet towel, and go forth with suffocated skin, and a sense of uncleanliness to be drilled by a fat little cadet, young enough to be my son … that indeed was misery. How I hated that little cadet! He was always so wide-awake, so clean, so interested in the drill; his coat-tails were so short and sharp, and his hands looked so big in white gloves. He made me sick.[10]

Nevertheless, the cadets were useful and dedicated to their task. The downside, of course, came when they were thrown into battle, where their academic expertise did little to keep pace with the realities of gunfire. At the Battle of Manassas in July 1861, the first cadets had faced enemy fire. Thomas D. Ranson, walking the spent battlefield, later remembered: "The nearest one killed to the cannon was a fair-haired boy in V. M. I. cadet uniform, hardly fourteen, who was shot through the heart … I shall never forget how brave and handsome he looked with his little dress sword clenched in his hand."[11] Jefferson Davis himself had warned of the dangers of sending the country's most promising youth into battle: "In making soldiers of them, we are grinding the seed corn."[12] So it was that after the Christmas holidays, Gus Smythe and his fellow College Cadets found themselves back in Columbia, tackling their lessons rather than the hated Yankees.

Meanwhile, General Sherman had spent the first four months of the occupation trying to carve out a viable role for the men under his command. His great hope was to see them occupy one of the important Confederate strongholds. His preference was Charleston, although he was willing to make an attempt on Savannah. This brought him into immediate conflict with Captain DuPont, who favored limiting action to the coastal fortifications that came within range of naval gun power. As early as 21 December 1861, Sherman had begged for men and equipment to take the city; he wrote to Simon Cameron, Secretary of War: "The operations on the main and towards Savannah were not anticipated in preparing the expedition. We have no cavalry yet, and are not sufficiently supplied with field artillery. We came prepared to take possession of certain harbors and fortify them; that is all."[13]

On 26 December, Sherman followed up his protest in a letter to General McClellan. Maintaining that the sinking of the Stone Fleet had rendered a naval attack on Charleston Harbor impractical, he pressed his own plan to take James Island and shell the city into submission. He urged haste, since the enemy, anticipating such a move, was fortifying the area around the island. His view was supported by the accompanying report from Captain Quincy A. Gillmore, chief engineer of the Expeditionary Corps: "If we have James Island we command and can even hold the city, and of course secure all the real advantages which its possession is supposed to confer, even if the forts in the harbor (that is, Sumter and Moultrie) remain in the hands of the enemy."[14]

One Confederate officer might have shared Sherman's assessment. Brigadier General Johnson Hagood's regiment, the 1st South Carolina Volunteer Infantry, was assigned to Cole's Island on the Stono River to guard the "back entrance" to Charleston as early as 28 August 1861.[15] They constructed batteries along the river and a causeway between Fort Pickens and Cole's Island, along with barracks and all other shops necessary for the support of a thousand or more men—providing "more of the character of garrison life in time of peace than of campaigning."[16] In late

February, Hagood proposed that this garrison should be further strengthened to become a self-sustaining fortress, capable of withstanding a prolonged siege directed at Charleston. He hoped to keep the enemy from using the Stono to move troops and supplies, but his requests for more guns and ammunition were denied. Eventually, he was forced to abandon his stronghold, leaving the route open to James Island.[17]

During January, DuPont's opinion prevailed; his record, after all, was one of proven success. Sherman made an honest effort to co-operate. General Lee and his Confederate troops had abandoned the Sea Islands off the coast of Georgia, withdrawing their defenses to Savannah. They had also blocked and mined all the smaller channels that led into the Savannah River above Fort Pulaski. Since the naval commander insisted that he could find no access to Savannah except through the main channel of the Savannah River, Sherman turned his attention to the problem of attacking Fort Pulaski on Cockspur Island at the mouth of the river. Because the Navy's ships could not sail in safety within effective firing range of the fort, land forces would have to fire on it from a distance of over two miles. Sherman and Gillmore devised an ingenious scheme of installing on Tybee Island the new and still experimental rifled guns, which had a range much greater than that of the smoothbores. Secretly, work began on the emplacements on 21 February 1862. At the same time, Sherman continued to protest his assignment to attack Savannah by submitting repeated requests for cavalry and artillery, which he deemed essential if he was expected to take control of the entire coast.[18] McClellan finally lent his support to Sherman's original proposals in a letter written on 14 February 1862:

> I do not consider the possession of Savannah worth a siege after Pulaski is in our hands … But, after all, the greatest moral effect would be produced by the reduction of Charleston and its defenses.

There the rebellion had its birth; there the unnatural hatred of our Government is most intense; there is the center of the boasted power and courage of the rebels. To gain Fort Sumter and hold Charleston is a task well worthy of our greatest efforts and considerable sacrifices. That is the problem I would be glad to have you study.[19]

Sherman would have been happy to comply; still, no naval orders were issued for the taking of Charleston. Unilateral military action was out of the question. Because of the watery nature of the terrain, the Army could not move among the Sea Islands without naval transport, and at the moment DuPont had other fish to fry.

While the leaders of the expedition sparred over objectives, and pundits speculated about events to come, the common soldier and the local citizens had little to occupy their concerns except the exigencies of daily life. And, as might have been expected, frustrations mounted on both sides. In a letter dated 15 Jan 1862, from a Confederate camp near Pocotaligo, Frank Middleton wrote to his sister Harriott, wondering at the changes of fortune that had taken place since the Yankees had arrived. He told her a story of three Confederate soldiers who were captured while scouting Port Royal: "They were sent on board a regular mail steamer to New York and met on board a Negro who was going to New York as a cabin passenger and who had formerly belonged to one of them. This Negro treated his former master with great politeness and lent him $5."[20] The story left Frank with conflicting emotions. He was surprised and pleased that the former slaves demonstrated no animosity toward their former owner, but at the same time he could not help but resent the role reversal that made benefactors out of slaves and beggars out of wealthy planters.

Harriott, too, was feeling the strain of not knowing what was to come. Harriott Middleton and Susan Middleton were cousins, both unmarried although well into their thirties, and still living with their parents. Susan's family moved to Columbia after their Charleston house on New Street was destroyed by the great fire of December 1861. Harriott, whose family home on South Bay Street had escaped the blaze, remained in Charleston until May 1862 and then moved to Flat Rock, North Carolina. She and Susan kept up a voluminous correspondence, often marked by Susan's accounts of the latest rumors and Harriott's stiff-lipped reassurances that all would be well. In early February, Susan worried that if Savannah fell, it would carry Charleston with it. Harriott's answer was almost impatient: "I don't know why you would think that the taking of Savannah would involve that of Charleston. I don't think it would at all assist it even. Port Royal is the best base of operations against Charleston, and if they can't take it with that base, Savannah would not assist." Susan had heard that Lee was about to make another retreat. Harriott denied it: "I have heard nothing of what you tell me of Lee's moving the base of operations to the Congaree. On the contrary I heard nothing would induce him to move further back than his interior line of defense."[21]

Despite all the troubles she witnessed, Harriott clung to whatever bits of normalcy she could find in her daily activities, but even she gave in now and then to feelings of discouragement. Her oldest brother Henry had been killed at Manassas, and her father had yet to recover from that shock. She wrote to Susan of her despair:

Our life from peculiar circumstances is such a quicksand that we cannot look to a day. We never know what Papa may next fancy so that it is impossible to expect or to hope for anything. I dare say to a person who has not experienced it that it seems but a trifle, but like the drop of water of the Inquisition, it becomes one of the heaviest burdens that life gives us to bear. It is so very hard to get on without hope—impossible without it to lead a healthful happy life. Henry was the one stable thing in our lives. I had for him the love that casteth out fear. I knew that if the foundations of the world gave way around me he could not change but would be the same calm, affectionate guardian, forgetful of himself and living only for us.[22]

Weather was another source of frustration and unfulfilled expectations. Winter months tend to drag out—cold, damp, and gloomy even in the South. The Pennsylvania Roundheads were used to harsh winters at home. They expected unrelenting cold, bare trees, dead-looking vegetation, and periodic snowfalls that made walking treacherous. They also understood the mess of slush that resulted from an occasional thaw. That was what they knew of winter, and in their camps they prepared as best they could for such conditions. But the South Carolina climate defied definition. In early January, the northerners found themselves surrounded by flowers and fragrant plants, under a warm breeze and the bluest sky many of them had ever seen.

The Middleton family had imported four camellia plants from Asia in the late eighteenth century, and cuttings from those plants were now flourishing all over the Charleston and Beaufort area.[23] Camellia bushes, some of them now almost twenty-five feet tall, were covered in fragrant pink, white, and red blossoms that challenged the beauty of the finest rose. The show began in late December and continued into spring. Violets bloomed in January, and other semi-tropical plants added to the display: japonicas and tea olives were covered in fragrant white blooms throughout the winter, and the evergreen leaves of the sweet myrtle added their distinctive scent. Rev. Browne sent his son Davey some leaves of the sweet myrtle bush and a mimosa blossom, along with some seeds, so that he could catch a whiff of the South.[24] Even the *Camp Kettle* waxed poetic over the weather:

It seems strange to us "northern vandals" here in Beaufort, to receive letters from dear ones at home, telling of sleigh rides, skatings and coastings, while we are siting before our open windows, in one of the deserted palaces, surrounded by shrubbery green as the leaves of June and the air filled with the perfume of roses that bloom in beauty all around us. As we write, two vases filled with flowers of every color, gorgeous as the dreams of fairy land, stand before us, and their graceful and brilliant hues, seduce our eyes ... Ah! "land of the sunny South," where summer lingers in the lap of winter, and impatient spring, with hurrying steps resumes her reign of roses. Eden was scarce more fair ... [25]

But a snake lurked in this Eden, too. Without warning the weather could turn cold and wet. Camellia blossoms, touched by frost, turned an ugly shade of brown, collapsed under the beating rain, and fell off the bushes in mushy wads. The rain itself mixed with the fine sand that covered the ground to form a viscous layer of mud that oozed into every crevice and squelched underfoot, threatening to suck the shoes off one's feet. Sweet flowery breezes lost out to the subtle reek of decaying vegetation and the fishy stench of the coastal waters. Many of the Roundhead soldiers were still housed in makeshift tents, described as "little pouchons—soldier's gum blankets weaved together by the eyelets, two of them elevated on poles with a slope each way, making a tent."[26] Water leaked through the holes, soaked everything inside, and allowed every loose grain of sand to attach itself to the soldiers sheltering there.

The weather, of course, affected everyone. Even Miss Emma Holmes, that indomitable young woman who was determined to put the best possible face on all situations, was known to complain that it rained every time she planned an outing.[27] Winter had one final blast to deliver in South Carolina. Robert

Moffatt described 7 March as "Snow storm in the morning. Snowed two hours. Quite thick ice. Very cold all day."[28] Then spring began to make an appearance. The Middleton family's river plantation was awash in azaleas.[29] The air now smelled of orange blossoms, and the seemingly carefree young women of Charleston began making regular visits to the Confederate camps outside of town. Emma Holmes played at sampling the soldiers' fare, although she frequently complained that the food was served on tin ware instead of china. At the Ashley Dragoons' camp, she tried the "famous camp pudding, of bread soaked in molasses & fried bacon … The latter with a little whiskey or 'kitchen wasser' poured over it, the gentlemen declared, tasted like mince pie, but a few mouthfuls soon satisfied me."[30] On other occasions, she and her friends were entertained with peaches and honey, fruitcake and champagne, and once with a dinner of "boned turkey, ham, lobster, salad … brandied greengages, fresh preserved peaches, jelly & pound cake and afterwards ice cream and of course champagne and wines."[31] On such occasions, war must have seemed very far away, but the pleasant socializing masked a harsh reality that neither Confederate soldiers nor civilians were willing to face.

For the Roundheads, there was no such avenue of fanciful escape, even for a few hours, and miserable weather was in some way the final blow that contributed to their own J-curve breakdown. The first signs of disaffection appeared in the correspondence of that pillar of the Presbyterian church, Robert Audley Browne. Like the rest of the regiment, Rev. Browne was fiercely loyal to his men and their officers, but by January he was having trouble pouring out the "milk of human kindness" for those he considered "outside of the Roundhead community." To be sure, he had not been shy of expressing his disapproval of Quartermaster Lilly as early as their days at Annapolis, and he had openly disapproved of General Sherman's decision to work the men

on the Sabbath. But by January and February, his letters to his wife became more and more vituperative. He described himself as becoming "misanthropical—a perfect man hater and woman hater!"

The chaplain's letters to his wife (and hers to him) make it clear that he had become suspicious of Nurse Nellie and her relationship with Col. Leasure. While the other nurses stayed with their fathers or husbands in camp, Nellie resided at the Leverett house with the colonel and his son. Moreover, she had the kind of forward personality that led her to take over the management of the house as if she were indeed its mistress. Browne had insisted on having his own house, and only visiting the Roundhead's staff headquarters on official business. He wrote of Nellie:

> I say this now in perfect persuasion this curse is going to be lifted off us in a short time. Arrangements are in progress to send her to some city hospital. If they can cure her character there, they will do more for it than has been done in any field, or post-hospital yet … My relations with Col. L. are of the friendliest character … But by my marked absence from H. Q., I have expressed my protest in an unmistakable manner to the relations existing there …[32]

Although there were some few people around him whom he admired, he resented the times he was expected to perform as a host for those he disliked: "If that means to have your time invaded, the sacred quiet of all you have for a home turned into the din and bustle of a Caravansara; and your table surrounded and your provisions eaten by uninvited and unwelcome, because intensely selfish, intruders, who don the hallowed mane of 'guests,' then do I hate social life with a most hearty hatred."[33] He was developing a particular hatred of General Stevens, whom he described as "a poor creature—dyspeptic, irascible, profane, partial and unprincipled as to his appointments and intemperate." He fairly gloated in a letter to his father when he discovered that both Gen. Stevens and Quartermaster Lilly were in trouble:

> Q. M. Lilly is under arrest, the order of arrest having been issued in view of the charges having been received …The charges and specifications are innumerable and the result is inevitable. It is also said that the last mail bro't intelligence that the Senate, instead of confirming the appointment of the offices of our Brigade, had *laid over* the question of the Brigadier Gen and Brigade Q.M. and Surgeon (Stevens, Lilly and Kimball) … Perhaps Stevens is objected to for carrying such a beast as Lilly on his back … he and Lilly have become each other's deadliest foes. Stevens has ordered that Lilly's confinement shall be so close that *the liar* shall see no one to tell his stories to … [34]

Browne also had some intolerant words for the 50th Pennsylvania Regiment, whom, he said, the Roundheads called the "dirty, dirty dutch" because they always seemed to be "unspeakably dirty" and came from the eastern part of Pennsylvania rather than their own fine western region.[35] In so doing, he revealed the Roundheads' penchant for remaining insular even in the midst of a civil war. He explained to his wife the reasons his men preferred the company of the 79th New York State Militia to that of their fellow Pennsylvanians:

> You know we Western Pennsylvanians, descended from the Scotch-Irish stock of the Anglo-Saxon family always enjoy the study of the originals of the stock that come to our country from the old historic land. These "Highlanders" are not exactly highlanders, but Scotch-Irish naturalized citizens chiefly from the city of New York, and their sudden assimilation with our *"country borns"* from Lawrence and surrounding counties is another illustration of the principle of natural affinities and shows the national adage true—"blood is thicker than water."[36]

Name-calling and in-fighting were not unusual during periods of enforced inactivity, but the Roundheads, while willing to dish it out, objected to any slur on their own characters. The *Camp Kettle* heatedly reported on an unfair court martial of four members of the Roundheads' Company E. According to the newspaper's report, two sets of brothers, the Hannas and the Locks, were assigned picket duty along a road hedged in by heavy brush.[37] Because they were ordered to keep out of sight, they were forced to lie or crouch under the bushes. When the Officer of the Day passed by, he thought they were sleeping on duty and arrested them. They argued that they were simply benumbed by the cold and slow to react because they had been on duty for so long. Ignoring their pleas, the

50th Pennsylvania Regiment in Parade Formation, Beaufort
Photo courtesy of Library of Congress

officer brought them to trial, where Col. Leasure stepped in and asked the court to acquit them. The editors of the camp paper indignantly protested the rumors that were going around about them and declared, "We are authorized to say that, as men and soldiers, they stand amongst the first and best in the regiment. Their friends at home may rest assured that no stain or reproach rests upon either of them."[38]

A more serious charge of mutiny was brought against some Roundheads in February. The proximate cause was again the weather. Several companies of the regiment, including Company H, were still living in leaky tents, and the constant rain had turned the floors of the tents into virtual quagmires. Apparently the company officers gave the men permission to go to town to get lumber with which to floor the their quarters. Now, ever since their first day of active duty, the Roundheads had efficiently employed their appropriating system to provide for their own needs, and this occasion was no exception. Finding no fresh lumber for sale in Beaufort, they turned to a couple of abandoned buildings and ripped up the planks to take back to camp. They had installed their new floors and were enjoying a touch of comfortable dryness when Gen. Stevens learned of their activities.

Descending upon their camp, he raged that they had violated the rules against destroying buildings, and he demanded that they immediately rip up the floors and return the boards to the town. Facing their first real reversal of expectations, the men reacted exactly as a J-curve would predict—they refused loudly and profanely. The crisis escalated rapidly, as Gen. Stevens, also realizing that his expectation of instant obedience was not to be realized, called out "three regiments of infantry, a battery of four guns, and two companies of Cavalry" to take away their officers' swords and surround the camp.[39] Eventually Col. Leasure was able to calm his

men, the boards were loaded back onto the wagons, and no one was punished. "Still," reported Lt. Applegate, "the curses that were heaped on General Stevens were not loud but deep."[40] Rev. Browne referred to the incident as "General Stevens' folly" and described it as "calculated to provoke a mutiny in our regiment under pretext of quelling one that had no existence …"[41]

The next letter from James McCaskey, written on 5 March 1862, did not mention these incidents, which might have upset the folks back home. But his words reflected the boredom of remaining encamped with little to do but wait for mail or go to town for a cheap cigar.

> Dear parent and brothers and sisters one and ol,
>
> I take my pen in hand once more to let you know that I am yet on the land liveing and in good health, and I do hope that these few scribled lines may finde you ol engoying the same blesing. I have began to think the time long to hear from you ol. I have not heard from any of you for the last month, but the reason of it is, I supose, is because the ship that saled from New York some time agow with a male went down at sea. At any rate she has not been heard of.
>
> It is geting prety warm down here. The darkeys is makeing garden here, and the flowers, gardens, and peach trees is in full bloom. I have nothing of importance to rite to you at presant--only that we hear acounts evry day or to of rebles being whiped out and taken prisners by thousand, and this is joyful news for us. Beaufort has become prety well setled up with darkeys and merchants. Thare must be five or six stores in it now, and we can get any thing we want, but the prise is vary hie. Stinken buter is only fifty cents a pound, and toby cigars five cents a peace, and other things in proportion. That is the way a solder's money goes--pop goes the weasel. You nead not send me any more stamps or paper, for I can get plenty of them here now.
>
> Or men is ol fat and harty, and ol sends thare best respects to you ol. This is ol at presant

but remain your dutiful son until death, James McCaskey

P.S. Please done forget to write soone and let me know how you ar ol getting along.

Several casual comments in this letter deserve amplification. The report of a missing mail ship seems to have been rumor rather than fact. The *New York Times* during the period from December 1861 to March 1862 contained no report of such a loss. Further, DuPont's correspondence shows that he received mail from New York on 17, 20, 21, and 26 February. There were, however, problems with the mail service. General H. W. Benham, who assumed command at the end of March, reviewed the situation in a letter to General M. C. Meigs, Quartermaster General: "Yet even this small boon of this weekly mail has been denied this department, mails having at several different times reached here only at intervals of three to four weeks, in one case having accumulated to the number, as the postmaster states, of over 83,000 letters, and since my arrival to between 60,000 to 70,000 at once."[42] For homesick soldiers with nothing else to occupy their thoughts, such a lack of mail must have been particularly distressing.

James had also mentioned the daily accounts reaching them that the southern forces were being "wiped out." Even allowing for the hyperbole of the camp rumor mill, such was indeed the case. The *Charleston Mercury* contained much bad news for the Confederates during the month of February. On Thursday, 13 February, it reported the attack and capture of Fort Henry on the Tennessee River. On the next day it carried the news of the Union invasion of North Carolina and the disastrous battle at Roanoke Island. On Wednesday, 19 February, came the news of the capture of Nashville, "the heaviest blow that has, thus far, been dealt us by our Northern enemies." The *New York Times* for 22 February brought word that 15,000 Confederate troops had been forced to surrender to General Grant at Fort Donelson.

Worse was to come. On 8 March, a defeat at Pea Ridge gave the Union control of Missouri. The Confederacy lost control of nine forts and forty-one heavy guns near New Bern, North Carolina, on 14 March. During the same month, the *New York Times* reported other Union successes: the evacuation of Manassas by Confederate forces, (12 March); DuPont's capture of Brunswick, Georgia, and Fernandina, Florida (15 March); and the surrender of St. Augustine and Jacksonville. Florida (20 March). An editorial in the *New York Times* for 13 March 1862 maintained that the Confederates were running out of both food and money. The paper therefore predicted that the rebellion could be assumed to be waning. The losses at Glorieta Pass on 28 March gave the Union control of New Mexico and drove the rebels back into Texas. At Fort Macon the last open channel to Beaufort, North Carolina, was threatened. In Virginia, confrontations at Hampton Roads, Kernstown, and Yorktown caused enormous loss of Southern lives, even when Confederate troops did not actually lose the battle. By the time Union armies snatched a last-minute victory at Shiloh Church, which gave them control of the Tennessee River on 7 April, and took control of the Mississippi at New Madrid on 8 April, southern soldiers and civilians alike faced their worst discouragement of the war.

Mary Chesnut's diaries record the defeats and her angst over them:

Jan 24: East Tennessee and the part of North Carolina which borders on East Tennessee is gone. How downhearted are we, who were so happy yesterday.

Feb. 16: Awful newspapers today. Fort Donelson they call a drawn battle. You know that means we have lost it! That is nothing—they (the Yankees) are being reinforced everywhere.

Feb. 17: I was crushed at a report that Cedar Keys is gone and that they have Nashville, with thousands upon thousands of our few and precious soldiers.

Feb. 20: … my Mercury contained such bad news. Fort Donelson has fallen, but no men fell with it. It is prisoners for them that we cannot spare, or prisoners for us that we may not be able to feed. They lost six thousand, we two thousand; I grudge that proportion.

Feb. 25: They have taken at Nashville more men than we had at Manassas; there was bad handling of troops, we poor women think, or this would not be. Mr. Venable added bitterly, "Giving up our soldiers to the enemy means giving up the cause. We cannot replace them."

Mar. 11: The worst of it is that all this [the Merrimac's victory] will arouse them to more furious exertions to destroy us. They hated us before, but how now?

Mar. 18: Today Mrs. Arthur Hayne heard from her daughter that Richmond is to be given up … Met Mr. Chesnut, who said, "New Madrid has been given up." It is bad, all the same, this giving up. I can't stand it.[43]

This litany of losses reverberated through the military as well as the civilian communities, and there was a widely based feeling that changes were overdue.

For the Confederate forces, the most pressing problem was one of manpower. Behind the original volunteer regiments lay some assumptions that had their roots far back in history. Southern gentlemen, who frequently saw themselves as old-world aristocrats, valued their military prowess as a solemn obligation. Just as medieval lords had earned their lands and titles through military service to the king, so the southern planter somehow felt that his large plantation holdings were a benefit to be earned through defending the land. The plethora of military academies in the south testifies to the tradition that sons, particularly oldest sons, were expected to be proficient in swordsmanship and close-order drill, as well as familiar with battle strategies from the great wars of the past. For the wealthy planters of the southern states, military service was both a privilege and a duty. When the first states seceded, these were the volunteers who flocked to serve the Confederacy. Given the nature of nineteenth-century warfare, however, they were also the first to fall in confrontations marked not by elegant battle lines but by the devastating fire of mortars and cannons. The casualty figures were staggering: nearly 15, 829 at Ft. Donelson; 10,694 at Shiloh; 6,134 at Fair Oaks; 2,582 at Roanoke; 5,200 at Pea Ridge; 19,000 in the Peninsula campaign.[44]

At the end of February, there was a flurry of activity as the reality of manpower shortages became apparent. The Charleston *Mercury* urged the formation of a "Charleston Battalion or Regiment … due to the history and position of Charleston, to the part taken by Charleston in promoting secession, and to the alacrity with which our brethren and friends of the up country have rushed to our aid."[45] Within days, the battalion took shape, as smaller groups of militiamen volunteered for twelve months' duty. They included the Charleston Riflemen, Sumner Guards, Calhoun Guards, Union Light Infantry, Irish Volunteers, the Charleston Light Infantry, along with four smaller groups: the Emerald Light Infantry, Sarsfield Light Infantry, Jasper Greens, and Montgomery Guards.[46] Among those already serving in the Confederate army, the end of one term of enlistment did not necessarily mean an end to duty. Milton Maxcy Leverett wrote to his mother: "I have volunteered again,—to serve in the Confederacy, and for any number of years, which will be of course for the war. I have thus volunteered unconditionally, and my trust is in God that 'unconditionally' won't come hard on me."[47]

During those early months of 1862, it became increasingly apparent that the war was not going to end any time soon, and that southern manpower losses could not easily be replaced without resorting to some form of conscription. Terms of enlistment for the wealthy planters who had signed up when the first shot was fired at Ft. Sumter were coming to an end, and many of the volunteers were heading home to oversee the planting of their crops. Other southern regiments had been cobbled together from men much lower on the social scale—men who had little understanding of the underlying issues of the war. Elizabeth Blair Lee, writing to her husband from Washington, DC, passed along an assessment from someone who had seen the Confederate prisoners taken at Fort Donelson: "they are emphatically poor whites *not one of all* the hundreds he spoke seemed to have any heart in the war & were generally ignorant of its causes or deceived and all nearly were men who could neither read nor write"[48]

President Davis demanded more troops from each Confederate state, establishing a quota of 12,590 more men from South Carolina. Accordingly, on 6 March 1862, the Executive Council of the State of South Carolina issued a resolution calling for "all the male citizens of the State between the ages of eighteen and forty-five, not now in active service, to be enrolled as soon as may be after the passage of these resolutions." Exemptions were to be granted only for those who could prove that they had already served honorably, or those who could prove that they had a bodily infirmity of a permanent nature that would keep them from serving.[49] The reality of conscription shocked many Confederates, whose faith in their own institutions had made them over-confident of the outcome of this struggle. It also had the effect of warning the civilian population that there would be no quick or easy solution to the presence of Federal troops on their land.

Mary Chesnut mused: "Conscription means that we are in a tight place. This war was a volunteer business. Tomorrow conscription begins—the last resort."[50]

Among the southern aristocracy, the "seed corn" argument continued. Just as European aristocrats had sent their younger sons off to monasteries to protect them in case they were called upon to succeed an older brother killed in battle, so the wealthy families of the south sent their younger sons to college to prepare for safe and distinguished careers in religious or legal professions. And as Pres. Davis had argued at the beginning of the war, they wanted to protect these young men who, it was believed, would form the heart of the new Confederacy. Others argued that the first priority should be filling the ranks with able-bodied men. On 12 March, Mary Chesnut wrote in her diary, "Today's paper calls enlisting students: 'exhausting our seed corn.' All right, but how about preserving land wherein to plant your corn? Your little corn patch seems slipping away from you. You need boys, yes and even women's broomsticks, when the foe is pulling down your snake fences."[51] A day later, she quoted her husband, who was being overwhelmed by requests to grant exemptions to college students: "Mr. Chesnut answers: 'Wait until you have saved your country before you make preachers and scholars. When you have a country, there will be no lack of divines, students, scholars to adorn and purify it.'"[52]

The discussion was in many cases purely rhetorical, for the "seed corn" had its own opinion and acted upon it. The boys still at South Carolina College in Columbia leaped at the chance to enlist before the state could draft them. The proclamation meant that they could be real soldiers, not just coddled College Cadets, and objecting parents had few arguments to counter their enthusiasm. Some families supported the new enlistments. Mary Chesnut noted, "Mrs. McCord, the eldest daughter of Langdon Cheves, got up a company for her son, raising it at her own expense. She has the brains and energy of a man."[53] The Smyths were more reluctant to have young Gus enlist, but could not fight against his determination. His mother wrote:

My dear Son, The will of God be done. I have striven hard, & strained every nerve, tried by all means to keep you from going into the camp, & to keep you at College, because I thought it best for you, best for your temporal as well as eternal interests, & best for your country, as you would by so doing be qualified to server her in higher capacities than the camp:—but if this is all overruled, & you cannot remain without disgrace, if our authorities call upon you in a way not to be misunderstood, you must submit. I make no further opposition … do not hastily unite with any company, take time to decide. My own decided wish is that you should be with your brother & Uncle, [brother Adger Smyth and uncle Joseph E. Adger] not from any preference for the company, but *to be with them*, in case of sickness, or of trouble, & for the pleasure and benefit of their society in health.[54]

Rev. Smyth may have felt some reluctance to have his son turn soldier, but he seems to have had little comprehension of what the war would mean. His attitude seemed to be one of "well, do what you feel is right and get it over with." Rev. Smyth was known as a bibliophile and art collector, and he may have disguised fears for his son beneath his concerns for his library. While Gus was packing to leave for the war, Rev. Smyth was preparing to send his entire collection for safe keeping to his wife's uncle, Dr. John Bailey Adger, a professor at the Columbia Theological Seminary.[55] Mrs. Smyth's worries were typically motherly. She dithered about what was to be done with Gus's clothing and bedding at the school, and worried about "all those books" he had taken with him:

And now what will you do with the pictures. Pity you unpacked them. Your Aunts will help you fix them up, & send them—where? to Uncle John's.[56] It would never do to leave them for a year in the College. And what about your clothes, too. The furniture is not much, your blankets bring *all* with you; bed & pillows—what? & what about your clothes?—The best you must pack up with camphor or tobacco, or black pepper, & leave. A change bring with you, & bring some of your lighter clothes from summer. If you have your light summer merino, or gauze flannel shirts, bring them. You will need them as soon as the weather gets warm. I don't know whether you or I have them. If you can't get your clothes packed to suit you, bring them all down, & I will pack & fix them here & then send them back by some one. But do not bring any books or papers or knickknacks, pack them all up there. I only fear the moths will get into your clothes … When you are arranging your room, remember you leave it for a twelvemonth. No one can be answerable for that length of time. *Put up your things. Take* time & do all right.[57]

While his mother fussed over trifles, hoping perhaps to delay his departure and reassuring herself that his active military engagement would last only a year, Gus was taking care of those things that mattered most to him. On Tuesday, he sent a volume of Longfellow's poems to Miss Louisa McCord, in appreciation of her "continued kindness during his college course." He suggested that the memory of numerous happy hours in her company would tend to cheer "many a weary moment in the dull routine of camp life, or of the lonesome pickets."[58] Then he was off to war. He had first enlisted in a company commanded by Captain Alex Taylor, the father of one of his college friends, but in obedience to his parents' wishes, he immediately requested a transfer to Company A, 25th South Carolina Volunteer Regiment, Hagood's Brigade. By 21 March, he was a soldier in fact as well as in title, and was beginning to learn what soldiering was really like:

> Here we are, safe & sound, tho' a little jaded by traveling & the labor of fixing up. We got all our truck down safely, & are now in a measure fixed up, tho' of course we do not feel settled. We were quite hungry aboard of the boat & had to open our haversacks. We are now on Goat's Island, but had to land on Cole's Island with our baggage, & then walk ¾ of a mile to the camp … there are too many sand-fleas & mosquitoes here for comfort.[59]

Despite the fact that he had his own slave, Monday, with him to do the cooking and washing up, Gus found less and less to like about soldiering. His letters to his mother tell of snakes and alligators, flies and ticks, "green, slimy water that promises malaria," and sand that was "everywhere, in eatables as well as everything else." Gus also complained of the short rations provided every three days for his mess, which included his brother Adger, his Uncle Joe, and Monday: hard tack, which the men called "floating batteries," along with 1 ½ oz. sugar, 6 gills of rice, some hominy and salt, and a fair amount of tough beef. Nearly every letter he wrote was filled with requests to send him things that would make his life more comfortable: mosquito "fixin's" [presumably some sort of repellent], fishhooks, "a little bunch of orange blossoms to perfume my tent, & a bundle of candy to sweeten my temper," along with warm socks and another uniform coat. His most unsoldierly request was for "a piece of homespun, or old table-cloth, or sheet, or anything in that line, that will do us for a tablecloth. The table is a little less than 2 yards long and about 3 ½ feet wide. It is very dirty however and unpleasant to eat off the boards fresh from contact with Monday's hat & our boots, etc."[60]

Apparently, no one told him to keep his feet off the table. Nevertheless, even such callow recruits were a welcome solution to the short-handed army. The Confederacy was entering a new phase of the war, when the harsh realities of warfare required all citizens, from dirt farmer to aristocrat, to relinquish their idealism and fight for their own survival. Under such circumstances, even very young soldiers grew up quickly.

During March, DuPont's policy of challenging the coastal defenses had continued to pay dividends. Southern towns and forts fell, one after another popping open before naval assault like so many corks from bottles. But for the Union Army there was only the drudgery of constructing the Tybee Island battlements by night and camouflaging the work by day. Rev. Browne worried about the effect of such inactivity: "What the Roundheads are to do besides eating rations and other ordinary camp duties I don't know. They are too fine a body of soldiers not to march them against the enemy."[61] He might have done better to worry about the changes the Roundheads were experiencing during the early months of the year. James McCaskey's March letter home had reflected a fairly high level of satisfaction: the news of union victories was "joyful," food and supplies were plentiful, and he and his friends were all "fat and harty." He seems to have had every expectation that those conditions would continue, but such optimism was about to implode.

Three groups of newcomers arrived, bringing with them new conditions that altered the lives of the men of the Expeditionary Force. The most benign of these were family members who came out to visit their loved ones, lured by the early spring weather and the deceptive lack of actual battles on the South Carolina coast. Rev. Browne wrote to his wife, who was nine months pregnant, proposing that she allow their son to visit Beaufort. He assured her that the place was quite civilized; it would be "just like a visit to

Mercer or Pittsburgh. Mrs. L. and Jimmy are coming, and Col. L. has a pass so that Willie can come with them."[62] In a separate note to Willie, he warned, "Should you make this trip at all, you must go in no dangerous places on shipboard. You must not climb the ropes or go any where else from where you might fall or be washed overboard." In February, Mrs. Leasure arrived with her younger children to spend a delightful few days in happy family reunion with the colonel and his oldest son, Geordie. Accompanying the Leasures was Rev. Browne's son, whose mother had just given birth to another son and was presumably happy to have Willie in his father's care for a while.

Gen. Stevens' wife came, too, with less happy results. Browne related an incident that occurred when Mrs. Stevens arrived for a visit and found the general on a "big drunk." According to Browne, Col. Leasure told him that Stevens had summoned him repeatedly "to tell him what a fine fellow he was and what a fine set of fellows the Roundheads were (I omit the expletives and qualifications). The last visit, he hugged the Colonel, who was afraid he was also going to kiss him, which would have been very disagreeable as his beard was quite slobbered over with spittle."[63] These family reunions may have lifted the spirits of those whose wives and parents could visit, but they only increased the homesickness engendered in other young men away from their families for the first time.

The second category of visitors included those sent by the government to deal with the cotton problem and those sent by various abolitionist groups to deal with the abandoned slaves in the area. The problem of what to do with the black population of the Sea Islands had frustrated General Sherman almost from the moment of his arrival. The able-bodied blacks had come to the Army looking for employment, and Sherman had tried to put them to work. But along with them came their families—wives, children, and aged parents—all needing food, clothing, and medical attention. He had repeatedly requested that the government make a policy decision on paying the former slaves to work the deserted plantations and that teachers and supervisors be sent to deal with the problem.[64] Lincoln's government was not ready to emancipate the former slaves. The president wanted to see them treated humanely, but he also understood that the stability of his own office depended upon pacifying the Border States, populated by those who were slave-owners as well as those who were not.[65] Thus, while the slavery question loomed over nearly every government decision, no one seemed willing to offer more than platitudes when pressed for a solution. Southerners watching events from Charleston recognized that the needs of the former slaves were enormous—more than the "gentlemen of large expectations and liberal ideas" were equipped to deal with.[66]

According to Sherman's estimates, there were at least 9000 blacks on Hilton Head, "daily increasing in numbers and daily diminishing in their resources …"[67] The description of their activities that James McCaskey gave in his letters reflected the attitudes of a born farmer. He had observed their fields, eaten their crops, and approved their farming methods; seeing crops maturing in March would have delighted someone used to a northern climate. This was one indication of the difference between the official reality of the army reports and the perceived reality of the common soldier. The official army description, forwarded to headquarters by General Sherman, failed to recognize the promise of the slave farms: "Hordes of totally uneducated, ignorant, and improvident blacks have been abandoned by their constitutional guardians, not only to all the future chances of anarchy and starvation, but in such a state of abject ignorance and mental stolidity as to preclude all possibility of self-government and self-maintenance in their present condition."[68]

Other observers of the South Carolina coast saw that huge amounts of money could be had from the abandoned cotton crops. True, some plantation owners had burned their fields and warehouses to keep the crop from falling into enemy hands, but not all had had time to do so. Much of the crop harvested in the fall of 1861 was still available if someone could coordinate its sale and shipment. There was also a certain amount of urgency involved in the need to replant. The fields were lying fallow and the labor was available. If a new cotton crop could be seeded by mid-February, the profits would go a long way toward financing the army and feeding the black workers at the same time.

As often happened, the financial opportunists were quicker off the mark than were the abolitionists. Lt. Col. William H. Reynolds convinced Secretary Samuel P. Chase to send him to Beaufort to oversee the cotton crops. He was in Beaufort by 20 December 1861, carrying orders that allowed him to take whatever he needed from the abandoned plantations. To him that meant that he could round up the slaves and put them to work again. It also meant that the possessions of the planters could be confiscated if they could be used to turn a profit. He soon alienated the army by carrying off furniture, tools, and other items that the soldiers had put to their own uses. A major confrontation flared over the books in the Beaufort Library. The army officers had hoped to reopen the library for their own use; Reynolds shipped the books off to be sold in the North.[69]

Because there was not yet any set governmental policy regarding the slaves, Secretary Chase also asked a young abolitionist lawyer, Edward L. Pierce, to go to Beaufort and assess the need for humanitarian aid. Pierce made a short trip to Port Royal in January 1862 and immediately realized that his goals and those of Reynolds were bound to conflict. Returning home fired by the need to rescue the former slaves through education, he turned to two organizations, the newly founded Boston Educational Commission for Freedmen and the American Missionary Society headquartered in New York. As he later described his goals, he sought people who would be dedicated to "the industrial, social, intellectual, moral and religious elevation of persons released from Slavery in the course of the War for the Union."[70] Working together, the two groups screened applicants and chose a band of fifty-three people willing to sail for Port Royal and do what they could to help. They departed from New York on 3 March 1862, and arrived in Beaufort on 9 March. William Channing Garrett was just twenty-two when he joined this band. He had recently graduated from Harvard and was struggling with a need to do something "good" with his life, even though his Unitarian father was too much a pacifist to allow his son to become a soldier. In his diary, he described his companions as a strange mixture of "clerks, doctors, divinity-students; professors and teachers, underground railway agents and socialists … white hairs and black … Unitarians, free-thinkers, Methodists, straitlaced, and the other Evangelical sects." Edward Philbrick, a Boston engineer, admitted that some of his fellow missionaries "look like broken-down schoolmasters" and worried about their practical abilities. Others saw them as distinctly seedy. John Murray Forbes, an industrialist from Boston, was a passenger on the same ship. He described them as "… odd-looking men, with odder-looking women." He was not sure "whether it was the adjournment of a John Brown meeting or the fag end of a broken-down phalanstery… ."[71]

The Gideonites, as they were sometimes called, meant well, but they received little welcome in the Sea Islands. Reynolds and his helpers already had last year's cotton crop well in hand and were organizing the slaves of several plantations to plant the new crop. They did not welcome a group of non-farmers, who seemed bent on taking over the production and training the former slaves for independence and full citizenship rather than obedience.[72] Most of the former slaves were willing to work on their food crops but had little interest in raising cotton. For them, the newly arrived band represented just another group who wanted to put them to work at a task that brought them no immediate benefits. The soldiers stationed on the islands also resented their arrival. Many companies had taken up residence on other plantations. James McCaskey and his fellows, for example, were quartered on Barnwell Island, in the former residence of William Henry Trescott. Rev. Browne described the house as "stylishly finished, oaked inside and painted drab without, with a veranda above and another below in front and heavy cornices." The men, he told his wife, spend their time "singing in the parlors and playing the fifes."[73] They were not eager to be evicted. General Stevens tried to cooperate with the Gideonites, but he had little faith in their abilities. The missionaries seemed to many soldiers to be just another obstacle in the way of their own progress.

The Gideonites responded with similar animosity, particularly toward the soldiers, whom they blamed for being a "demoralizing influence on the defenseless Negroes." The soldiers, a few of them believed, demonstrated feelings of superiority to the Negro and treated them with contempt, even to the point of beating up the men for their own amusement and raping the women. Others were upset that the soldiers had told the slaves that they were "free." And nearly all the missionaries blamed the soldiers for appropriating the material goods of the plantations, which represented the homes of the slaves as well as of the planters. In some cases, the Yankee soldiers had appropriated the food supplies laid in for winter and even (literally!) ground the seed corn.[74] While some of these accusations were based on fact, the soldiers resented the criticism and let it fuel their already growing disenchantment with their war effort.

Meanwhile, the Department of War was becoming increasingly dissatisfied with Sherman's lack of accomplishment. The feelings against him were summarized in a letter written to Secretary Stanton by Colonel Edward W. Serrell:

> In reply to that part of your letter requiring my judgment of the means wanted "to produce a successful and speedy result," I have the honor to state: 1st. That in my opinion the most essential requisite is an intelligent, vigorous, energetic general, in whom the Army would have entire confidence, who would counsel with his principal officers, and act promptly upon any decision he might form, and who, having orders, would concentrate his efforts on some particular object and accomplish it.[75]

On 15 March 1862, Adjutant General L. Thomas ordered a reorganization of forces: "The States of South Carolina, Georgia, and Florida, with the expedition and forces now under Brig. Gen. T. W. Sherman, will consti-

Gen. David Hunter, USA
Photo courtesy of Mikel Uriguen

73

tute a military department, to be called the Department of the South, to be commanded by Major General Hunter."[76]

General Sherman remained in command for the rest of the month and continued to fortify Tybee Island. During this interval he pleaded his case, still insisting that he could take Savannah if only the Navy would cooperate, but his pleas went unanswered. Major General David Hunter assumed command of the new Department of the South on 31 March; on the same day, he assigned command of all Sherman's forces to General Henry Washington Benham. Benham had graduated first in his class at West Point in 1837, when he was only twenty years old. Before assuming command of the troops assigned to the South Carolina Expeditionary Corps, he had served in the West Virginia Campaign under McClellan.[77] DuPont, whose lack of cooperation was largely responsible for Sherman's replacement, seems to have felt a pang of regret. In a letter to his wife written

immediately after the change of command, he commented: "General Benham came out with General Hunter to relieve Sherman, giving more point to the recall, or rather *making it recall* which was unnecessary if not unjust; I believe *both*, and I think it came from the influence of the *extreme* men."[78] It was his custom to lapse into French when he felt inclined to make very personal comments, and his estimations of the two new military leaders were not for public consumption. Of General Hunter he observed, *"Mon impression n'est pas très haute."*[79] DuPont also found General Benham *"a beaucoup de moyens, mais avec un caractère très difficile."*[80]

March had been a difficult month for the officers of the Expeditionary Force, and their feelings undoubtedly had an effect on the men who served under them. On 1 April, James wrote to his fifteen-year-old brother John; his words took on a new tone of discouragement:

> Dear Brother,
>
> I seat my self down for the presant to inform you that I received your vary welcome leter of the 18 of March yesterday evening. I am not vary well at presant. I have a vary bad cold, but I am excused from duty at presant and am on the mend. I am a litle nervous and cant write vary well, so you will have to excuse a few scribled lines for the presant.
>
> I was vary sorry to hear that grand mother met with such an accident, though I hope that she will get well again. And another thing makes me feel vary bad is that you have such friendly neighbours so close. I dident think it would ever come to that--that my nearest and dearest friends would ever give them selvs up to such work as that. I use to think that I would like to go home to sea you ol, but sense it has come to this, I donte think it would bee a vary plesant trip or site to sea one's friends in such a plight in times of war. However, this is anuff of this for the presant.
>
> We ar ol geting along vary well at presant and evry day or to hearing of victories gained buy our armies evry whare. And we ar exspection

Gen. Henry W. Benham, USA
Photo courtesy of Mikel Uriguen

evry day to have a scratch with the rebles our selvs. The rebles ar firing on our pickets evry day or to, and we ante going to stand that kinde of work vary long til we will gow over and setle up with them.

It is geting vary warm down here, and the darkeys have been planting corn and potatoes here for the last month. And thare is such reports that the war will soon be over. And I donte think that it can last vary much longer my self, for I rather think that the rebles is geting in rather close quarters to thrive vary well at presant. Tel father that I would like to hear from him once more, and please write soon your self again.

The evident discouragement James felt may have been partially the result of his illness. Beaufort was considered one of the healthier locations on the South Carolina coast and had at one time been used as a health resort.[81] Still, the Union forces suffered greatly from the climate and the diseases so prevalent there. During the month of March 1862, there were 17,821 men stationed on the Sea Islands. Of these, 665 suffered from diarrhea and dysentery, 156 from diagnosed malaria, 183 from remittent fevers that were probably malarial, 150 from colds and bronchitis, and 138 from typhoid. Robert Moffatt's diary records that he suffered a bout with mumps for ten days in March[82]

Another 2,472 men were ill from wounds and other undiagnosed ailments.[83] Thus over twenty percent of the troops were incapacitated at some period during the month. In view of James's comment that he was "a little nervous" and having trouble writing, he may have been suffering from one of the intermittent malarial fevers that produced a marked shaking of the hands.

Nevertheless, there was more going on here than can be accounted for by blaming it on illness. The Roundheads and the other regiments in the Expedition had experienced a series of blows to their expectations, and in some ways, they, too, were being "ground down" by circumstances. They had come to fight, but they almost had to manufacture an excuse to take a potshot at the enemy. Men were dying, not from battle wounds, but from diseases brought on by a hostile climate. Strangers were replacing the officers in whom they had placed their trust. Newly arrived missionaries, who did not understand their situation, were accusing good Presbyterian boys of multiple sins. Home seemed very far away, and it was becoming more and more difficult to envision an end to a war that had not, apparently, even started for the Roundheads and the other regiments of the Expeditionary Force.

CHAPTER 6

This Cursed Soil of South Carolina

With all the bristle and bustle of a new broom, General David Hunter took charge of the Department of the South at the end of March 1862. In a letter written to Secretary Stanton on 3 April 1862, he announced his intention to take Fort Pulaski as soon as he felt his forces properly augmented and equipped. Displaying a somewhat clouded understanding of the conditions under which the abandoned plantations struggled, he proposed recruiting some 50,000 "loyal volunteers," by which he meant former slaves, from the South Carolina countryside. To this end, he requisitioned 50,000 muskets and 50,000 pairs of scarlet pantaloons to make his new troops, whom he had yet to identify or recruit, instantly recognizable. The letter ended on a note of admirable but simplistic confidence: "By the next steamer I hope to be able to announce to you the fall of Pulaski. We then shall be able to hold the Savannah River with a small force and to concentrate on Charleston."[1]

The task of taking Charleston and Savannah lay upon five officers with very different dispositions and ideologies. It was an assignment made even more difficult by their conflicting personalities. Despite his assurances of cooperation, Captain DuPont remained convinced of the Army's incompetence. His assistance would be available but always less than whole-hearted. General Hunter, at age sixty, was desirous of victory and a staunch abolitionist at heart, but he was past the point

in his career when he could afford to take chances. He preferred conciliation to controversy and hesitated to take any action on which not all could agree. His second in command, General Benham, was vastly different. Young and eager to the point of brashness, he already had a reputation for acting upon his own initiative without stopping to consider the consequences. General Wright, an engineer who was more comfortable overseeing construction than supervising men, proved dangerously over-cautious when in command of the First Division. General Stevens, commanding the Second Division, was a competent military leader; officials in Washington were considering him as the next commander of the Army of the Potomac.[2] More experienced than his commander, he deeply resented Benham's arrogance and allowed his animosity to cloud his military judgment. Such lack of harmony among the commanders diminished the possibility for unified action.

Of all the high command, General Henry W. Benham was by far the most troublesome member. He had a brilliant military mind combined with a personality that irritated nearly everyone with whom he came in contact. Alfred G. Gray, captain of the Union transport *McClellan*, needed only a few moments to size him up, calling him "the most headstrong and foolish General that I met with during the war." Perhaps fittingly on 1 April 1862, Gray's task was to deliver the newly arrived general to Beaufort. He described an April Fool's Day of strong winds and high seas. Nevertheless, Benham ordered him to go alongside the *Atlantic*. The captain was sure there was some mistake in the order, but Benham insisted. The result was that the waves washed the two ships together, and the *McClellan* suffered damage to "paddle box, rails around the quarterdeck, etc." As the transport neared Beaufort, Benham complained that the boat would have to pull right into shore so that its passengers would not get their feet wet as they disembarked. One of the ship's officers asked Benham "if he thought a ship would float where shore birds could walk." Eventually the crew managed to get "General Benham and his lady friends" to land at Beaufort, but Captain Gray observed that the effort had cost the government "several thousand dollars." He also reported that even as they landed, Gen. Benham "had to find fault with the officers of the boat … which General Benham knew nothing about."[3]

Meanwhile, General Hunter turned his attention to Fort Pulaski, which most had believed to be invincible because of its isolated location on Cockspur Island. Even though Federal gun ships managed to cut off all supply lines to the fort, it was prepared to withstand a long siege. It was manned by 385 Georgia troops, with forty-eight cannon and a six-month supply of rations that could have been stretched even further if necessary. Its walls, made of brick and backed by massive masonry piers, were seven-and-a-half feet thick. General James Totten, the U. S. Chief of Engineers, had observed, "You might as well bombard the Rocky Mountains."[4] The nearest landmass from which a bombardment could be mounted was on Tybee Island, well over a mile away from the fort and nearly two miles in some places—a seemingly insurmountable distance for effective cannon fire. In the months leading up to the final battle, Captain Quincy A. Gillmore had erected eleven batteries and installed some thirty-six guns in the marshy terrain of Tybee Island. Several of these were heavy Columbiads that could shake the wall of Fort Pulaski, along with heavy thirteen-inch mortars. But the jewels of his armament were five heavy rifled James guns, ranging from forty-eight pounders to eighty-four pounders, capable of penetrating the massive walls with their new cast-iron lined barrels and conical, powder-filled shells.[5]

Rumors of a pending attack on Charleston and Savannah had been circulating for some time, and the Roundheads hoped that this time they could be in on the action. When Col. Leasure received orders to be ready to move out on 10 April, no one knew for sure where they might be heading. Some thought they would go to Tybee Island for the attack on Fort Pulaski, while others expected to attack the railroad line that connected the two major cities of the Low Country. Rev. Browne wrote "I think we are now going to move soon against the foe. I surmise our first point will be the railroad, and that the enemy will give us but little fighting to do. We (the 100th regiment only) march tomorrow. It is an experimental move to discipline the men—the Col. thinks we will be back in a day or two, but that we *may* be marched forward without returning at all. Our preparations are made accordingly."[6] Whatever their destination, the Roundheads were ready. Up at 5:00 A.M. on the morning of their departure, they struck camp, packed knapsacks with two days' worth of cooked rations and forty rounds of ammunition, and set out. After a march of about four miles, they set up a new camp in what one soldier described as a beautiful field; they dubbed their new location "Camp Experiment."[7] Off in the distance, some claimed to be able to hear the guns bombarding Fort Pulaski. They were correct.

Hunter had been wise enough to adopt Sherman's deployments and to retain Quincy Gillmore to direct the planned bombardment of Fort Pulaski. The attack began at sunrise on 10 April, just as the Roundheads were moving off in the opposite direction. The Union guns were manned by detachments from the 7th Connecticut, the 3rd Rhode Island Artillery, the 46th New York, and the 8th Maine.[8] The strategy so carefully worked out by Sherman and Gillmore proved astonishingly effective. At the end of the first day of the battle, the Union forces could not tell that their efforts had accomplished much, but that was only because they were too far away to see the extend of the damage. Inside the fort, however, the damage was all too evident. Nearly every gun had been dismounted or put out of operation. One whole section of the wall had been chipped away until it was less than half its original thickness. When firing resumed the next morning, the full ex-

were now sailing through those holes to land dangerously close to the fort's powder magazines. The eager General Benham planned to lead a direct assault on the fort, but before he had a chance to move, the young Confederate commander, Col. Charles H. Olmstead, raised a white flag of surrender. At 2:00 P.M. on 11 April 1862, the "invincible" walls of Fort Pulaski had crumbled, both literally and figuratively.

The Roundheads waited at Camp Experiment for two days, and then packed up, formed a line of battle, and marched back to Beaufort.[9] Once again, the Pennsylvania regiment had missed a chance for battle, and their enforced idleness seemed to be wearing on them. "Idle hands are the Devil's playthings," more than one Scotch-Irish mother had

Damaged to Parapet of Fort Pulaski
Photo courtesy of Library of Congress

tent of the destruction was apparent even to the Yankee observers. The inside of the fort itself could be seen from Tybee Island through two large holes in the wall, and shots

preached to her sons, and the Roundheads were learning at first hand about the truth of that aphorism. No other instances of mutiny had occurred, but individuals seemed to find a myriad of ways of getting into trouble. John McKee, Company F, simply reveled in his leisure time and the abundant food that was just ready for the taking. On 27 April, he wrote to his parents:

> "I have very good times here. We have plenty of every thing—even to fish. The drum fish is first class—they weigh from 25 to 100 lbs. And have a delicious taste—the bones are not much trouble to pick out. I had a mess of fine blackberries on Saturday—the Island is covered with them, and the soldiers, I can assure you, are enjoying them. Corn is over two feet in height, and squash vines fully as long. You would be surprised to see the different sizes of peaches that are on the same tree—some are coloring, others are no larger than peas, and blossoms in abundance. When nearly ripe, if I have an opportunity I will send you a small box full for a taste or rarity. The figs are growing rapidly—the large oranges are beginning to color, and I think they will soon be fit for use, and as soldiers are expected to take care of themselves, I will endeavor to get my share.[10]

Marius McDowell of Company F told of pulling the ivory off the keys of a piano they found in an abandoned plantation house and using it to carve numbers for their campaign hats. Others were appropriating the berries they found growing wild on the island, leading, according to one author, to the death of a soldier who picked the wrong berries.[11] All were growing cranky and impatient with those in charge.

Immediately after the uneventful march to Camp Experiment, Rev. Browne wrote to his wife, deploring the decline he observed in both morale and moral behavior:

> There is considerable profanity and not a little card-playing—connected with the latter is some gambling, which is promptly punished as soon as discovered. My soul is sick of the insights I get here into the unblushing contempt of God which poor, debased, corrupt and *damnable* human nature indulges so soon as petty human restraints are withdrawn or one low wretch sets an example for another of mean impiety. And when I think that all this is in the Roundhead Regiment, one of the best morally considered among seven hundred or eight hundred now in their country's service, I am filled with feelings exceedingly varied, but all of them painful.[12]

On the subject of Nurse Nellie Leath, however, Rev. Browne had mellowed considerably. He had suffered during the early spring from an attack of malaria that threatened his life. In this emergency, Col. Leasure had moved him to regimental headquarters, so that Nellie could care for him. As others had before him, Rev. Browne fell under the spell of her kindness and gentle care. Soon he was praising her efforts to his wife: "Nellie … undertook making some transfers of furniture in the house … The room allowed in my apartment by the change greatly increases my comfort. Nellie has also had my room floor entirely covered with matting and a fine rosewood table put in."[13] He even posed for a regimental photo, which showed John Stevenson, Dr. Ludington, Col. Leasure, and Rev. Brown standing on the lawn outside the Leverett House. Nellie sat in a chair in front of them and Bob

Roundhead Headquarters Staff at Beaufort, SC
Photo courtesy of USAMHI

the Negro cook stood behind her, to remind them all of South Carolina.

The Federal victory at Fort Pulaski was more good news for the North and further discouragement for the South. Elizabeth Blair Lee, safely ensconced in the family home outside Washington D.C., took great pleasure in the news of the fight and its outcome. On 15 April, she wrote to her husband, "Fort Pulaski is taken at last our guns broke the Walls off it so says the Telegraph."[14] For the Yankee teachers and missionaries newly arrived on St. Helena Island, however, their first exposure to the realities of war was frightening. Susan Walker, assigned to Pope's plantation, wrote: "Heavy firing all morning yesterday and commenced again at 10 last evening, still continued till about 2 P.M.—probably cannonading Fort Pulaski 30 miles distant—so heavy as to shake our house. If Sesech gain, we will hang from the highest tree. I look at these tall pines in the grove near my window and wonder which branch will hold me."[15] On the Confederate side, Mary Chesnut realized how serious the loss was. In her diary, she wrote, "Pulaski fallen! What more is there to fall?"[16] Emma Holmes, that staunch daughter of the Confederacy, was shocked by the news. On 15 April, she wrote in her diary: "Willie Guerard has just arrived & says that [Fort] Pulaski has really fallen which many doubted. But nothing further is known as none of the garrison have escaped as was reported. We only know that the detested flag of U.S. now waves over it …"[17] Later, refusing to believe that the Union forces could be stronger than those of the Confederacy, she tried to explain the loss away: "Our men fought gallantly … but the fort was in such a dilapidated condition that the walls trembled and tottered."[18]

Confederate soldiers, too, recognized the blow that had befallen the Southern cause. Gus Smythe commented: "No news except for the fall of Pulaski! What a blow to our cause! & on the 12th of April, too [the anniversary of the taking of Fort Sumter]. We are in good spirits, however, on the whole, tho' this bad luck has staggered us somewhat."[19] Milton Maxcy Leverett admitted that the fall of Pulaski caught him by surprise and blamed it on "treachery or cowardice." He warned his family that the fall of Savannah was now "only a question of time." He had not heard a full explanation of the Federals' use of the new rifled guns, which might have made him even more morose about the outcome. He still thought that the shells had been from mortars, fired into the air "very much like a monkey dropping a cocoanut out of the tree on the ground in order to burst it."[20]

The Federal commanders rejoiced in the significance of this battle. Exalting in his success, Hunter wrote to Stanton:

> The whole armament of the fort— 47 guns, a great supply of fixed ammunition, 40,000 pounds of powder, and large quantities of commissary stores have fallen into our hands; also 360 prisoners, of whom the officers will be sent North by the first opportunity that offers.
>
> The result of this bombardment must cause, I am convinced, a change in the construction of fortifications as radical as that foreshadowed in naval architecture by the conflict between the Monitor and Merrimac. No works of stone or brick can resist the impact of rifled artillery of heavy caliber.[21]

DuPont, however, noted the unfairness implicit in Hunter's taking credit for a victory in which so much had depended upon Sherman's careful preparations. In a letter to his wife, he commented, "General Hunter has not been a week hardly before he took Pulaski. Nearly three months of heavy toil produced the result."[22]

Now that he had accomplished his first objective, General Hunter turned his attention to making sweeping changes in the organization and administration of the new department. Certainly, improvements were needed. The men had been idle far too long, and for all of the Union forces there, the war must have seemed more like rumor than reality. Hunter was determined that his forces would shortly see their share of action. In an attempt to speed up the coming assault on Charleston, he jettisoned the plans General Sherman had made to take out the railroad line between Charleston and Savannah before moving on either city. But in the eyes of James McCaskey, the changes he introduced were not an improvement. James wrote on 4 May 1862:

> Dear father and mother,
>
> I seat myself to inform you that I am well at presant, and I hope that these few scribled lines and miz spelt words may finde you enjoying the same blesing. I have not heard from either of you for some time, so I thought that I would gist set down and write to you, and then mabe you would write to me.
>
> I have nothing of any grate importance to write to you at presant. Only we heard that the Mississippi River was clear and clean red out from one end to the other, and New Orleans is ours. And I hope before vary long that the hole thing will be ours, and that the war will soon bee over. And we will return home out of this cursed soil of South Carolina, and once more bee free from Uncle Sam, or rather from some of his offisers hoo rather thinks that thay ar Uncle Sam them selvs. This is one grate fault that corupts our army to a grate extent, and that ante ol of it. It olways will bee the case while the world stans.
>
> It is geting prety warm down here at the presant time. I supose that it is as warm here now as it generally gets in the north whare you live. And dear knows how much warmer it will get here yet before the solders will leave here.
>
> I would like to hear from you both vary much at the presant time, and know how you are geting along and what kinde of times thare is in that part of the land under the presant surcemstances of affares. This is ol at presant. Father, please write soon and let me know how you ar geting along.

> From James McCaskey
>
> Good by for the presant.
>
> This eight Mishigan regiment is one of our brigade.

Once again, accurate news about the war was reaching the men of the waiting South Carolina Expeditionary Force. New Orleans had fallen to a joint military and naval attack under the leadership of Flag Officer D. G. Farragut and Major General B. F. Butler on 2 April 1862. The New York Times referred to New Orleans as the "great commercial and financial emporium of the south. It is to the Gulf coast what New York is to the Atlantic coast."[23] The Charleston Mercury described the loss as a "deplorable calamity," a "disaster," and a "heavy misfortune."[24] After a ferocious battle, the Union forces had emerged victorious at Shiloh by 7 April and were moving into Mississippi; by 29 April, Gen Beauregard withdrew from Corinth. On 8 April 1862, Commodore A. H. Foote, commanding the naval forces on the Mississippi River, had taken possession of the rebel stronghold at Island No. 10 on the Tennessee border. Five thousand Confederate troops surrendered and 585 remained unconditional prisoners of war. He had also taken possession of eleven earthworks, seventy cannon and four steamers. This action effectively opened the Mississippi River to the Union forces.[25] All of this should have been, and was, good news to the boys of Pennsylvania. Still, the frustration of inaction continued to take its toll.

For the first time, James complained about the conditions under which he was living, but many others had also noted the drawbacks of the climate on the Sea Islands. Early scouting reports had emphasized the impenetrable jungles and marshes.[26] The correspondent who accompanied General Hunter upon his arrival at Port Royal wrote back to the New York Times about the palmettos and rattlesnakes.[27] And as early as 10 December 1861, General Sherman had written to General Meigs about the health hazards: "This is not a healthy climate; not nearly as healthy as the Potomac. The actual temperature has but little to do with it; it is the deadly malaria that arises from the swamps and the very sudden changes from hot to frosty cold. The mortality is alarming, considering the season of the year."[28] Although no exact records exist of the temperatures that spring and summer, the heat caused severe problems. On 23 May 1862, General Benham wrote to the Quartermaster General to ask why his requisition for hats for the men had not been filed: "The greatest heats of the Southern sun are now impending, and the men have no head covering but those little cloth caps."[29] Dr. Steiner reported that in a review held on 9 July, one out of every four men dropped out from heat prostration.[30]

James's complaints about the climate were not therefore surprising; more noteworthy was his comment on certain officers who "corrupt the army." All soldiers complain now and then about their commanders, and during the Civil War the inexperience of the officer corps elicited many such derogatory descriptions.[31] In this case, however, James's unhappiness is in sharp contrast to his earlier complimentary references to Colonel Leasure and Captain Cornelius. James was not a belligerent draftee who resented orders from his superiors; he was an eager volunteer who had regarded his officers almost as father figures. His uncharacteristic outburst might well have arisen from the removal of General Sherman and his replacement by the less popular General Hunter.

For his part, General Hunter continued to struggle with the solution to the problems of his southern command. But military matters tended to be overshadowed by the immediate demands of the civilian community. As the young Gideonites moved onto the abandoned plantations of the Sea Islands, they confronted a myriad of situations for which their college educations had not prepared them. They had arrived with high expectations of cooperation from the local authorities in their efforts to prepare the slaves for freedom. They were dismayed to discover that those seemingly in command could not even cooperate with each other. One new plantation superintendent, Edward S. Philbrick, reported that he had trouble getting the crops handled, because of interference from two sources. Gen. Hunter was trying to call up recruits for his new volunteer troop, and

Slaves from J.J. Smith Plantation, Beaufort, SC
Photo courtesy of Library of Congress

the cotton agents were hiring the men away for fifty cents a day. Philbrick complained that the blacks would wonder off and then return several days later, expecting to see their families and then go back to work: "They are nearly all active young men and are pleased with this roving sort of life, but you may imagine how fatal such a state of thing is to my efforts at organization"[32] Susan Walker also commented on the clashes over conflicting authorities: "I fear the cotton agent, Salisbury, stationed here is not a good man. The Negroes complain of him, and they all look so neglected it is quite evident he has done no good upon the plantation. He drives the finest horses I have seen in Port Royal or St. Helena, gives good dinners, entertains largely, has appropriated all the furniture and nearly all the teams about the place and refuses to give anything to the superintendents placed there by Mr. Pierce."[33]

Such complaints and others reflected the various misapprehensions under which the missionaries and other Northern authorities labored in their early efforts to handle the problems of the abandoned slaves. Susan Walker found her duties frustrating. Her first impression of her pupils was that they were "ragged and dirty" but polite, welcoming, more eager for books than for clothes.[34] She was a teacher by training and an abolitionist by conscience, and the abolitionist in her believed that to hand out charity to the blacks would be to deny them their inherent equality. At the same time, she could not ignore the lack of "social graces" that set them apart from other students she had known. She was encouraged on the one hand by their receptiveness but repelled by their lack of basic hygiene. Soon she was sending at least half of them home from her makeshift classroom each morning to wash their hands and faces before she would teach them. Not long after her arrival, she visited the Jenkins' plantation, about eight miles away, where she met a very pregnant slave woman whose problems overwhelmed her. "Katy has 7 ragged, dirty children—what shall be done? No husband and *nothing*. Some clothes are given for her children—one naked, and must have it at once. Is Katy lazy? Very likely. Does she tell the truth? Perhaps not. I must have faith, and she must at least cover her children."[35]

Philbrick's reaction was somewhat more admiring, although he recognized that his wife might have reservations about working with the former slaves. He warned her that she could not bring a servant with her if she chose to join him: "There are plenty of servants here, which you are supposed to teach not only to read but—what is more immediately important—to be *clean* and industrious. If you feel any hesitation about coming in contact with them you shouldn't come, for they are sharp enough to detect apathy or lurking repugnance, which would render any amount of theoretical sympathy about worthless."[36] Perhaps because he looked for signs that a slave was fully capable of full citizenship, he found much to commend: "Think of their having reorganized and gone deliberately to work here some weeks ago, without a white man near them, preparing hundreds of acres for the new crop! The Irish wouldn't have done as much in the same position."[37]

Two habits of the former slaves seemed particularly to confound those who had come to help them make the transition from slavery to full citizenship—their distinctive religious ceremonies and their deference toward whites. The missionaries did their best to teach the lessons of Christianity and to re-introduce regular worship services on each plantation. The blacks were attentive and respectful, but when the official services were over, they pushed back the furniture and organized their own religious celebration known as the "Shout." Sometimes the whites were invited to observe, although never to participate, and several of the missionaries tried to describe what they saw:

… when the "sperichil" is struck up, [they] begin first walking and by-and-by shuffling round, one after the other, in a ring. The foot is hardly taken from the floor, and the progression is mainly due to a jerking, hitching motion, which agitates the entire shouter, and soon brings out streams of perspiration. Sometimes they dance silently, sometimes as they shuffle they sing the chorus of the spiritual, and sometimes the song itself is also sung by the dancers. But more frequently a band, composed of some of the best singers and of tired shouters, stand at the side of the room to "base" the others, singing the body of the song and clapping their hands together or on the knees. Song and dance are alike extremely energetic, and often, when the shout lasts into the middle of the night, the monotonous thud, thud, of the feet prevents sleep within a half a mile of the praise-house.[38]

Disapproval was widespread. Some of the easily shocked missionaries called the practice "the remains of some old idol worship," "the most hideous and at the same time the most pitiful sight I ever witnessed," "savage," or "barbarous." Other observers considered it an "amazing and primitive manifestation of the Negro spirit … Some 'heel and toe' tumultuously, others merely tremble and stagger on, others swoop and rise, others whirl, others caper sideways, all keep steadily circling like dervishes …"[39]

What many failed to recognize was that the "Shout" served important purposes. It was a chance for slaves to escape the rigors of the workday, and to exercise a bit of creativity and self-expression. The adults might disapprove of young people dancing "out in the world," but in the "Shout" they could turn a natural inclination into a form of worship. The songs were improvised but very creative, and provided a chance to articulate the longings that masters would not allow under ordinary circumstances. They expressed a desire for escape, even if it was through death. The best of the missionaries saw in the "Shout" a unique combination of ancient cultural traits and the new faith of Christianity. The worst ones could not come to terms with what they did not understand.

The second major problem facing the missionaries was their inability to reconcile their relationships with the abandoned slaves and their preconceived abolitionist ideals. For almost every one of the teachers and plantation managers, the goal was to train the blacks for full freedom, equality, and citizenship. Yet, they found themselves cast in the roles abandoned by the former slave owners. The women teachers discovered that they were more warmly welcomed in the slave quarters than were their male counterparts, primarily because they were taking the place of the plantation mistress. The blacks found the white women stabilizing and reassuring, a source of medical "learning," and conveyers of the education that was the key to freedom.[40] The white men, on the other hand, were seen as the labor bosses. Because the newcomers knew little or nothing about raising cotton, they had to rely on the former slaves, first to teach them what needed to be done, and then to do it. However, that put the blacks into their old roles as workers and automatically cast the whites as the masters.[41] The blacks' reluctance to work in the cotton fields made the problems worse. They labored readily enough when they were planting food crops, because they understood that they were thereby feeding themselves. But few appreciated the value of cotton because they had never shared in the rewards of the crop.[42] So when the plantation manager ordered them into the cotton fields, the natural response was, "Yes, Massa," and the work was just as backbreaking as it had always been.

Despite their best efforts, the Gideonites were failing to communicate their basic message that whites and blacks were equal. Philbrick and the others remained convinced that the blacks could be trained for full citizenship, but they had not counted on having to overcome the deference that the blacks expressed toward whites simply because they were white. The frustrating problem resulted from the missionaries' failure to understand the slave culture under which the blacks had lived for so long. As one study explains, "The

Negroes had long dwelt in a strict hierarchy in which the ideal white man not only lived upon the labor of his slave but also accorded him a kindly protection … The ingratiating dependence of 'Sambo' had been a superb defense for the helpless slave." The Gideonites did not understand that this dependence and deference was "one of conscious playacting."[43] They simply interpreted it as another obstacle to be overcome before the slaves were ready for full emancipation. Susan Walker described the attitude of the slaves in one of her letters:

> With a few exceptions, the laborers have gone about their work as in the master's time. All understand the planting better than we can teach them, but they need encouragement. They have not yet become self-reliant. Many are well-disposed and work willingly when made to understand that the corn, which they so willingly plant, is to furnish them food, but the cotton must also be planted for Government, and for this planting wages will be paid them and with their wages they must buy clothes, sweeting and tobacco or have none.[44]

General Hunter's solution was quicker, more expedient, and far less attuned to the anti-abolitionist sentiments still prevalent in much of the Union. He simply emancipated the former slaves. In an order issued from Hilton Head on 9 May 1862, he wrote:

> The three States of Georgia, Florida, and South Carolina, comprising the Military Department of the South, having deliberately declared themselves no longer under the protection of the United States of America, and having taken up arms against said United States, it became a military necessity to declare martial law. This was accordingly done the 25th day of April, 1862. Slavery and martial law in a free country are altogether incompatible; the persons in these three States, Georgia, Florida, and South Carolina, heretofore held as slaves, are therefore declared forever free.[45]

Both the North and the South regarded the proclamation with disapproval. The *New York Times* dismissed it as absurd: "His declaring freedom to all the slaves in three States, when he has no power to free a single one outside of his camp, is regarded in Washington as an act of stultification highly discreditable to any one holding the rank of General, supposed to have ordinary intelligence."[46]

On St. Helena Island, the missionaries were as surprised as anyone else to learn of the emancipation, and their reaction reflected their ambivalence toward the former slaves' preparation for independence. Philbrick did not think that the emancipation decree was a very good idea, and he seemed to expect Hunter to lose his job over it. As for the blacks, he called the effect of the proclamation " … inconsiderable. They don't hear of it, to begin with, and if they did they wouldn't care for it."[47] On the day the emancipation was announced, however, Harriet Ware overheard one of the house servants tell someone, "Don't call me 'Joe'; my name is Mr. Jenkins."[48] It was a lovely expression of what freedom might mean to former slaves, but the reality was something quite different.

Hunter immediately followed up his proclamation with an intensified drive to recruit soldiers from the newly emancipated slaves. On Sunday, 11 May, "Capt. Hazard Stevens arrived at Pope's Plantation on St. Helena Island, bearing an order from General Hunter notifying the plantation that on Monday morning 'all colored men between 18 and 45 capable of bearing arms shall be taken to Hilton Head'—no explanation."[49] Susan Walker was particularly horrified to discover that her duties as plantation manager required her to provide a list of all those who qualified: "I write the names almost as signing their death warrants. The saddest duty I ever performed."[50] The next day she described the scene as Stevens came back for the men, lining them up at gunpoint. "The men were called from the field and thus hurried off without time for coat or shoes or a good-bye to their families … Women wept and children screamed as men were torn from their embrace. This is a sad day throughout these islands … Mr. Pierce has gone to Hilton Head to see General Hunter about it."[51]

The same order to call up able-bodied Negroes came to Pine Grove Plantation on 12 May, and Harriet Ware described the pain it causes her: "You never saw a more wretched set of people than sat down to our breakfast table. I *could not* eat, for about the first time in my life."[52] Here, however, the blacks were treated more gently, with the soldiers cheering up the blacks by telling them of the money they were going to make and the fine uniforms they would receive. They also allowed some house-servants and drivers to remain for the "good of the plantation."[53]

Edward Philbrick joined Mr. Pierce on his trip to Hilton Head to confront Gen. Hunter about this latest move. They received a plausible explanation of what was going on, although many did not believe it. Hunter had not gotten the black volunteers he sought, they were told, and so these were temporary measures, designed to give the men a taste of military life and drill, in hopes that more of them would be willing to volunteer. Harriet Ware was one of the doubters: "If we can have blacks to garrison the forts and save our soldiers through the hot weather, everyone will be thankful. But I don't believe you could make soldiers of these men at all—they are afraid, and they know it."[54] William C. Garrett echoed her sentiments: "Negroes—plantation negroes, at least—will never make soldiers in one generation. Five white men could put a regiment to flight; but they may be very useful in preventing sickness and death among our troops by relieving them of part of their work, and they may acquire a certain self-respect and independence which more than anything else

they need to feel, if they are soon to stand by their own strength."[55]

Hunter's effort to form a regiment of black soldiers immediately encountered almost insurmountable problems. Neither the military hierarchy nor the civilian missionaries and cotton agents had a full understanding of what the "land" meant to those who worked it. Northerners harbored an assumption that newly freed slaves would eagerly leave the plantations where they had worked against their will. The Gideonites were there to offer training for such freedom, and General Hunter and his staff offered immediate employment in the Union army. None of them seemed to understand that while the slaves might have resented their inferior status, they regarded their little cabins and the plots of land they worked as home—the only home most of them had ever known. Being free did not mean a chance to flee; it meant a chance to manage the land as they saw fit. They had refused to leave the Sea Islands in November when their masters had fled before the arrival of the Expeditionary Forces. They refused to leave in May when Gen. Hunter tried to lure them into military service.

Another difficulty Hunter faced was the lack of administrative support. Since his scheme did not have official governmental approval, he had to scrounge for staff officers. Some of the Roundheads, invited to help with the formation of the black regiment, witnessed at first hand the unit's problems of leadership and organization. John H. Stevenson reminisced:

> This was called the 1st South Carolina Volunteers, though the fact of volunteering was far from being a fact, as many of the slaves were brought in as recruits by squads of armed white soldiers. [I] was tendered a commission, but Col. Leasure dissuaded me from accepting the same, though quite a number of "Round Heads" were accepted as captains [and] lieutenants, and this regiment was sub-

sequently disbanded as the government did not seem to be ready for such a bold scheme.[56]

The real problem was that the Federal government was not yet ready to accept emancipation, and President Lincoln acted quickly to repeal Hunter's decree. On 19 May, he issued the following statement:

> I, Abraham Lincoln, president of the United States, proclaim and declare, that the government of the United States, had no knowledge, information, or belief, of an intention on the part of General Hunter to issue such a proclamation; nor has it yet, any authentic information that the document is genuine. And further, that neither General Hunter, nor any other commander, or person, has been authorized by the Government of the United States, to make proclamations declaring the slaves of any State free; and that the supposed proclamation, now in question, whether genuine or false, is altogether void, so far as respects such declaration.[57]

Lincoln went on to explain that he would encourage any state to consider the gradual emancipation of slaves and would offer the cooperation of the federal government in such efforts, but Hunter's decree was effectively dead. Most of the blacks rounded up in the recruitment drive of 12 May were home within ten days.[58]

For one slave, however, that ten-day period of freedom provided both the opportunity and the determination to make a permanent impact on the course of the war. Robert Smalls was a twenty-three-year-old slave who had worked on ships in Charleston Harbor since he was twelve. In the spring of 1862, he was employed on the side-wheeler *Planter*, flagship of Brigadier General Roswell Ripley, deputy commander of all Charleston defenses. This shallow-draft boat, 150 feet long and 46 feet wide, supplied Confederate outposts along the coasts because it could carry heavy

loads of armaments through the shallow passages of the Sea Islands. In the days just prior to Hunter's emancipation proclamation, the

Robert Smalls
Photo courtesy of Library of Congress

captain, C. J. Relyea, and his crew of three whites and eight slaves had been helping to evacuate General Hagood's troops from their base on Cole's Island. Smalls was a better seaman than the ship's captain, and often worked in the wheelhouse, actually steering the ship while the captain struck a swashbuckling pose on the deck. Ripley and Relyea trusted Smalls but gravely under-estimated his intelligence. They freely discussed military orders, strategies, passwords, and secret signals in front of the slaves, wrongly assuming they would not understand or remember what they heard.

As Smalls watched the developments on Cole's Island, he stored away every tidbit he could gather, always looking forward to the day when he could make an escape. By 10 May, when Hunter announced that he was freeing the slaves, Smalls had his plans well organized. He had taken into his confidence the other slaves in the ship's crew, promising them that he could take them, along with their families, safely into Union hands. Smalls' wife and young children were in hiding, along with several other wives, on a boat concealed on a nearby island. Everyone was waiting for the chance to present itself.

On the evening of 12 May, the *Planter* docked at Charleston. Captain Relyea and the other white officers left the ship to visit their homes, and Gen. Ripley was attending a party in Charleston, leaving Smalls in charge of the ship. Smalls made no move until 3:00 A.M. Then he hoisted the Confederate flag and sailed out into the harbor, observing every protocol as it would have been carried out under Relyea's command. The ship made one quick stop to take aboard the five women and three children who were huddled in their small boat and then sailed straight for Fort Sumter. To further the subterfuge, Smalls put on the captain's braided jacket and trademark straw hat, taking on the captain's jaunty stance on the deck and hoping that the shadows of early dawn would hide the difference in pigmentation. As they passed Fort Sumter, he gave the secret countersign by blowing the whistle in a pre-arranged code. It worked. Waved on by the Officer of the Day, the *Planter* sailed out into the harbor mouth. Then it made a quick turn, hoisted a white flag of truce, and headed straight for the nearest ship in the Union fleet that had been blockading the southern coast ever since November. When officers of the *U. S. Onward* boarded the smaller ship, Smalls announced proudly, "I have the honor, sir, to present the *Planter*, formerly the flagship of General Ripley … I thought they [its armaments] might be of some service to Uncle Abe."[59]

He delivered to the Yankees the four cannons that were aboard the *Planter*, but his more important contribution was his knowledge of what the Confederate forces were planning. He knew that on 16 April, the Marion Rifles and the Eutaw Battalion had joined the effort to evacuate Cole's Island. They had constructed footbridges across the Stono River as an avenue of escape in case the road was cut off along the Stono to Battery Island. Then, to "keep up appearances," they had placed dummy cannon where they had removed the real ones. The flag still flew and the men simulated complete military occupation although there were only about thirty soldiers there. All buildings were prepared for destruction by burning when fired upon by the federal fleet.[60] That news meant that the way was open for Union troops to move onto James Island via the Stono River in preparation for the taking of Charleston itself.

James Island lies on the south side of Charleston Harbor. Its major fortification, Fort Johnson, formed a triangle with Fort Sumter and Castle Pinckney to provide vital protection for the city. Union officials generally recognized that Fort Johnson was the "key to Charleston."[61] General Sherman had proposed a plan to bypass Charleston Harbor by taking James Island shortly after the arrival of the Expeditionary Corps, but no one had worked out the logistics of such an attack. Now General Hunter, flush with his first success, felt a need to follow up the victory at Fort Pulaski with one of his own design. Charleston was an ideal target. The most serious obstacle to such an attack was the need for close cooperation between the Army and the Navy and DuPont's reluctance to provide assistance. The solution came from an enterprising young naval officer in his first real position of command.

John B. Marchand commanded the small fleet of ships blockading Charleston Harbor. From his vantage point offshore, he daily observed the difficulties involved in attacking the city from the water. The major channel into the harbor was open but defended by Forts Sumter and Moultrie on the east and Fort Johnson on James Island to the west. He recognized, as naval officers further removed from the scene did not, that, if military forces

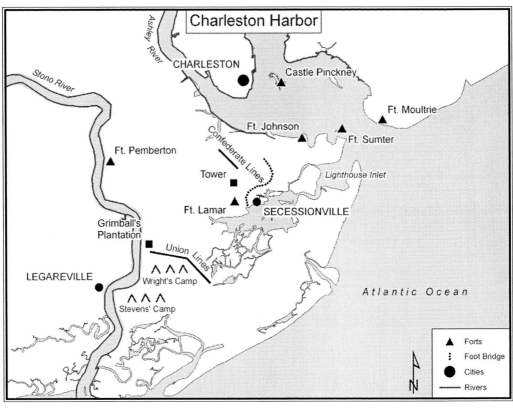

Fortifications on James Island and Charleston Harbor
Map by Anna Inman

could take out the guns at Fort Johnson from the rear, the Navy would have a much easier time penetrating the harbor defenses. Marchand turned his thoughts to this problem and shortly discovered the solution. The mouth of the Stono River lay out of sight of Confederate defenses. If navy ships could find a way to cross the bar that blocked access to the river, army troops could land on James Island.

After several abortive tries, Marchand succeeded in getting several boats of shallow draft across the bar on 20 May 1862. The few Confederate soldiers left behind to guard the shores of the river set fire to their outposts and fled at the sight of Marchand's gunboats. The Confederate commander at Fort Pickens described the retreat in honorable terms as a prudent withdrawal, but Marchand's journal recorded that they "took to their heels and ran for their lives."[62] A bit farther up the river,

Marchand's men had an even more pleasant surprise. Mr. Paul Grimball, a Union sympathizer, owned a plantation on the banks of the river; he was willing to facilitate the landing and encampment of the army. The logistics were in place; now it was finally time for the Union troops to move to James Island.

Meanwhile, Charleston itself was in turmoil. At the beginning of April, James Island had been still in the hands of the Confederates and considered safe enough for Miss Emma Holmes and her friends to visit the soldiers for picnics. For the young women of Charleston who spend the early spring of 1862 riding, sailing, dancing, and attending the dress parades at the Citadel, James Island was a particularly romantic spot. Many of Emma's friends were getting married to the young Confederate soldiers stationed there, and she remarked, "The war seems rather incentive to love than a check."[63] But now that

Hagood had been forced to give up his post on Coles Island, possession of this strategic outpost was no longer assured. Worse was the news of Robert Smalls and his defection. On 14 April, Emma wrote:

> The news of yesterday and today is so dreadful and so discouraging that I really feel despondent ... We were horrified by learning that the negro crew of the Planter which, besides being armed with a 32 & 24 pounder, was laden with four heavy guns for Fort Ripley, the new fort on Middle Ground, had carried her over to the fleet; the captain, mate, & engineer, all white men, being absent as they ought not to have been, nor was there a guard on board as ought certainly to have been to protect the very valuable guns & ammunition. [64]

The fall of Fort Pulaski had triggered new fears of imminent invasion, and the withdrawal from Coles Island and the defection of the *Planter* simply intensified those fears. Family after family packed their valuables and fled inland, many of them finding refuge in Columbia and the surrounding countryside. The Leveretts, who had felt it necessary to abandon their plantation and Beaufort home in November, now found it prudent to leave Charleston for "The Farm," a 64-acre plantation on the outskirts of Columbia. There the women of the family did their best to restore some pattern of normalcy to their lives, even to the extent of raising chickens in the yard. But for the usually gentle Rev. Leverett, this last upheaval inspired him to new levels of hatred for the North:

> The villainous Yankees ... are a rascally set from Lincoln down. I feel ashamed to have been born in New England & denounce the people as the meanest criminals that every disgraced humanity. Liars, thieves, robbers, adulterers—villains generally. They have not a redeeming qualification. My only wonder is that such wretches have been al-lowed to pollute the land so long. But patience—the day of retribution will arrive, & God will strike with a vengeance suited to their criminal career. [65]

The Middleton cousins, too, were beginning to revel in the psychological relief that hating Yankees produced. In April, Harriott wrote to Susan about an article she had read in the *Quarterly Review*. In it the author had quoted a letter from someone named Robert Chisolm, who was sending his mother a drinking cup made out of a Yankee skull. [66] Harriott purported to be shocked by the slander, but Susan enjoyed the story. She wrote:

> I have heard nothing of it, but I should not wonder if it *is* genuine ... and I am "savage" enough not to be very much surprised, or shocked either, at the idea of a Yankee skull drinking cup. Compare it with any one of the million atrocities daily committed by *them*, whenever *they* have the power to insult, injure, or desecrate, they have somewhat dulled out refined sensibilities, and hate and revenge, such as *such* an enemy inspired, can scarcely be expected to be over-delicate, or squeamish.

After confirming that there really was a Robert Chisolm from Coosaw, she went on to report that she had heard tales of Alabamans decorating their tents with enemy skulls and a Confederate general who wore spurs made of Yankee jaw-bones. [67]

Emma Holmes remarked upon the general exodus from Charleston. As early as 2 May, she noted, "Everybody in town has a face 'two miles long.' They report an attack upon the city is expected very soon & gentlemen are sending away their families" [68] Harriott's family, like many others, held out in Charleston until May, but then set out to take shelter in Flat Rock, North Carolina. Just before they left, she wrote to Susan, "There was a great panic in town and Frank thought there might be some foundation for it and if there was it would become still greater and we might find many inconveniences. The agitation among the servants in town was becoming very unpleasant and we did not care to subject ours to it any longer."[69] From her temporary home at "Albermarle," outside Columbia, Susan replied: "How lucky you all are in having a comfortable home in a fine climate ready for you! There is so much difficulty here, in this mean little town, in finding a place of refuge, even at an exorbitant price, the extortions which are practiced upon the low-country refugees, by the so called *best people in Columbia*," are enough to disgrace the place forever ... "[70]

Other families remained in Charleston even longer. The family of Rev. Thomas Smyth resisted leaving the family home at Number 12 Meeting Street, although Mrs. Smyth's Adger family had all departed for their lands near Pendleton. Rev. Smyth suffered from some form of paralysis, which not only made it difficult for him to contemplate a move, but also made him irascible and contrary. His long-suffering wife wrote to her daughter, "He wishes everything packed up, this however we cannot do as long as we remain, for we are very apt to put up just what he wants, & then all has to be unpacked again. This was done ... again this evening with a box in which his silk and woolen undergarments were put."[71] To her the situation was grim: "They tell me the streets are quite deserted. I have not been out myself, but I know few persons are to be seen from our windows except the soldiers, & the houses are all closed. All looks deserted & sad."[72] Before even a shot had been fired in an attempt to take the city of Charleston, the Northern invasion of the South Carolina coast had destroyed the idyllic lives of the wealthy plantation owners and their Charleston compatriots.

The Confederate forces in South Carolina were also in disarray. The first Confederate enlistments had run their course, and the draft instituted in March had failed to replace the numbers of those who, having served out their pledged term, now returned to ci-

vilian life. Mary Chesnut complained that the middle-aged men of South Carolina had been perfectly willing to send their young sons off to war. They had been willing to serve as officers if needed. They had not even complained overmuch when they were asked for money. But they found horrifying the idea that they or their slaves should be recruited for military service in the ranks.[73] "War seems a game of chess," she observed. "We have knights, kings, queens, bishops, and castles enough, but not enough pawns; and our skillful generals whenever they cannot arrange the board to suit them exactly, burn up everything and march away."[74]

The commanding officers were indeed part of the problem. Maj. Gen. John C. Pemberton had replaced Lee as commander of the Department of Georgia and South Carolina in February. He was a West Point graduate and experienced enough, but he arrived with one huge strike against him. He was a Quaker from Philadelphia, and despite the

Gen. John C. Pemberton, CSA
Photo courtesy of Mikel Uriguen

fact that his wife was a Virginian, South Carolinians saw him as an outsider. Mary Chesnut commented: "Men born Yankees are an unlucky selection as commanders for the Confederacy. They believe in the North in a way no true Southerner ever will, and they see no shame in surrendering to Yankees. They are half-hearted clear through; Stephens as Vice-President, Lovell, Pemberton, Ripley. A general must command the faith of his soldiers. These never will, be they ever so good and true."[75] It was an unfair judgment, perhaps, but one that resonated in the hearts of Southerners, from the lowliest citizen to Gov. Pickens himself. Complicating Pemberton's reception in South Carolina was that fact that under his command were four Confederate officers, each of whom had recently suffered an embarrassing reversal of fortunes and all of whom were now more eager than ever to defend their own strong opinions.

Gen. Johnson Hagood and his 1st South Carolina Volunteers had been in the front lines, doggedly fortifying Coles Island until they was ordered to abandon the site on 13 April 1862. On 11 May, Gen. Pemberton declared martial law in Charleston and put Hagood in charge of enforcing it. No one seems to have known what that meant, but Pemberton's explanation was not much help. Hagood grumbled, "He expected such a system of police that a dog could not enter the town without the knowledge of the provost marshal and his ability to lay hands upon such dog at any moment was required."[76] Enforcing martial law called for a large number of troops, most of whom lacked both training and discipline. Hagood observed that the officers assigned to him were to be found in the hotels and barrooms of the city while the enlisted men were inflicting "outrages of a flagrant character" on the city. Hagood reacted on 12 May by outlawing the manufacture or sale of liquor in Charleston, particularly to any member of the military—a move that did not endear him to the citizenry.[77]

Col. Arthur M. Manigault, before the war a wealthy Charleston rice planter, was in command of the First District with headquarters at Georgetown. On 25 March, Pemberton ordered the men and equipment at Georgetown to move to Charleston.[78] Those who had relied on Manigault's forces to protect South Carolina from any land invasion north of Charleston were horrified. Susan Middleton reported: "Pemberton is much censured. The 1,000 men at Mars Bluff cannot protect the property wh[ich] his removing 200 from Georgetown Fort left exposed."[79] After the Battle of Shiloh, Manigault and his men were transferred from Charleston to actions in Kentucky and Tennessee, a move that Manigault surely did not oppose.

Brig. Gen. Nathan "Shanks" Evans, commander of the Third District, was responsible for the Sea Islands south of Charleston and

Gen. Nathan "Shanks" Evans, CSA
Photo courtesy of Mikel Uriguen

all the way to Savannah. "Shanks" Evans was a rough and tumble South Carolinian, known for hard drinking and hard fighting. He seldom looked the part of a general; Harriott Middleton reported that one of her friends had met him and mistaken him for a brick-layer.[80] After the loss of Fort Pulaski, Pemberton systematically withdrew Evans' men from the southern Sea Islands, moving them north to protect Charleston from invasion via the Edisto River. Despite Evans' attempts to explain his tactical plans for the Third District, Pemberton ignored his wishes and eventually brought him all the way north to defend James Island.[81]

Brig. Gen. Roswell Ripley was in charge of the Second District centered on Charleston. He was another West Point graduate, originally from Ohio but a longtime resident of South Carolina, his wife's home. From the beginning of the war, Gov. Pickens had relied upon him to oversee Ft. Sumter and to protect Charleston. He developed a reputation for being insubordinate when he outspokenly disagreed with Gen. Lee's plans to withdraw from the coastal islands and protect only the major cities. He would have preferred to establish the defensive line as far from the city as possible. Now, serving under Pemberton, whom he considered his inferior, only made him more opinionated and contumacious. When Pemberton ordered him to abandon the batteries on Coles Island in order to construct new lines of defense on James Island, he obeyed and put in charge of James Island a talented new Brigadier General, the aptly named States Rights Gist. Then, assured that the defenses on James Island were in competent hands, Ripley immediately put in a request for transfer. Despite the fact that he was quite possibly the only man who fully understood the nature and extent of the Confederate defenses around Charleston, Ripley departed the state on 23 May, bound for a new command in the Army of Northern Virginia.

The task of defending James Island and the route to Charleston fell primarily to the 24th South Carolina Volunteers, led by 24-year old Lt. Col. Ellison Capers, and the Charleston Battalion under a much older and experienced Lt. Col. Peter Galliard. Gen. Gist su-

Gen. States Rights Gist, CSA
Photo courtesy of Mikel Uriguen

pervised their activities and put them to work constructing a defensive line that ran across the middle of James Island from the Wapoo Cut of the Stono River to a small summer resort town of Secessionville. Gus Smythe was by now a part of the 25th South Carolina, and he found himself camped on Goat Island, just across the marsh from the spot where Col. Lewis Hatch was constructing a tower and small fort to protect the Secessionville peninsula. Gus spent his days, and more often his nights, on picket duty. It was, he told his sister, "not very pleasant work"—dark, rainy, windy, and relieved only by breaks in a "holy" tent that allowed wind, dirt, and fleas to pour in.[82] Other detachments of his regiment were camped on Sol Legare Island, also known as Battery Island during the war. From these spots deep in the marshes around James Island, the Confederate outposts could keep track of Yankee incursions on the Stono. During the last two weeks of May, Federal gunboats frequently sailed up the Stono River as far as Grimball's plantation but avoided going so far as Fort Pemberton, where they might come under damaging fire. Periodically the crews of the *Pembina* and the *Unadilla* exchanged shots with the rebel forces in the marshes, but little damage occurred on either side.

As Gen. Pemberton tried to fulfill his mandate from Gen. Lee to protect Charleston, "street by street, house by house," his subordinates continued to second-guess his decisions.[83] With Ripley gone, Pemberton was forced into a complete reorganization of his divisions. He moved Gen. Evans back into his former Third District, replacing him in Charleston with Hugh Mercer. William S. Walker and Thomas Drayton received new districts between James Island and the Savannah River. Gov. Pickens, however, still wanted Pemberton removed, and the resulting dissention meant that Confederate preparations moved slowly and in a random fashion. One symptom of this lack of unity was that the Confederate troops were engaged in two simultaneous building programs—erecting defensive barriers, but also building escape routes across rickety causeways for fear their fortifications would not hold.

The terrain of James Island was also partially to blame for the problems faced by its defenders. Much of what looked like grassland was actually pluff mud. The characteristic soil of the Sea Islands was the result of rotting sweet grass and other salt marsh vegetation, mixed with broken oyster shells and the detritus of sea life in the shallows. At high tide, the seawater mixed with the fine soil to produce a soft, dark mud that resembled chocolate pudding.[84] At low tide, the mud could bake hard, giving up as it did so the unmistakable odor of hydrogen sulfide. In one particularly disastrous episode, General Gist sent out a detachment of artillerymen under the command of Captain C. E. Chichester to establish a battery of four guns on Sol Legare Island. Within two days, the men managed to lose three of the four guns in the sticky pluff mud that bordered the Rivers Causeway. Those who struggled on James Island during the last few days of May to complete construction of defensive barriers that would stop the advance of Benham's invading army had as much reason as the Yankees to grumble about the "cursed soil of South Carolina".

CHAPTER 7

Onward to Charleston!

As both Confederate and Union generals began to focus on James Island as the key to Charleston, so too did the paths of several pairs of individuals begin to converge on that swampy piece of land. Some were career army officers, like Gen. Pemberton and Gen. Benham, both 1837 graduates of West Point, whose years of education and training had spawned rivalries that were about to be played out on the battlefield. Some were family members, like the Drayton brothers or the Campbell brothers, whose differing ideologies or different career paths had placed them on opposite sides of the conflict. Others were strangers whose lives had nevertheless been following separate but parallel paths. James McCaskey and Gus Smythe were both first-generation Americans, Scotch-Irish by blood and Presbyterian by faith. Their respective regiments had entered the war at approximately the same time and for exactly the same reasons. They had witnessed their first conflict from opposite sidelines, had sat idle while others fought what seemed to be exciting battles, and now were about to come face to face on James Island. Each of these paired individuals might have voiced the same sentiments as did Union Gen. Henry Hunt to Confederate General Braxton Bragg in 1861: "How strange it is. We have been united in our views of almost all subjects, public and private. We still have, I trust, a personal regard for each other, which will continue whatever course our sense of duty may dictate ... yet here we are, face to face, with arms in our hands, with every prospect of bloody collision. How strange."[1]

On both sides of the conflict, soldiers waited eagerly for their chance to become a part of the war. Gus Smythe, already safely encamped behind the fortifications near Secessionville, was restless and worried about his family in Charleston as he waited for something to happen. Several times, he set off for a short visit home, only to be called back to camp when Union shells threatened. On 31 May, he wrote to his mother:

> Yesterday evening I had to drive a wagon down to Fort Johnson for some of our men, and it did seem hard that I should be within sight of home & yet not able to reach it ... There is another alarm this morning ... I do not know what will be the end of it. Uncle Joe just says that the couriers report the Yankees landing on Dixon's Isl where we were on picquet ... As far as the men are concerned, we would rather go forward & attack them than retreat.[2]

On the Union side, rumors of the move to James Island circulated through every camp. Captain William Lusk, of the 79th New York Regiment, served as an adjutant to General Stevens, which placed him in a position to know about impending moves. At the end of May, he wrote to his mother: "At length a prospect is before us of active service. The long dreamed of time has arrived, and the word 'Onward to Charleston' has been spoken."[3]

DuPont, who had been promoted to rear admiral after the fall of Fort Pulaski, was still not convinced of the Army's ability to attack Fort Johnson from the rear, but he now offered "every facility in my power toward their operations."[4] General Hunter, for his part, was eager to commit his troops to the taking of Charleston. Minimizing the problems involved in conducting a military maneuver during a southern summer, he suggested that "our men are all the better for a little occupation and a change of scene."[5] General Benham was now in command of the troops of the South Carolina Expeditionary Corps and ready to move. He considered the plan to attack Charleston by way of James Island "perhaps the most daring project for so many troops that has been proposed in the war."[6]

The men under Benham's command were in two divisions led by Generals Horatio G. Wright and Isaac I. Stevens. Benham proposed a two-pronged occupation of James Island. Gen. Wright led the First Division.[7] Their orders were to assemble on Edisto Island, cross the Edisto River by boat, and then march across Johns Island to the abandoned town of Legareville on the southern bank of the Stono River. General Stevens' Second Division was to proceed to Hilton Head by ship, where they would pick up the 46th New York and the 28th Massachusetts, and from there sail to the mouth of the Stono River, where the 7th Connecticut would join the brigade.[8]

The Confederates had been immediately aware of the movement of Union troops and what their arrival presaged. A flurry of messages on 2-3 June showed that General Pemberton was trying desperately to organize his defenses.[9] Near the small settlement of planters called Secessionville, in the center of James Island, stood the beginnings of a fort. Secessionville itself was little more than a widened spot in the road, approximately seven miles inland and six miles from Charleston. The Union forces called the unfinished

Union Gunboats on Stono River
Sketch courtesy of Harper's Weekly

earthwork just west of Secessionville "Tower Fort" because of its proximity to a lookout tower that was visible from their camp; the Confederates called it Battery Lamar.[10] Near Secessionville the rebels quickly strengthened the earthworks and installed guns able to shell the areas where the Union troops were likely to camp. Pemberton ordered stockpiles of ammunition, moved heavy guns from the Citadel and Fort Sumter to James Island, and requested permission to call up troops from Savannah. On 2 June, he received a telegram from Gen. States Rights Gist at Secessionville: "Seven additional gunboats in Stono, five at anchor outside, and others in sight. We may look out for the attack at any hour. Two of the vessels are reported transports." Pemberton passed the notification on to Gen. Mercer, calling on him to be "ready to move at a moment's notice." He warned, "If the enemy attempts to land he must be attacked tonight or whenever he leaves the cover of his gunboats."[11] His message to President Jefferson Davis, however, was much more alarmist: "Twenty vessels are in and off the Stono and increasing in number. If they attack it will be by land and water. If you say risk it, I will order 5,000 men from Savannah, but I think it will be dangerous."[12]

In Late May, George Webb, assigned to Col Hagood's command, had written to his mother from Fort Fever at Mr. Lawton's Place on James Island. Watching the first forays of the Union boats, he referred to sentry duty along the Stono River, as "a lovely sport." But a second letter written from Fort Pemberton on 2 June, revealed that his flippant attitude had undergone a serious revision. He wrote, "The day for the great battle around Charleston is at hand." He reported heavy firing at Fort Johnson, and said that the Union had "far superior force to ours both in artillery and men."[13]

On Monday, 2 June 1862, the troops of the Second Division began their approach to James Island with little difficulty; Marchand's shallow-draft boats proved more than equal to the task.[14] They sailed up the Stono River as far as Legareville. There, two companies of Roundheads, C and M, disembarked on the far side of the river to secure the abandoned town. James McCaskey had been delayed one more time on his way to James Island. Company C must have been disappointed to remain behind again, as the rest of the Roundheads moved on to James Island itself. It would be several days before James and his comrades would cross the Stono to join the rest of Stevens' Division in their effort to penetrate the Confederate batteries barring the way to Fort Johnson and Charleston. The rest of the division moved on to Battery Island, now called Sol Legare Island, which was not really an island at all but a narrow strip of high ground between two marshy creeks, not far from where the 24th South Carolina Volunteers were attempting to strengthen the defenses at the unfinished "Tower Fort."

The Confederate pickets were alert, and the batteries, however poorly constructed, were ready to repulse any troops on the ground. Sporadic and unpredictable fire from the Union gunboats, however, was so deadly that about all the Confederate troops could do was duck and cover when the shots came near their positions. The order book of the Eutaw Battalion, kept by Capt. C. H. Simonton, reported on 2 June that "the fire from the gun boats became grand and terrific ... [We] took possession of River's outbuildings, which in some measure protected us from the fury of the shots during the night."[15] Young Gus Smythe was getting his first taste of combat and finding that he did not much like it. In a scratched-out letter to his mother on Wednesday morning, 4 June, he wrote:

> Just got back safe & sound from a 20 hrs. experience of rain, hard marching & Yankee shells, & although completely broken down, I write these few lines to relieve your mind of all anxiety on my account. We had a very hard time, especially

five of us, who, in addition to marching all day, had to go out all night on piquet … We drove back the Yankees when they attempted to land, with our artillery, but tho' we were exposed to all the shelling, only ¼ of a mile from the vessels, we did not even have the privilege of getting a shot at them.[16]

From the camp behind the fortifications at Battery Lamar, John Sheppard stood guard and listened to the firing. He wrote to his mother, too, to reassure her that he was unhurt: "Shells falling around & over but not in our camp … We are safe; in fact, do not be alarmed when you hear the 'Big Guns'; they

Maj. James H. Cline, USA
Photo courtesy of Michael Kraus Collection, USAMHI

make a great noise but hurt nobody. One man in a Cavalry Co. was thrown from his horse & broke his arm, one horse had his leg broken, which I believe is the extent of damage done so far."[17]

The Union forces had been drilling and training for warfare for nine months, but they were still untested troops, unfamiliar with the

realities of the battlefield. That was about to change. Around midnight on 2 June, a reconnaissance troop, composed of forty men each from the Roundheads' Companies A, D, I, and F, under the command of Captain James Cline, joined two companies from the 28th Massachusetts and two from the 79th New York. Their orders were to explore the rest of Battery Island and to clear it of any Confederate outposts. Sgt. Robert Adler of Company F later recalled his initiation to combat. Capt. Cline had ordered him, along with fifteen of his men, to set out and discover how close they could get to Fort Sumter. True to his rural origins, he soon decided to climb a tree and look around. To his horror, he spotted a line of Confederate troops less than half a mile away and moving in his direction. His reaction was immediate and instinctive:

> I thought my squad and I were doomed to have our home in Dixie for a while. I don't think I was very dignified in my orders to retreat. It was "git boys!" I set the example, dropping at once out the tree and making a "MAUD S" [modest] speed for the negro shanties, bringing away my gun and all my accoutrements, minus my cap, and if I do say so myself, getting in ahead of the men, two-thirds of whom threw away guns, cartridge boxes, and everything else.[18]

At about the middle of the "island," the rest of Capt. Cline's troops came upon the abandoned Legare Plantation, where the open ground provided easier walking but left them exposed and vulnerable to anyone lurking in the woods to the north near the Rivers Causeway. The Roundheads searched the plantation grounds and outbuildings, while the men of the 28th Massachusetts advanced toward the woods. Two companies of the 79th New York, led by Captain William Elliot, brought up the rear and secured the left flank. Suddenly gunfire erupted from amongst the trees. The Roundheads formed a ragged battle line near the plantation house as the Massachusetts men came running back, chased by Confederate soldiers.[19] The rebel troops were under the command of Lt. Col. Ellison Capers of the Eutaw Battalion, who had been sent out to try to recover the guns lost in the mud by Capt. Chichester.[20] Captain Cline led a small troop of Roundheads out to hold the right flank, expecting the New Yorkers to move into the gap between his men and the plantation. But when the Rebels turned to concentrate on this smaller group, the 79th fell back, leaving twenty-two Roundheads outnumbered and cut off. The trapped Roundheads put up a credible struggle before they surrendered to Capt. Ryan of the Irish Volunteers, who later wore Cline's sword "as a trophy of his gallantry."[21] Rev. Browne described the scene dramatically:

> Capt. Cline was in the act of cleaving down with a sword, a man who had laid hold of Gilfillen and almost cut the rebel's arm in twain, when half a dozen of the foe fell on him and pulled him down. He refused to hand up his sword, but flung it and the scabbard on the ground. "You will have a hard reckoning for the day's work," said he "when you meet the Colonel of the Roundheads."[22]

As the Confederates marched the captured Roundheads off toward Secessionville, the other men of the reconnaissance force made their way back toward the safety of the Union line and the cover of the gunboats in the Stono River.[23] Their retreat took them close to the Rivers Causeway, a bridge that connected Battery Island and the Legare Plantation to the mainland of James Island and the Rivers Plantation. And there in the sticky pluff mud that surrounded the causeway, they spotted the three guns left behind by Capt. Chichester and his Gist Guards when they had failed to erect their battery on Battery Island.[24] Several enterprising New Yorkers from the 79th Regiment joined the Roundhead effort to pull out two of the three guns. Another contingent of Roundheads

and Connecticut artillerymen worked feverishly to free the third gun, but came under fire and had to abandon the effort. Still, they made a gleeful procession of it as they returned to camp dragging two brass cannons from the Confederate arsenal. The next day, young George Leasure wrote to his mother, bragging of the escapade:

> Our men Roundheads took three pieces of a battery which belonged to the Rebels. One of them stuck in the mud, one had one wheel broken off and had to be left behind, but the other two are now in camp, and Papa and I slept under one last night, as our tents are not here yet. After our boys had run up and seized the guns and hauled them out of their position, some of the 79th helped draw them in and claimed the honor of taking one of them but they did not.[25]

The Yankee appropriating system had often served the troops well, allowing them to scrounge meals when mess provisions failed, to add variety in what would have otherwise become a terribly monotonous camp diet, and to make their accommodations more comfortable and homelike with the loot gathered from abandoned plantation houses. Only infrequently did it get them in trouble, as it had when they tore down houses to provide tent flooring. But never was the morale boost as high as when they were able to appropriate the enemy's own artillery right under the noses of the Eutaw Battalion, whose commander assumed that the cannons being dragged back to camp were Union guns in ignominious retreat.[26] Col. Leasure was delighted with the story. He wrote to his wife that night, "Just think of it, about fifty of them charged right smack up to a battery of siege guns and actually hauled off two of the guns by hand while the enemy from another battery just rained the shells among them, hitting everything but them. They (guns) are enormous 8 inch Howitzers. In all this they never lost a man or received a scratch."[27]

For the young soldiers of Stevens' Division, who had been waiting for a "scratch with the rebels" for almost ten months, this first day of actual fighting had been both terrifying and exhilarating. But the day held yet another surprise for one of them. As they made their way back to camp, the men of the 79th New York "Highlanders" managed to pick up a prisoner, 2nd Lt. Henry Walker of the Charleston Battalion, who had a superficial wound in the leg. He was from Scotland and seems to have felt much at home with the Highlanders; he talked to them freely about his unit. It was through him that Alexander Campbell learned that his brother James was on the island and that they had been fighting against one another that very morning.

The Campbells had emigrated from Scotland in the 1850s. Alexander had found work in New York City as a stonecutter, while James went on to Charleston, where he worked as a drayman. Alexander had tried his luck in Charleston for a few months, and in the period before actual war broke out, both brothers had signed onto local Charleston militia companies. But in 1859, romance drew Alexander back to New York City, and by April 1861, he joined the 79th New York Regiment of the State Militia. Meanwhile as South Carolina approached secession, James became a member of the Union Light Infantry. Alexander's regiment joined the South Carolina Expeditionary Force in October 1861; James's militia unit entered active duty in March 1862, as the 1st South Carolina Infantry, Charleston Battalion.[28] After a long talk with the prisoner, Alexander wrote to his wife about this unexpected encounter: "He was a Luetenant and belonged to the same company that Brother James is in … So you see we are not farr from each other now … This is a warr that there never was the Like of before Brother against Brother."[29]

Captain Cline and his men were taken to the fortifications near Secessionville, where they were apparently accorded all due respect as prisoners of war. On 5 June, the captain received permission to write to his commander. He reported, "We have been very kindly treated by the citizens and soldiers among whom we have been. I do not lay the blame of our capture upon any one officer in particular. I would just say, that had we been properly supported when the charge was made, we might not have been taken …"[30] Four days later, the prisoners had been transferred to Columbia, South Carolina, and Capt. Cline wrote again, hoping for rescue: "We have been in captivity but a short time as yet, but only those who have experienced it know how galling it is to be deprived of the society of friends and immured within the walls of a prison. Col., I hope you will use every exertion to secure our exchange."[31] Unfortunately for the captured Pennsylvanians, their predicament would have to wait until the Roundheads were in a better position to negotiate.

The quick arrival of the First Division might have made a huge difference in the outcome of the taking of James Island, but General Wright had been characteristically hesitant to move. Plans called for him to march his division over land and join those transported by water at Grimball's plantation. Fearing reports of Confederate forces on John's Island, Wright refused to cross the Edisto River until the navy could provide him with the protection of gunboats.[32] Even after DuPont dispatched the requested covering fire, Wright's caution delayed his arrival until 5 June. Worried that his men were not strong enough to withstand a forced march in the excessive heat, Wright had ordered that whiskey be provided for those who faltered. As a member of the 3rd New Hampshire reported, "Many fell to the rear, apparently exhausted for the sake of the whiskey. Consequently, a few were very much overcome by the relief and could not march."[33] By the time the First Division arrived at the rendezvous point, the men were so overcome by Wright's solicitous precautions for their well-being that they required an additional three days to recover from his remedies.

The weather, too, played its part in delaying the arrival of Wright's First Division. Col. Edwin Metcalf and his 3rd Rhode Island Infantry experienced all the misery of Wright's march across Johns Island. With tongue firmly planted in cheek, Metcalf described the plan of attack:

A short victorious march to Charleston, and the whole sea coast is ours! How simple, easy, natural—how well contrived, how impossible to fail! Alas! No; success was very certain—if it should not rain, and it did rain. In June, rains will come in South Carolina and when they come, men's plans always fail if they won't stand drowning … How the water did pour! How the road deepened and lengthened …"[34]

After joking about his horse, which did not drown only because "it was born to be shot," and his own childhood near drowning, the colonel turned deadly serious. "Our little army was floundered," he wrote. "I saw the hardiest in my command, proud, self-reliant officers and men, sit down and cry like children while they cut off their shoes, and then dragged themselves along to shelter."[35]

The weather remained the principal victor for the next week or more. The rain came down in sheets, accompanied by gale-force winds and blinding lightning. Complaints about soaked clothes, moldy tents, and soggy sleeping arrangements prevailed in almost every soldier's letters during this period.[36] Those who thought they could find shelter from the storms in farm buildings discovered that the fleas had beaten them to the best resting places. When the sun did come out for a while, so did hordes of "long-nosed mosquitoes" that "bled us day and night."[37] But over and under everything else was that ubiquitous pluff mud, spreading with each high tide, fed by torrents of rain, and churned up by tromping boots and falling artillery shells. For the

northern soldiers it was particularly treacherous, for expanses of sweetwater grass looked deceptively like pleasant wheat fields until one took a single step into them and discovered that the grass actually grew in bottomless muck. Southern soldiers, too, struggled to figure out what was really solid ground and which pathway might give out beneath them without warning. Crisscrossing James Island was a network of narrow roads and makeshift causeways; the ground beyond those paths might be permanent pluff mud, or pluff mud just drying out from the last tidal flood, or silty soil just about to make the transition back to pluff mud. Unfortunately, both Union and Confederate battle plans were just as muddy as the terrain. If there was any equalizing factor, it was that neither side was particularly familiar with the topography of James Island, and neither military staff had a clear idea of how to go about taking control of the muddy land.

The Drayton brothers were once again among those who were preparing to face the coming battle. Gen. Thomas Drayton was in command of the Sixth and Fourth Military Districts under Gen. Pemberton. He and his regiments were headquartered at Hardeeville, just north of Savannah, where they were awaiting orders to march to the relief of Charleston. Commander Percival Drayton was in command of the small group of gunboats that Marchand had sent to cruise the Stono River in preparation for an all-out attack on Charleston. Although neither brother voiced any hesitancy about opposing one another yet again, they must surely have remembered the Battle of Port Royal and their mother's lament that they had had to shoot at one another. Percy, certainly, had his doubts about the chances for a Union victory:

The troops have been gradually transferred to the James River [Island] side, and may be considered only to-day to have sufficiently recovered from their wetting and exposure to be in a proper condition for battle. Nearly the same positions are now occupied that were on the first day, and every attempt to penetrate farther into the island has as yet been unsuccessful, and they everywhere meet the fire of artillery, the position of which they half the time can not exactly discover … although the Army of the South has been so long spoiling for a fight it does not seem to me that the spirit that leads to victory is prevalent, but rather a despondent tone is the prevailing one, nor do I think that Benham commands the confidence of his subordinates. Of course all advantage from a surprise has been lost, partly from the delay in Wright's arrival, partly from the horrible weather.[38]

By 7 June, the Confederates knew something about the Union plans. Major General J. C. Pemberton, who was in charge of the defense of Charleston, sent an urgent message to Jefferson Davis: "A prisoner taken tonight says the enemy has landed a division and three light batteries and a siege train on James Island and a division on John's Island; also cavalry and artillery. The generals are Stevens and Wright. Says his division (Stevens') is 10,000 strong."[39] Estimates of Union troop strength, however, varied enormously from observer to observer, and since there was no clear pattern in the Union forays into the interior of James Island, Pemberton and his staff were pretty much at a loss as to how to prepare their defenses. One of his orders, sent under the name of his adjutant, Maj. J. Waddy, alerted Gen Drayton on 5 June, "Have your command ready to move in any direction should it be required."[40]

Pemberton kept up requests for additional troops from Georgia or North Carolina, but his needs went unrecognized by a general staff that was preoccupied by the concurrent battles raging in Virginia. This exchange of messages on 11 June between Pemberton and George Randolph, the Confederate Secretary of War, illustrates the problem:

Pemberton to Randolph:
> "My force is very inadequate to the defense of both Charleston and Savannah. Exclusive of garrisons of forts, at this time I have not to exceed 10,000 effectives to defend Charleston, including Evans' command, and to defend Savannah not more than 5,000 effectives, including Drayton's; some of these are unarmed; many badly armed. Can I not get some troops from North Carolina?"

Randolph to Pemberton:
> "Movements of an important and decisive character are practicable if we can get re-enforcements from the South. Send them if you possibly can without too much risk to Charleston."

Pemberton to Randolph:
> "I not only cannot spare any more troops from this department, but there is danger here unless I am re-enforced."[41]

Pemberton did not deserve full blame for such conflicting demands and the resultant troop shortages. His failure to engage the trust of the governor and citizens of South Carolina, however, complicated his situation. President Davis seems to have assumed that the citizens of Georgia and South Carolina would rise to their own defense, and Pemberton, too, expected his officers to be able to draw upon the citizens of Charleston to defend their city. On 4 June, the *Charleston Mercury* editorialized, " The day of trial is upon us … Our people are calm, and prepared for a desperate resistance." [42] Unfortunately, the citizens of Charleston were really neither willing nor able to respond. When the Union forces landed on James Island on 2 June, Gen. Hagood reported in his *Memoirs*, Gen. DeSaussure called upon every man under the age fifty to enlist in the effort to defend Charleston. Only one man volunteered. Eventually Hagood was able to find some 150 old men who were willing at least to stand guard. Most of the other able-bodied men had packed up their families and moved to safer locations.[43]

So Pemberton floundered, and his orders tended toward confusion, if not contradiction. He approved a change of command on the very day the Yankee troops assembled on James Island in force. Responding to a call from President Davis, he released Gen. Alexander Lawton from his command in Savannah to move to Richmond; Gen. Mercer, who was busy trying to defend James Island from invasion, was to be sent to replace Lawton in Savannah; and Brig. Gen. William Duncan Smith, freshly arrived from Savannah, would take over command at Secessionville. Then, inexplicably, he delayed all the transfers, so that no one was quite sure who was in charge.[44] At one point Pemberton sent these confusing instructions to Brigadier General Smith: "I wish the large woods west of Secessionville strongly occupied with troops, and field artillery on the road or in easy communication with the road. It is of the first importance to hold this wood. You will give strict orders to prohibit the roads being blocked up with wagons, artillery, or any other obstruction to the movement of troops."[45] No record seems to exist to show whether Smith disobeyed orders by placing his guns on the road or by placing them off the road.

The situation worsened when Pemberton sent conflicting orders to a general who was already confused. Gen. "Shanks" Evans received orders to set up camp at Adams Run, from which location Pemberton ordered him to attack Legareville (to the west) and to defend Seabrook Island (to the east).[46] Evans' report revealed that he had no knowledge of where the enemy troops might be located: "I have the honor to report that I have yet been unable to ascertain the exact intentions or designs of the enemy ... There are about 1,500 on Seabrook Island, and are being re-enforced from Fenwick's and Edisto Islands. There is also a small force at Legareville ... I have just directed Colonel Dunvant, First Regiment

Infantry, to attack the enemy at Seabrook tomorrow morning. The attack will not probably take place until the afternoon."[47] In fact, at that very moment, there were few if any Yankees at Seabrook, but Gen. Wright's entire First Division was at Legareville and preparing to cross the Stono River. Little wonder then, that one Confederate soldier wrote to his father:

> Our coast is well fortified and our men are brave and determined, and my only fear is the incompetency of our Generals. I am sorry to say it, but it is nonetheless true, that our lines on the coast are badly provided for in the way of Generals. A rumor is current and in all probability correct, that Col. Means and Col. Slaughter of Ga. and other Cols. intend reporting Gen. Evans for incompetency. The last few days has fully developed his incapacity for a high and responsible military position, and it is galling to men of patriotism and genuine worth, who have so much at stake, to see their privileges abused and liberties trembling in the balance, solely on account of an incompetent General.[48]

As it happened, the rumors were wrong. On 12 June, Pemberton rewarded Evans by recalling him from his outpost and stationing him and his regiments on James Island, a move that effectively demoted the clever and competent General Smith to second in command.[49]

Whatever his other failings, General Pemberton had no illusions as to the seriousness of the Union threat to Charleston. His correspondence in the following days was filled with pleas for assistance. He requested additional troops and ordered extra rifled guns and twelve-pound howitzers, percussion caps, powder, friction tubes, 700 rounds of rifled ammunition, and 100,000 rounds of ammunition for smooth-bored muskets. He requisitioned ferryboats and passenger trains from the Charleston and Savannah Railroad to move troops and supplies. The men stationed at the earthworks were ordered not to waste ammunition but to double their efforts to complete the fort and entrenchments.[50] Still he was not satisfied with the preparations. On the evening of 15 June, he wrote to Governor Francis W. Pickens: "You should be fully acquainted with the fact that the troops at my disposal for the defense of Charleston are inadequate for that purpose … On [James Island] I have not at this moment to exceed 6,500 men."[51]

General Pemberton at least understood his situation; the Union generals seemed to lack that basic understanding of what they were about to face. Federal troops had occasional skirmishes with the island's defenders in the days after they arrived on James Island, but such confrontations tended to be brief and without long-term results. On Sunday, 8 June, Col J. H. Morrow led a detachment of men from the 46th New York and the 1st Massachusetts regiments to explore the land east of Grimball's plantation near the Presbyterian Church. They walked into an ambush laid by four companies of the Eutaw Battalion; two men were killed and five were wounded. The next day, Gen. Wright moved his troops to Grimball's plantation in force. The Eutaw Battalion observed the move, but Pemberton had ordered Lamar not to waste his ammunition by firing at them. A more serious conflict erupted on Tuesday, 10 June. The Yankees formed a defensive line in front of Grimball's and held off an attack by Georgia troops for nearly two hours before the gunboats pitched in and drove the Confederates back. Casualties were high. The Georgia regiment lost over seventy men killed or wounded, and Gen. Wright reported that he had taken at least eight prisoners. The Union regiments lost three dead and nineteen wounded.[52] Units might brag about their small victories, but neither side was accomplishing anything more than an occasional, and very temporary, morale boost.

On 8 June General Benham had issued preparatory orders for an attack on the gun emplacements near Secessionville. The men were to be ready by the evening of 10 June. Each soldier was to carry two pounds of cooked meat, hard bread, filled canteen, blankets or oilcloths, and sixty rounds of ammunition. They were to move into position silently by moonlight, rest until 3:00 A.M., and then attack. General Stevens' division was to be the attacking force, while General Wright's men served as a supporting column and Colonel Williams's brigade acted as a reserve.[53] The attack did not occur. Sporadic shelling of his camp had convinced General Wright that they were hopelessly outnumbered, and he was able to communicate his fears to Benham and Hunter. Hunter concluded that the taking of Charleston was unlikely to come off in the near future and abandoned the plan. Gen. Stevens was furious. In a letter to his wife, he raged that Hunter was an "imbecile, vascillatory, and utterly unfit to command." Benham, he said, was "an ass—a dreadful man of no earthly use except as a nuisance and obstruction."[54]

Shortly thereafter, General Hunter decided to return to Hilton Head, where he had left a few troops literally "holding the fort," and where Mrs. Hunter was waiting for her husband to come back. This decision left him vulnerable for later criticism. Even Admiral DuPont, who invited the Hunters to dinner aboard his flagship on Sunday, 15 June, later wrote to Mrs. DuPont, "Mrs. Hunter has followed her husband everywhere, having no children … While I like them both, and think the General a most estimable person, his military course puzzles me … General Hunter returned here from Stono, which everybody will say he did because his wife was here—though it is his headquarters … "[55] Hunter, however, thought he had left his troops in good hands because he had issued the following order to General Benham:

In leaving the Stono River to return to Hilton Head I desire in any arrangements that you may make for the disposition of your forces now in this vicinity, you will make no attempt to advance on Charleston or to attack Fort Johnson until largely re-enforced or until you receive specific instructions from these headquarters to that effect. You will however provide for a secure intrenched encampment, where your front can be covered by the fire of our gunboats from the Stono on the left and the creek from Folly River on the right.[56]

This order only served to delay the inevitable confrontation to the detriment of the Union forces.

General Benham continued to plan an attack. Stressing the portion of General Hunter's order that instructed him to "provide for a secure intrenched encampment," he determined that the guns threatening the camp had to be removed. On the evening of 15 June, he called a meeting of his officers to announce his intention of attacking the earthworks at Secessionville that very night. As he must have anticipated, both Gen. Wright and Gen. Stevens were opposed to such a move. Wright seems to have believed that any offensive action was contrary to orders and bound to be unsuccessful. Stevens favored the attack only if it began in the afternoon, after shelling had weakened the defenses. In the official records, Gen. Wright outlined his objections in the form of interrogatories directed at Gen. Stevens:

First interrogatory: "Have you impaired the strength of the enemy's works at Secessionville by the firing of your battery?"

General Stevens' answer: "Not in the least. I have driven the enemy from his guns by my fire and I can do it again, but as soon as the fire ceases he returns. I have not dismounted a gun, and we shall find him in the morning as strong as ever."

Second interrogatory: "Do you know of any instance where volunteer troops have successfully stormed works as strong as those which defend the approach to Secessionville?"

General Stevens' answer: "I know of no such instance."

Third interrogatory: "Have you any reason to believe that the result in the present case will be different in its character from what it has invariably been heretofore?"

General Stevens' answer: "I have no reason to expect a different result. It is simply a bare possibility to take the work."[57]

Their protests duly recognized, General Benham nonetheless ordered an immediate attack. His plan was the same as the one he had outlined a week earlier. The men were to make their approach at dawn. In a letter to General Hunter, he defended his decision:

It was indispensable that we should destroy or capture the fort and floating battery of the enemy at Secessionville ... as these batteries covered with their fire the whole of the position and camps of General Wright on our left and the advanced post of General Stevens on our right, and as these were the only or the lower positions that secured a footing upon the main portion of James Island and a direct route on firm land to Fort Johnson, which, when required, gave us the command of the city and harbor of Charleston.[58]

The Pennsylvania Roundheads themselves were ready for action. They approached their first real battle with the same religious fervor that had inspired their reputed Cromwellian ancestors two hundred years earlier. Certain of God's protection and of the rightness of their cause, they might well have echoed Cromwell's own *Catechisme* when he asked about the considerations that made a soldier courageous. Among the answers Cromwell had expected were these: "The goodness of the cause ... The promise of God to help his

107

church and people … The assurance that not a hair can fall from our heads without the providence and permission of God … The danger of faint heartedness; he that would save his life in such times as these shall lose it."[59]

The regimental chaplain, Rev. Robert Audley Browne, wrote to his wife just two days before the battle. Bolstered by his Presbyterian belief in predestination, he expressed his confidence in the coming victory. Not yet sure when the battle would begin, he wrote, "When it comes, the enemy are foredoomed to be beaten back, and that without much loss of life on our part … You may be sure Sumter, Moultrie and Charleston are destined to fall … If, however, it becomes a matter of personal prowess in the field—of coolness and bravery—let us be thankful our troops and I think I may say confidently, our Roundheads will inevitably conquer."[60] Similar confidence came from the men. Capt. Thomas J. Hamilton, Co. D, wrote to his wife from James Island on 15 June:

I don't anticipate much trouble here on the Island, and when we get this we can approach Fort Sumter … When we get our Gun Boats in range of Charleston I think they will skedaddle in a hurry… The prisoners we have taken say that they expect that Charleston will be taken. We see dense volumes of smoke this morning; it is supposed they are burning the cotton and destroying their property. This looks as though they expect to be taken, which they certainly will. I think the city is ours without much trouble if it is managed right.[61]

Even George Leasure wrote to reassure his mother: "We will take this Is'd and Charleston by siege. We intend to plant large guns and take it *inch by inch* and hold it as we go."[62] The reality, of course, would be quite different.

CHAPTER 8

Grape, Canister, Shot, and Shell

As in any such tumultuous event, accounts of the battle at Secessionville on 16 June 1862 differ according to the position and emotional involvement of the observer. In the ensuing days, each officer submitted to his immediate superior a report of the actions of the men under his command. Understandably, these accounts tended to emphasize the hardships faced by each unit and the courage with which the men met their particular challenge.[1] The Confederates, for example, reported three distinct assaults; the Union commanders regarded it as one sustained attack that came in waves only because the front was too narrow to allow simultaneous troop movements. When one reads all of the official reports, however, certain salient points become clear.

The Union forces obeyed orders to form their lines in silence during the night. Each man was to carry sixty rounds of ammunition but to advance with fixed bayonets and unloaded rifles, since surprise was the key to a successful attack. The regiments lined up in this order: the 8th Michigan, the 7th Connecticut, the 28th Massachusetts, the 79th Pennsylvania, the 100th Pennsylvania, and the 46th New York. General Wright's division was on the left to protect the leading troops from a flank attack. They were ordered to remain one-half mile to the rear and to provide support. The troops assembled at various times between 1:00 A.M. and 3:30 A.M. They were to move at daybreak.

A major discrepancy in the accounts concerned the time at which the attack actually began. General Stevens reported that they moved before dawn. "It was," he said, "a very dark and cloudy morning. I moved at 4 o'clock. It was so dark that one man could not follow another except at very short intervals, it was much darker than on usual starlight nights."[2] Col. Joseph R. Hawley, 7th Connecticut Infantry, whose men were near the forefront of the advance, maintained that he was able to see clearly for a distance of over 75 yards when the attack began.[3] Most accounts place the time of the attack between 4:00 A.M. and 5:00 A.M.; observers variously described the morning as overcast, cloudy, or foggy. The question of available light became important in later attempts to understand what went wrong with the attack, for surprise was only possible if the approach were made under cover of darkness. On 16 June 1862, at latitude 33 degrees, sunrise occurred at 4:51 A.M. More significant, the beginning of morning nautical twilight, which permits observation of objects on the ground at 400 yards, came at 3:45 A.M.[4] It seems evident that the approaching forces were easily visible from the fort.

The Union forces faced a march of two miles. The front was approximately 200 yards wide, narrowing to some thirty yards in front of the earthworks. The ground was sandy and ridged by old cotton furrows and stubble. Trisecting the field over which the Union army had to march were two ditches lined with hedgerows that provided some meager cover. On either side of the approach to Battery Lamar (Tower Fort), pluff mud and salt marshes lined the narrow finger of navigable ground.

General Isaac Stevens described it this way:

> The front on which the attack occurred was narrow, not over 200 yards in extent, stretching from the marsh on the one side to the marsh on the other. It was at the saddle of the peninsula, the ground narrowing very suddenly at this point from our advance. On either hand were bushes on the edge of the marsh for some little distance. The whole space at the saddle was occupied by the enemy's work, impracticable abatis on either hand, with carefully prepared torus de-loup on our left and in front a ditch 7 feet deep, with a parapet of hard-packed earth, having a relief of some 9 feet above the general surface of the ground. On the fort were mounted six guns, covering the field of our approach. The whole interior of the work was swept by fire from the rifle pits and defenses in the rear, and the flanks of the work itself and the bushes lining the marsh on either hand were under the fire of riflemen and sharpshooters stationed in the woods and defenses lying between the work and the village of Secessionville [5]

Thus, although technically outnumbered, the Confederate troops possessed a tactical advantage by virtue of their strongly entrenched position.

The Confederates themselves, however, were not at all sure that their defenses would prove adequate. Although they were aware that attack was imminent from their observations of Union troop movements, they were not yet fully prepared for battle. On the

night of 15 June, they had stationed pickets 800 yards in front of the earthworks to alert them to any advance. Most of the rebel soldiers had worked through the night on the entrenchments. They had not fallen asleep until 3:00 A.M. Then, at 4:00 A.M., the pickets were captured, and the defenders found themselves rudely awakened and plummeted into battle. The original 500 men stationed

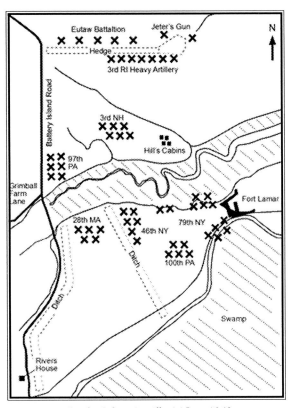

Battle of Secessionville, 16 June 1862
Map by Anna Inman

on the earthworks were armed with an eight-inch Columbiad loaded with grape and canister, two rifled 24-pounders, two 18-pounders, and a mortar. Defensive forces were not complete until the arrival of General Evans, commanding the Pee Dee Battalion, the Charleston Battalion, and the Louisiana Battalion. These troops had not moved until alerted by the first sounds of gunfire; encounters with their own troops further delayed the Eutaw Battalion along the way.

The Union army had begun their attack just as Confederates were finally going to sleep. The 8th Michigan under William Fenton was first out, designated, according to Pat Brennan, to serve as "bait" in the "forlorn hope" that they might attempt such a daring assault and live to tell about it.[6] The *New York Herald* published a lengthy eyewitness version of the battle, which the *New Castle Courant* later reprinted. Their correspondent began his account:

> The forces of Gen. Stevens were formed in perfect quiet at his outer pickets at 2 ½ yesterday morning. The men fell promptly into line, having been at that hour first apprised of the movement they were to undertake. The morning was cold, and the entire sky was overcast with black, heavy clouds, so that in the darkness the task of maintaining silence and avoiding confusion was one of no little difficulty. We moved at half past four, no accident occurring to interrupt our progress. Col. Fenton's brigade consisting of the 8th Michigan Volunteers, under Lieut. Col. Graves; the 7th Connecticut, under Col. Hawley, and the 28th Massachusetts, under Lieut. Col. Moore—was in the advance.—Col. Leasure's brigade comprising the 79th Highlanders, under Lieut. Col. Morrison, the 100th Pennsylvania, under Major Leckey, and the 46th New York, Col. Rosa—was in support, together with Rockwell's Connecticut Battery, Captain Sears' company of Volunteer Engineers, and Capt. Sargeant's company of Massachusetts cavalry. A storming party consisting of two companies of the Eighth Michigan, led by Lieut. Lyons, Aid-de-Camp to General Stevens, with a negro guide was in the extreme advance.[7]

General Stevens led his forces very quietly as far as Rivers Causeway, where he stopped to let stragglers catch up. Shortly thereafter, they ran into Confederate pickets from the Charleston Light Infantry. The Charleston paper the next morning reported, "The enemy, about daylight Monday morning, made a sudden move upon them, capturing some three or four and driving in the remainder. The alarm was immediately given, but the enemy had also pushed rapidly forward and had got within three hundred yards of the battery …"[8] *The New York Herald* correspondent made the encounter sound more dramatic:

> Our route lay over an extensive cotton field, or rather a succession of cotton fields separated from each other by hedges and ditches. The ground was broken by these ridges peculiar to the plantations in this vicinity, and the passage over the uneven, billowy surface, marching as we were upon the "double quick" was excessively fatiguing; yet we moved forward very rapidly. Although our line was formed within rifle shot of the enemy's pickets so quietly were the troops maneuvered that they were ignorant of it, and a rebel lieutenant and four privates were surprised and captured.—Orders had been given to move forward by the flank, regiment following regiment. In no event were we to fire, but to press on and forward into line by regiments. When the enemy should open upon us, we were to use the bayonet on him and endeavor if possible to gain possession of the works.
>
> These orders were faithfully executed. Reaching the open fields about a mile from the rebel fortifications, Fenton's brigade directed its attack against the right, and Leasure's against the left of the work. These two brigades now pushed forward with great rapidity, the regiments keeping within supporting distance of each other and the Michigan regiment keeping close to the storming party.[9]

Inside the fort, confusion reigned for a few minutes as sleeping Confederate soldiers came awake to the reality of a battle already in progress. Captain R. L. Crawford, of the 1st South Carolina Volunteer Infantry, described the scene:

> I suppose by the time you get this, you will have seen an account of the battle day before yesterday. We had a hot time of it for about 3 or 4 hours. The battle commenced about 5 oclock in the morning and lasted until 9. The enemy had for nearly two days and a night been fighting our batteries at Secession Ville. Finding that they could not silence them, they finally concluded to take them by storm. They ceased firing about 8 oclock at night. When the firing stopped, Col Lamar ordered his men, who wer nearly exhausted from the long continued fight, to go into the rat holes and rest. pickets wer then thrown out, and every thing thought to be secure. Next morning however they wer completely surprised. The enemy passed our pickets and advanced under cover of a thick skirt of woods, and when the sentinel at the Fort discovered them they wer not more than a hundred yards off, he fired his gun and gave the alarm. Capt Reid [sic] who was in command of one of the companies ran out, and to his utter surprise found the enemy in strong force about forty yds from the fort, he immediately leveled our piece and fired into them. By this time one of the sergeants had got to another gun, but was unable to sight it, he called to Capt Reid to send some one to sight his gun, he jumped to the gun saying he would do it himself, just as he was getting the piece into position, he was shot through the head, the sergeant was also severely wounded. By this time Col Lamar had got to another gun and fired it with his own hands, he too was wounded in the face and back of the neck. The whole command was now in the fort but as they had no small arms and the Yankees had begun to come up the breast works their

condition was truly critical. Determined however not to give up their works they gathered the large sticks they use to put their pieces in position, and succeeded in clubbing them back as they would come up. they must have done good work from the quantity of brains which I saw on the breast works.[10]

Confederate guns on either side of the breastworks fired down the center of the field, causing the Yankees to veer both left and right.

The New York Herald described the design of Confederate defenses:

> When within about four hundred yards of the fort a terrific fire of grape and canister was opened on our columns from the work, and from the woods, abattis and rifle pits on our right. Four heavy guns on the enemy's parapet sent their murderous charges through the files of our brave men; masked batteries, of whose existence we had no knowledge, poured their terrible missles against us; sharp-shooters stationed all along the rebel line selected our officers for targets, and many a gallant leader fell at their first volley, while the men in the ranks dropped by scores.[11]

The Union Army was supported by naval gunfire from the *Ellen* and the *E. B. Hale*. These gunboats were located in Lighthouse Inlet, separated from the battlefield by a mile of woods; therefore, they could only take aim from the sound of cannon fire. Their assistance was of dubious value, since the gunners could not see whether their shots were hitting the earthworks or falling among their own men.

The Union troops advanced unarmed through a devastating fire of grape, canister, and musketry that swept the entire battlefield. The 8th Michigan, leading the assault, held a position in front of the fort for approximately twenty minutes. Some of these men actually managed to scale the parapet and engage in hand-to-hand combat. Behind them, the men

Pluff Mud Swamp at Edge of Fort Lamar, Secessionville
Photo by Floyd Schriber

of the 100th Pennsylvania advanced to within thirty or forty yards of the breastworks. Col. Leasure, who was serving as brigade commander, led the 79th New York into the attack. In a letter to his daughter, he described it this way:

> I advanced with the left flank of the Highlanders, cheering them to the charge, till when within about one hundred yards of the works three immense guns bellowed out a perfect cloud of grape, canister, old chains, empty porter bottles, nails, and even brickets, and just cut the regiment in two leaving one half to go to the right and the other to the left. Still the two portions passed on till when about thirty paces from the parapet, the rifles and musketry opened on us, and in less than two minutes I was the only man left on his feet.[12]

The Highlanders scrambled to rush the wall of the earthwork, and some actually managed to get into the fort, or at least to the top of the wall, where the fight became one not of artillery but of rifles, rifle butts, and fisticuffs. Next in the Union line came Hawley's 7th Connecticut, who headed toward the northern arm of the fort, following what they thought was an open path, and ending up stuck in the pluff mud along the causeway. The 28th Massachusetts followed them straight into the muck. While they were milling around in total disorder, the 8th Michigan was still near the wall but now receiving fire both from the fort and from the Union troops behind them.

Meanwhile, the Confederates were receiving some much-needed reinforcements. On Sunday night, two battalions had been sent out from Fort Lamar to erect a new battery of heavy guns that could reach the Yankee encampments. When they received the alarm that the Yankees were moving to attack Fort Lamar itself, they abandoned the new works and hurried to help fend off the attack. The 9th South Carolina "Pee Dee" Battalion, led

113

by Lt. Col. Alexander D Smith, arrived over a footbridge that approached the fort from the rear, and their additional manpower helped to drive the Yankees back. Lt. Col. Peter Gallaird and his Charleston Battalion followed the Pee Dees. Lieutenant James Campbell was among them, although he had set out from the work detail so abruptly that he had forgotten his gun. The *Charleston Daily Courier* praised his actions, singling him out as one of the "individual instances of courage and resolution … almost beyond commendation … Lieutenant Campbell having no other weapon at first, seized a large log of wood which, from the rampart, he threw down the side, rolling off several stormers, taking one of their own rifles, and continuing to fight with that."[13]

In front of the fort, the 79th New York arrived to join the battle, but they were forced to struggle over the bodies of their comrades. They directed their charge toward the south side of the fort, and Alexander Campbell defiantly planted their flag in front of the fort. Shortly after the battle, while flags of truce were allowing free passage between the lines to facilitate the recovery of the dead and wounded, Alexander received a letter from his brother who served in the Charleston Battalion:

> Dear Brother,
>
> I was astonished to hear from the prisoners that you was colour Bearer of the Regmt that assalted the Battrey at this point the other day. When I first heard it I looked over the field for you where I met one of the wounded of your Regt and he told me that he believed you was safe. I was in the Brest work during the whole engagement doing my Best to Beat you but I hope that You and I will never again meet face to face Bitter enemies in the Battle field. But if such should be the case You have but to discharge your deauty to Your caus for I can assure you I will strive to discharge my deauty to my country & My cause.[14]

Alexander was unable to reply before the period of truce ended, but he wrote of the incident to his wife: "Its rather too bad to think that we should be fighting him on one side and me on the other for he says he was in the fort during the whole engagement. I hope to god that he and I will get safe through it all …"[15]

Once again the 79th New York attempted to scale the wall of the fort, but without much success. Right behind them came the Roundheads, led into this battle by Maj. David Leckey because Col. Leasure was acting as brigade commander. Maj. Leckey later explained that he had only half the Roundheads with him.

> The morning report of the 15th instant showed 583 privates present for duty. Of these 300 and some odd, with the necessary officers, went on advance picket duty at 4 o'clock on the evening of the 15th, which left me about 280 men, with the necessary officers, to go into the field.
>
> On arriving at the picket headquarters, about 3 o'clock on the morning … About 130 men of the picket, including the two companies of the reserve alluded to as being on fatigue duty, joined me on the march or after we had got under fire.[16]

The Roundheads were told to support the 79th, and they were double-timing across the cotton furrows trying to catch up when the Confederate artillery opened up on them. Company C took the brunt of the blow as Leasure turned around and watched in horror:

> Within fifty yards of me on the right and looking to the left, I saw a whole regiment, lying in the bushes behind a kind of bank that led up to the left of the fort. I had barely time to see this and to see the right of the Highlanders wilting under a similar fire of small arms and the 100th coming up gallantly to

their support, when again the storm of missiles from the huge guns leaped out with tongues of fire, darkening all the air with the projectiles with which they had been crammed to the muzzle. Quick as thought I dropped flat on the ground and let the iron hail pass over me, and when I rose it was to see the ground strewn with Roundheads crying, dead and wounded, in all sorts of mangled horrid forms, and the Regiment cut in two, just as the other had been.[17]

Sgt. James McCaskey died in this barrage, although his fate would go unnoticed until the battle was over. By the time the Roundheads had arrived in front of the fort, the scene was chaotic. The darkness of the early morning mixed with the smoke of the big guns to obscure vision. The soldiers double-quickstepped across deeply rippled furrows and jagged stalks left by cotton crops. The ground, even where it was solid, was rapidly becoming slippery with blood. The topography of the field, narrowing sharply as one approached the fort, acted as a funnel, pushing the men toward the center from either flank, crowding them into an ever-decreasing space. Cannonballs flew overhead from the fort in front, from the union artillery behind the advancing line, and from the gunboats in the river. Soldiers who had already tried to storm the earthworks were moving back to the shelter of one of the ditches, hoping to regroup and mount another attack, but their paths led them straight into the middle of the new regiments moving forward. Occasionally, a retreating soldier stopped to lend a hand to someone who was only slightly wounded, but there was no time to pick up and carry one who was unconscious. The dead and wounded lay wherever they fell, while advancing troops could only try to avoid tripping over them.

The 46th New York arrived on the north side of the field, but too late to save what was turning into a rout. Gen. Stevens ordered his troops to back out and reform behind the two hedges, mainly because Wright's troops, who had been expected to provide artillery support from the rear were not yet in position. Col. Leasure obeyed the order:

> … I now saw the utter futility of attempting to form a line of battle there, and keeping my face toward the fort, I walked bareheaded and called my men to follow me slowly. Slowly, deliberately, doggedly they followed me step by step, till we reached the dyke about three hundred yards in front of the fort, where I halted them and put them in safety till I should return to them.
>
> Having mounted my horse, and Geordy [his son] having remounted, I commenced the task of rally my command under fire, and over that field we rode from end to end and from side to side, gathering up the men and forming the different regiments in their proper positions behind the dyke three hundred yards in front of the battery.[18]

The retreat allowed the Confederates to relax for a moment. Battery Lamar was by this time nearly out of ammunition, and its defenders had been reduced to firing scrap metal, stones, and anything else they could find. They were still hoping for reinforcements. Soon, troops from Gen. Wright's First Division, late as usual but ready for a fight, began a new attack along the north arm of the fort. They were under the command of Col. Robert Williams, who had been ordered by Gen. Benham to join Stevens' forces and fill their decimated ranks. The 3rd Rhode Island Heavy Artillery, under Major Edwin Metcalf, and the 3rd New Hampshire, under Lt. Col. John Jackson, moved up Battery Island Road and then eastward toward the fort, only to discover that they were separated from it by a marshy barrier of pluff mud. Also separating them from the fort was a line of felled timber and impenetrable thickets, while from behind them they could hear approaching gunfire from a new source. Desperately the New Englanders brought their artillery to bear on the fort, and for a few minutes the defenders of the fort seemed doomed. Then suddenly, the Yankees found themselves encircled by the arrival of the 4th Louisiana Infantry Battalion, only 250 strong but ready to take on the entire Northern army if the situation demanded it. After a quarter of an hour of confrontation, the Union soldiers retreated. The men from Rhode Island managed to move their artillery further north, but the New Hampshire troops were surrounded. They left behind on their particular little battleground 104 men dead or severely wounded.[19] Lt. Col. John McEnery of the 4th Louisiana could not help but boast of his men's prowess as they drove off this much larger force:

> I went into the action with 250 men and succeeded in putting to route twice that force of the enemy on the right. I think that this force of the enemy would undoubtedly have completely flanked the battery but for our timely arrival. The small band of brave men in the fort, exhausted and broken down in their almost superhuman exertions in repelling the foe in front, must have been unequal to the task of successfully engaging the enemy in front and on the right.[20]

Lt. Col. Charles Simonton's Eutaw Battalion and Col. Johnson Hagood's detachment from the 1st South Carolina had also marched from their camp on Dill Branch Road. They made their way to Artillery Crossroads and the Presbyterian Church, and then headed south on Battery Island Road toward Secessionville. Lt. Col. Ellison Capers and his detachment manning the battery at Clark's Point joined the march. Along their route, the Confederates discovered some of Gen. Lamar's men with a cannon but no knowledge of how it worked. Ellison Capers quickly gave them a lesson. He later reported:

> Meanwhile the enfilade battery in front of Clark's house was silent, and had not fired a shot. Its position enabled it to rake the front of the Secessionville work, and to fire right into the rear of the force at and beyond the negro houses. Colonel Hagood ordered me to gallop back to the battery and order fire at once. This I did with all possible speed, and found Lieutenant J. B. Kitching's 15 or 18 men there, belonging to Lamar's regiment. To my demand why he was not firing on the enemy, the lieutenant said that he and his men had but just come from the country, had no orders to fire, knew nothing of the service of the guns or ammunition, but would gladly fire the guns if I would direct them how to proceed. I at once loaded, sighted, and fired the right piece, the lieutenant and his men springing to the work in gallant style. The shell we fired [had the desired] effect on the enemy, delighting us all.[21]

Arriving within view of Secessionville, the Eutaws took up a position behind a hedge, but were told not to fire because their own men were in front of them. Eventually, they discovered that the troops were really the 3rd Rhode Island and attacked, driving the Yankees back toward the fort within range of the Confederate guns. Gus Smythe later described the action in a letter to Mrs. McCord:

> We were aroused early in the morning & double-quicked to the place of action, where our position was assigned us behind a hedge with the Yankees on the other side. Scarcely had we got into our places & the order given & obeyed to crouch down when a volley of balls past over our heads & continued for nearly three quarters of an hour & which killed four & wounded seven or eight in our company alone, besides knocking up the dust around the rest of us. I could see several fall & bury themselves not six inches from me in the ground. The worst of it was that Hagood thinking Stevens' [Col. Clement Stevens, 24th South Caro-

lina] men were in front ordered us not to fire & it was not until some of the Yankees had come through the hedge that we discovered our mistake & fired a volley killing & wounding some twenty or thirty.[22]

Both the 3rd Rhode Island and the 3rd New Hampshire had suffered heavy losses. Gen. Wright's forces could only cover the retreat while the wounded were taken to a field hospital at Rivers House. Meanwhile Col. Leasure was still trying to rally the survivors of his brigade for another attack. He had them reorganized at the second hedge, but had to delay while word was sent to the gunboats to stop firing into their midst. And while they waited, Gen. Benham called everyone off, declaring the whole battle a mere reconnaissance exercise. The *New York Herald* article continued:

In the mean time, though the casualties had been frightful, both in nature and number, the troops of the division were in good order. Their confidence was still unshaken. Their courage was unbroken. Like veterans they waited for the word to charge. But at this juncture Col. Williams command, which had occupied a position on the left, from which they threw a galling fire across the marsh into the position of the enemy, were compelled in consequence of the falling of shells from our gunboats, to fall back, and thus the main attention of the enemy was given to the front.—Under these circumstances it was deemed useless waste of life further to protract the contest, and the order was given to withdraw the troops. This was done in the most admirable manner. Rockwell's battery taking the lead, & the various regiments following in line of battle, with flags displayed.[23]

Col. Leasure's memory was somewhat different:

At about half past seven o'clock the enemy had expended all their ammunition, and the troops began to carry off their wounded over the causeway in the rear of the fort toward Charleston; and as I sat and watched them through my glasses the troops themselves began to cross over by the hundreds, when all at once they stopped, hesitated, and began turning back to the fort. On looking over to my left I saw *Wright's and Williams' brigades withdrawing* from the field, and presently an order came to me to fall back. Oh God forgive me, the bitterness engendered by the disappointment of that hour. "Old Benham" without seeing the field at all, relying upon the reports of his frightened young squirts of aides, gave the order to *retreat*. When to have held still for one more hour would have taken the fort without firing another gun.

That fort was mine, but for the contrary order. My men were fresh. They had stood to be slain. Where they could not fight, they would not give ground, till I gave the word, and they rallied like heroes under a most terrible fire. But why dwell on the sickening details of a day of useless slaughter, made useless in the first place by the incompetency of the planner of the attack and, when the skill and bravery of the army redeemed his blunder, made useless again by his untimely order to fall back.[24]

Once the battle was over, the thoughts of Col. Leasure and Rev. Browne turned immediately to the care of the wounded.[25] The chaplain described the scene in the makeshift hospital established at Rivers House:

A sad and painful experience it was to me to minister in the hospitals and assist the surgeons. Many of the poor fellows were dying, many suffering most acutely … Some were wounded in the head and face, some in the breast and bowels. A discharge of grape with old chains and other miscellaneous missiles of iron, glass, etc. was specially destructive to our men, chiefly shattering their legs. They lay most of them moaning in the hospital till the impressive service of the surgeons began. Every pain was calmed with chloroform, and there the mangled limb was removed ... I had spoken to all then, poor fellows, and directed them kindly to the Savior.[26]

And as they died, he "pronounced a sad brief service" over their graves.

The real hero of the hospital, however, was Col. Leasure, who immediately turned over his weapons and other soldierly trappings in favor of his former professional life as a doctor. One of his men remembered that the young field surgeons, overcome with the enormity of their task, called upon Col. Leasure for help.

He threw off his sword and coat, and in a few minutes every surgeon was at work under his direction and assistance, in relieving, dressing, and amputating. While thus engaged, General Stevens entered the hospital and seeing one of his commanders in superintendency of the wounded, Stevens went up and silently grasped his hand for a moment and while the big tears rolled over his cheeks, with great emotion he remarked, "God bless you, you brave soldier and good man."[27]

Not surprisingly, Col. Leasure himself did not mention this incident in his letters to his wife and daughter. It was not an action in which he would take pride; he was simply doing his duty, as any of the Roundheads might have done in similar circumstances.

The Battle of Secessionville was over. The retreat had been orderly, but no amount of flag waving or close order march could disguise the fact that the Union army had been soundly defeated. The casualty list horrified those who read the newspaper account:

The losses in Gen. Stevens' division have been very heavy. Nearly 200 of the eighth Michigan were ... cut down, and of ten company commanders who went into the field, only two returned with their commands. The 79th, whose gallantry at Bull Run we all remember, sustained a terrible list of casualties, as they accompanied the Michigan boys in the assault. The losses in the Twenty-eighth Massachusetts are also heavy. Many other officers in the second division were mowed down by the hellish storm, whose fury and whose terrible effect, during the thickest of the fight, no feeble rhetoric of mine can aid me to portray.[28]

Battle figures tend to be unreliable. The official report of the battle written by General Stevens indicates that the Union forces numbered only 3,562 men, while the Confederates had approximately 3000.[29] But another section of the records show that General Wright alone commanded 3,728 men and officers who were held in reserve while General Stevens had 6,411.[30] A modern account lists 6,600 Union forces.[31] The report of Brigadier General Nathan G. Evans indicated that Confederate strength was very weak at the beginning of the battle and did not reach 2000 until the second assault.[32] Similarly, the counts of casualties varied. The official Union record listed 107 killed, 487 wounded, and 89 missing.[33] Newspaper accounts stated the casualty total—killed, wounded, and missing—as 668.[34] Yet the Confederate reports stated that the bodies of 509 Union soldiers had been buried on the field of battle. Of the wounded, forty-three Union soldiers were known to have fallen into the hands of the Confederates.[35] Another fifty-seven Union men were so severely wounded that they were evacuated to New York on the U.S. transport *Ericsson*.[36]

In the next few days, both sides needed to take stock of what had just happened and to finish the onerous duties that accompanied such a vicious and deadly battle. Hundreds of wounds demanded attention. The dead had to be collected, identified, and decently buried. Prisoners awaited transport. Officers had their reports to fill out, and all those who were still able to write wanted time to notify their families that they were safe.

The difficult task of clearing the battlefield fell to the Confederates. Gus Smythe and a small detachment were sent out almost immediately after the battle to gather up weapons and tend the wounded. Gus was horrified by the sights he faced:

Such a scene I wish never again to witness. Twenty or thirty men lay stretched out on a small field, wounded, dying & dead. One must have been in the act of loading his gun when a grape shot took out the whole of his back, for he lay dead with this hands raised, just as if he were even then loading. Another lay close by with his leg entirely shot away, & only a piece of skin connecting his knee & his thigh ... On the other side of the marsh where Lamar's battery could play upon them, the slaughter was, of course, immensely greater. After bringing in the arms we were again sent out with litters to bring in the wounded, & we had to carry them nearly two miles to the ambulance.[37]

The bodies of the dead presented an even greater logistical problem. Sanitation concerns and the heat of mid-June demanded that they be buried quickly, which did not allow for identification of every body. On 18 June 1862, Brigadier General Isaac I. Stevens wrote to the commanding general of the Confederate forces on James Island: "In the action of the 16th it is known that some of our dead, and it is probable that a few of our wounded, were left at or in the rear of your works ... I have determined to send a flag of truce to ascertain the names of the killed and of the wounded, and if practicable to recover the bodies of the dead."[38] On the same day Brigadier General N. G. Evans replied: "The information desired as to the names and condition of your wounded ... will be cheerfully furnished you at an early hour. The wounded having been sent to the city of Charleston, it is necessary to communicate with that place first. I have also to state that your dead as far as found have been decently interred."[39] Among the Confederate reports is one from Lieutenant Colonel J. McEnery that his men had buried 168 unidentified Union soldiers on the field.[40] Another from Colonel Lamar states that 341 men were buried in front of his batteries.[41]

Perhaps the most difficult task of all entailed notifying the families of those who had died. In the absence of any formal process, letters of notification during the Civil War might be written by a soldier's companions, an attending physician, the unit chaplain, or one of the junior officers. But no matter who wrote the letter, it tended to follow something of a standard format. Drew Gilpin Faust, who has conducted a study of such letters, found that "it seems almost as if their authors had a checklist in mind, enumerating the necessary details."[42] Her findings suggested that the most important feature of such a letter was to demonstrate that the soldier had died a "Good Death: ... the deceased had been conscious of his fate, had demonstrated his willingness to accept it, had showed signs of belief in God and in his own salvation, and had invoked the idealized domestic deathbed scene by leaving messages and instructive exhortations for those who should have been at his side."[43] Such a letter might have provided some solace to the Calvinist families who waited for news of the Roundheads. Unfortunately the nature of the battle of Secessionville, with all its confusion, suddenness of death, and the anonymity of bodies abandoned on a blood-soaked battlefield, left the writers struggling to offer consolation while giving an honest account of what had happened.

Lt. Philo S. Morton was assigned to contact the McCaskey family with the news that their son was missing and presumed dead:

Mr. Jn. McCaskey,
Dear Sir:

Gen. Benham appointed the morning of the 16th as the time for our forces to move on "Tower Fort" near "Sesesha" Ville, which is in sight of Sumpter, and about 2 miles from the City of Charlestown.

We left Camp at 1 A.M. and at daylight marched up to the Fort under a galling fire of Grape, Cannister, Shot, and Shell. I was in Command of our Company. Men were falling on every side. Whilst near the Ft. a Shower of Grape came in our ranks, one of which struck your Son, James, and we think tore off one of his legs, near the body. He fell! This is the last we saw of him. The "Liter-bearers" of Gen. Wright's Div. must, I think, have carried him off the Field.

I have searched and searched for him but in vain. We all feel confident that he is dead. Jacob Leary fell at the same time and is also missing. James was a noble young man and a brave soldier—was beloved by all his associates. He was like a brother to me, and I lament his loss. You have my sympathy and prayers in your deep affliction.

The loss in our Co. was 4 killed and 71 wounded. We fought with great disadvantages and in consequence lost heavily.

If it can possibly be done I will send his Knap-Sack and traps home to you, as I have no doubt you would like to possess them. His Watch and what Money he had, were on his person.

If any further intelligence of his fate can be had, I will inform you in due time.

Yours truly,

Lieut. Philo S. Morton[44]

This account, when paired with the letter written by Gus Smythe, offers an intriguing possibility. Was the young Union soldier, who, Gus Smythe said, "lay close by with his leg entirely shot away, & only a piece of skin connecting his knee & his thigh," the same James McCaskey whose wound Lt. Morton described as a shot that "tore off one of his legs, near the body?" Perhaps not. The wound

was a common one, as Rev. Browne pointed out from the field hospital. Still, it is not out of the realm of possibility that these two young men, whose lives had paralleled each other for over a year, might have had one last encounter on the Secessionville battleground. In this strange war that pitted brother against brother and brought to opposing sides people with many shared convictions, no pairing was too bizarre. Capt. Percival Drayton, USN, could steer his ship to fire upon the fort commanded by his brother, Gen. Thomas Drayton, CSA. Pvt. Alexander Campbell, USA, could plant a defiant New York flag near the breastwork of a confederate fort while his brother Lt. James Campbell, CSA, rolled logs over the edge of that work to drive the Union soldiers away. West Point classmates General Henry Benham, USA, a New Englander through and through, and Gen. John C. Pemberton, CSA, born a Pennsylvania Quaker, could lead their armies to battle against one another on an obscure South Carolina island. So, too, could Corp. Augustine T. Smythe, a member of South Carolina's Washington Light Infantry, have stumbled across the body of Sgt. James McCaskey, a Pennsylvania Roundhead, on the battlefield they shared, just as they shared their Scotch-Irish ancestry, their Presbyterian faith, and the course of their military careers.

There is no evidence that the McCaskey family received further official notice of what had happened to their son's body. A family tradition holds that a fellow Roundhead had seen James propped up against a tree, wounded but alive. He had tried to help James to safety, but James had urged him to go ahead, assuring him that he would be all right where he was. Such a tale might have served as consolation that James had indeed died a "Good Death." It demonstrated his courage, his concern for others, and his awareness and acceptance of his own fate. There was also some reassurance in the news that other local boys who enlisted with James had survived the battle. Several months later, Corp. Frederick Pettit, Company C, wrote a letter to his sister, erroneously reporting, "It now appears James Mc[C]Haskey who was reported killed at the battle near Charleston was only wounded and taken prisoner."[45] But acting against whatever shreds of hope might linger were the facts: the horrifying description of the battle itself and the knowledge that hundreds of unidentified bodies had been pushed into a makeshift mass grave in front of the Secessionville fort.

Some six days after the battle, John P. Wilson, who had mustered into Company C along with James McCaskey, wrote to his sister Eleanor, describing his impressions of the Secessionville battle. Eleanor took the letter to John and Jane McCaskey, who carefully preserved it along with the few other mementos of their oldest son's military experience.

Dear Sister,

I embrace this opportunity to let you know that we are al well at present except Jim Mc-Caskey and Hugh Wilson that you knowed. We had a big fight on the 16th of June. We attacked a fort close to Fort Sumpter. We had about 5000 men, and we had about 1000 killed, wounded and missing. Among the wounded was Hugh Wilson, but they think he will get well. He had one of his eyes shot out by a musket ball. Jim McCaskey and Jacob Leary fell dangerously wounded close to the fort, and we did not get the fort, and we could not find them, and we dont know whether they are dead or if the rebels have them. They have some of our men and we have some of thers.

We run up close to the fort, and the rebels were raining showers of grape, cannister, chains, and musketballs, but I did not care for them a bit more than if it had been a shower of rain. Henry Guy has 3 holes through his blouse, but he is not hurt. There was one ball struck my bayonet. I was the only one standing for several rods around for a while. The rest laid down to avoid the grape, but I wanted to see where it was coming from. Several that laid down never got up

again, but there was not one of the balls touched me. We could not get in the fort when we got to it. We stayed for over an houer and then we got the order to retreat. And I know you never saw a lot of men walk so slow, and every little bit they would stop and look back. I did not hear the order to retreat, and I did not go back until the Colonel told me to fall back to the regiment. And when I looked around I could not see only about 20 of our regiment. And I walked 3 times along in front of the fort, but the rebels did not hit me, but balls was flying as thick as hail.

But I exspect you will have read all about the fight in the papers before you get this. And I think we will have the fort and maybe Charleston soon. We have the batteries pretty near finished that will knocke the fort clean off the ground.

General Benham is under Arest for taking the men in the way he did. General Wright is in command now. But I must close for this time, so good bye, Elli. I will write soon.

To E. A. W.

—J. P. W.

You must not be uneasy about us, for we want to try it again soon.

J. P. W.

John Wilson's letter must have aroused very mixed emotions in the McCaskey family. His reaction to danger smacks more of bravado than good sense, but it clearly portrays the chaos, danger, and frustration experienced by the Roundhead Regiment. It also reveals the curious conviction of invulnerability that energized not just John Wilson but all of the Roundheads. He did not care about the barrage of ammunition coming his way "a bit more than if it had been a shower of rain." His curiosity kept him on his feet because he "wanted to see where it was coming from." Every good Calvinist knew that his fate was preordained and that nothing he did would change the end God had already assigned him. John's observation that "Several that laid down never got up again" simply went further to prove his point. Wrongheaded though it may appear to a modern reader, John's letter echoed what he had been taught in sermons all of his life. Rev. Browne himself sometimes explained that he did not run when someone shot at him, because to do so might put him in the path of a bullet God had predestined for someone else. For the McCaskeys, it may have helped them to believe that James had died unafraid and at God's will.

Comments in John Wilson's letter raised important questions about the conduct of the battle. According to Colonel Leasure, the order to retreat came from General Stevens' aide, Captain Stevens. The Roundheads were first told to regroup behind the first hedge and then ordered to fall back still further so artillery could fire over their heads. By 7:30 A.M. they were told to retire to the road.[46] John Wilson's bitterness at the retreat was echoed by a member of the 79th New York, whose journal account was published in *The New York Times*: "Shot down by unseen enemies, and without having an opportunity of returning the fire with any effect, the men got discouraged, but remained stubbornly on the ground until the order was given to withdraw—an order, let me say, which was only rendered necessary by the shameful fact that, notwithstanding the strong force within supporting distance, no support came."[47]

James McCaskey had fallen during a battle marked by poor judgment, mismanagement, botched orders, and missed opportunities. Newspaper accounts such as this editorial could have been of little comfort to his family:

Our batteries did not open until we were repulsed. Was this not reversing the usual order of things? The enemy was not taken by surprise. We had a broad space to advance over, in full view of the fort, and they could shoot us down as rabbits are shot at a battue. Why shot and shell were not piled before an infantry attack was made, I am at a loss to imagine. Is siege artillery henceforth to be used only in covering a retreat, and is the bayonet, after all, the most formidable weapon which can be brought to cope with modern engineering science? If piles of dead bodies are to be our scaling ladders, muskets our sole stay and support against rifled cannon and wide-mouthed mortars, it will take a large and devoted force to capture Charleston.[48]

Even more significant was the bare mention of General Benham's arrest. The charges against General Benham were made in a letter from General Hunter to Stanton on 23 June 1862:

I gave positive orders to General Benham that no advance should be made until further explicit orders had been received from these headquarters. General Benham disobeyed these positive orders and clear instructions, and the result, I deeply regret to say, has been a disastrous repulse … I have felt it my duty to arrest General Benham and order him North by the steamer conveying this letter.[49]

The change of command spelled an end to hopes that "we will have the fort and maybe Charleston soon." Within a month the Union army withdrew from James Island, while Charleston itself remained in Confederate hands until February 1865.

CHAPTER 9

A Pity He Was Not Hung in Virginia

Contemporary observers of the Engagement at Secessionville recognized that the outcome had been a fluke; they could only muse on what might have been. Charles Cawley, a Union naval officer, believed that "had the same force assaulted these works a month earlier … the result might have been different."[1] General G. T. Beauregard, viewing the battle from the Confederate side, also recognized that the victory could have gone the other way:

> The truth of the matter is, that the point attacked by Generals Benham and I. I. Stevens near Secessionville was the strongest one of the whole line, which was then unfinished and was designed to be some five miles in length. The two Federal commanders might have overcome the obstacles in their front had they proceeded further up the Stono. Even as it was, the fight at Secessionville was lost, in great measure, by lack of tenacity on the part of Generals Benham and Stevens. Their troops outnumbered ours more than two to one, and fought with considerable dash. Some of them, in the impetus of the assault, went even inside one of the salients of the work. It was saved by the skin of our teeth.[2]

More recently, E. Milby Burton engaged in similar conjectures:

> If the Battle of Secessionville had been a Union victory, and if the victorious troops

had pushed forward across James Island and captured Fort Johnson from the rear, there is no telling what would have happened to Charleston. Had Charleston fallen in 1862, the entire course of the war could have been changed, and in all probability it would have been greatly shortened.[3]

But all of this is mere conjecture. The fact remains that nothing was accomplished by this brief period of carnage. Neither side lost or gained a foot of territory. The Union Army was no nearer its objectives, nor was Charleston any safer from the threat of attack. When the dust of battle cleared, all that remained were abandoned cotton fields littered with spent ammunition, newly dug graves, and individual lives that were forever altered.

For the Union generals, the days and weeks following the battle were spent vainly scrambling to repair damaged reputations. General Wright, newly appointed commander of the forces on James Island, at last realized the potential advantages of his position and the capabilities of his men:

> I have no reason to think that the occupation of James Island with our present force even, is now untenable. Every indication is to the contrary. We can hold on for a long time, if it be necessary, against any force that the enemy is believed to have in our vicinity, and we can only be reached by batteries which the enemy

must yet establish, his present ones not being within effective range.[4] This was a far cry from the attitude of impending defeat he had shown only days earlier, but his burst of confidence came too late. Within a week, his command would be abolished. Wright continued to serve in the rank of general until the end of the war. He would be given other commands, but they would always be peripheral to the action.

Admiral DuPont's worst fears about the incompetence of the Army had proved themselves correct, but he could take little pleasure in having been right in such an instance. His own career was soon to founder in the same location. In April 1863 he was ordered to attack Charleston Harbor with his naval forces alone. He did not approve of the plan but followed orders. When he was defeated, he asked to be relieved of his command. He, too, spent the remainder of the war serving on boards and commissions; he died on active duty in June 1865.

General Stevens, whose Second Division had suffered gravely during the battle, took steps to shift the blame onto other shoulders. In what might be considered an unprofessional move, he argued his case in the court of public opinion. On 15 July 1862, a copy of his official report appeared in the *New York Times*. Among his assertions were these: "I considered myself as obeying orders to which I had expressed the strongest possible objection … The very thing happened which is to be feared in such an attempt … The fault is not in my orders or arrangements, but in having a fight there at all under such circumstances."[5] Stevens moved to Virginia and died in action at Chantilly during the Second Battle of Bull Run on 1 September 1862. Although his death was a great loss to the Union Army, he thus escaped the embarrassment of being found partly responsible for the defeat at Secessionville. On 26 June 1863, the Judge Advocate General sent to President Lincoln his findings on the battle: "Had the officer charged with conducting the assault arrived, as it was intended he should, earlier, and directed personally and in proper order the march of the troops in their advance, and had he not ordered the troops under Colonel Hawley to fall back, the attack would have been successful."[6] In deference to an officer who had died in the line of duty, he did not mention Stevens by name, but the report leaves no doubt as to his share of the culpability.

The onus of defeat fell heaviest on General Benham. Benham's military career included early promotions and command successes in the Mexican War and as chief engineer of the Department of the Ohio under McClellan. But in September 1861, he had angered Gen. William Rosecrans, who accused him of insubordinate behavior and public drunkenness and blamed him for Union losses during the battles at Corrick's Ford and Carnifex Ferry, Virginia.[7] Benham's penchant for failing to obey orders continued through October and November of 1861, when his troops faced battles at Kahawha and New River, West Virginia. Dispatches between Rosecrans and Benham clearly demonstrated that Rosecrans was going beyond the call of duty to excuse Benham's mistakes and deliberate failures. Even as he wrote the final report, Rosecrans stated, "It has been with great regret that I have found it necessary to censure a general officer for the failure to capture the rebel forces who were justly ours."[8] Rosecrans eventually removed Benham from command and sent him from Virginia back to Boston, where for a while he worked on the defenses of Boston Harbor.

Many of the men under his command had scorned him from the moment he arrived in South Carolina, for rumors of difficulties in this previous command had preceded him. William Lusk, of the 79th New York, wrote of the troops' dissatisfaction just days before Secessionville:

The fact is, I believe Gen. Rosecrans was not far wrong when he charged Genl. Benham with cowardice, drunkenness, and lying. He was Court Martialed and acquitted, and sent down here to take charge of our little army. Right or wrong, all despise him. No one trusts him. If we take Charleston it will not be his fault. This is rather bitter, but it is a shame to put such men in command.[9]

The same estimate, of course, was apparent in the private correspondence of Benham's associates and staff. Gen Stevens had called him "imbecile, vacillating, and utterly unfit to command."[10] DuPont had predicted that it would be "literally impossible for him to conduct this military department."[11] And even Col. Leasure, whose judgments of others were usually kind, referred to him as "the old fool."[12]

Immediately after the battle, the correspondence of ordinary soldiers revealed that almost everyone blamed Benham for the defeat. Capt. Lusk was so angry that he fired off a letter asking an uncle in Connecticut, Benham's home state, to help get Benham removed from power:

> Let there be no mercy shown to one who shows no mercy. He must be crushed at once, or we are all lost, and even as it is, God only knows whether his folly may not involve us in destruction before any action can be taken. I will not enumerate half the examples of imbecility he has shown, or the wickedness of which he has been guilty. The last act is too real. His folly has culminated in one damning enterprise which must make him eternally infamous … the blood of the murdered men cries out for vengeance …

> When the action was over, Genl. Benham tried to say that it was only a reconnaissance. If this be so, let us have a General in command, who can recconoitre without the sacrifice of an eighth of the force engaged. 799 killed, wounded, and missing! Let the dead who died nobly have a voice, I say. Let the wounded lying on their beds of pain, plead their sufferings. Let those who lie in the prison houses of the enemy cry all shame, shame to a General who makes such a reconnaissance![13]

Benham was arrested on the evening of 19 June 1862, by order of General Hunter, on the grounds that the attack on Secessionville was a direct violation of orders. On 7 August, Secretary of War Stanton and General-in-Chief H. W. Hallack agreed without a formal hearing to muster Benham out of service as a brigadier general of volunteers. He was reduced in rank to major of engineers and once again assigned to supervise the building of fortifications around Boston. For the next several months, Benham wrote increasingly desperate letters to Hallack, Stanton, and Lincoln, asking for a chance to have his case reviewed in a public hearing. The Judge Advocate General's office, when it finally took up the matter in January 1863, reached the following conclusions:

> … the attack on the earthwork was not in fact, and was certainly not intended to be, a violation of orders; nor was it an ill-digested or criminally rash movement, but one which was made from a sense of duty, which should have succeeded, and which failed from no fault of General Benham, but from causes which he could not control …

> Over-aggressiveness has certainly not been so prevailing a vice in the military service during the present war as to call for such an example as the sudden dismissal of this officer presents. Rashness and over-eagerness to strike the enemy may certainly become culpable and be fraught with disaster, but the inaction of military men is often yet more to be deplored …

> General Benham should not be condemned as incapable or unfaithful, pre-

cipitately or without a hearing. His restoration is respectfully recommended.[14] The Army quietly restored Benham's rank on 6 February 1863, but he never held another combat command. During the remainder of the war he was assigned to bridge construction.

General Hunter, on whom responsibility for the Union defeat should have ultimately devolved, had moved quickly to cut his losses. His immediate dismissal of General Benham served to focus public censure on his second-in-command. Then, on 27 June 1862, lest his forces suffer further humiliation, he suspended operations and ordered a complete withdrawal from James Island. Concern for the health of the troops was his justification: "The great number of men prostrated on James Island by bilious and low typhoid fevers, and the increasing sick list, attributed to malarial debility, gave warning of what we might have expected had the occupation of our position there been continued."[15] Hunter never again commanded troops. He spent the remaining years of the war serving on boards, commissions, and courts-martial. He retired in 1866.

For the slaves whose owners had abandoned them, and for the missionaries who had come south to help prepare them for freedom, the defeat of Union troops meant a great shift of authority. Even before the Army's departure from the South Carolina coast in mid-July 1862, trouble was brewing. Because the Gideonites and the government cotton agents under Reynolds continued to clash, Samuel P. Chase took steps to correct the problems created by establishing dual authorities in the Sea Islands. He appointed Brig. Gen. Rufus Saxton "to take possession of all the plantations heretofore occupied by rebels, and take charge of the inhabitants remaining thereon within the department" and to make "such rules and regulations for the cultivation of the land, and for the protection, employment and government of the inhabitants as

circumstances seem to require." He was responsible only to the War Department and to Gen. Hunter.[16]

Under Saxton's administration, more money for equipment, food, and clothing for former slaves became available. Superintendents of plantations received regular salaries, and the sale of cotton financed future needs.[17] Accommodations for the missionaries improved after the cotton agents left, and the missionaries recovered many of the items the agents had confiscated. Given that summer was coming, food was more plentiful, and ex-slaves were more willing to work when they were assured of being paid.[18] Saxton did his best to correct the problems, but working against him were other factors. He knew little about growing cotton, he had arrived at the height of the malaria season when illness threatened everyone, and the entrenched military command was unwilling to cooperate with him because he was a newcomer. The missionaries saw that he could not stand up to military interference and soon lost faith in him.[19] Charles P. Ware complained that "though affairs have of course been improved by his presence and authority, very little in proportion to our hopes and our needs has been accomplished. We need a civilian, who is a first-rate business man, —of force, of forethought, of devoted interest in this undertaking."[20]

Saxon offered Edward Pierce a position on his staff, but Pierce refused to stay on after June. His overt reason was that he needed to return to his neglected law practice on Boston because he was not rich enough to continue to finance his stay in the south.[21] As for the other Gideonites, some determined to remain through the summer, only to be felled by the fevers that plagued them all. Several died, while others had to be evacuated home to recover. Some, including Susan Walker, who decided she was not suited for this type of work, simply lost their enthusiasm. Still others had to be sent home for general incompetence, for taking advantage of the situation to line their own pockets, or because they were unhappy that they could not achieve their own sectarian agendas.[22]

In a further development, Edward Philbrick and a group of other superintendents from the Boston area decided that they could operate more efficiently if they could get out from under government control entirely. They proposed buying several plantations to demonstrate the efficiency of real "free labor" working the land. In this proposal, Philbrick would hold the land in his name and manage it, paying six percent interest to those who contributed to the venture. He would claim one-fourth of the profits for his own and assume all responsibility for losses. Despite accusations of self-interest, the partners were able to purchase, on 9 March 1863, eleven cotton plantations and to lease two others from the government. This gave the new company over 8,000 acres of cropland, a third of St. Helena Island, and control of almost 1000 workers who lived on these lands. Philbrick had expenses of somewhere between $41,000 and $50,000 during their first year of operation. These included cost of land, labor costs, teachers' salaries, interest paid to subscribers, and the cost of transporting and marketing the crop. He produced 73,000 pounds of ginned cotton, which he sold for $1.50 to $2.00 a pound, netting $81,000 for the year's operation.[23] Those who had come to offer the slaves independence ended, in this case, by exploiting them.

For the slaves themselves, their situation improved only after Lincoln began to move toward freeing the Negroes. On 22 July 1862, Lincoln read a draft of his Preliminary Emancipation Proclamation; he officially announced it on 22 September 1862.[24] Under its provisions, no fugitive slaves were to be returned to their former owners. Negroes who served in the military were freed, along with all members of their families. On 5 October, Philbrick commented, "The President's proc-lamation does not seem to have made a great deal of stir anywhere. Here the people don't take the slightest interest in it. They have been free already for nearly a year, as far as they could see." Their only concern was whether "they would be given up to their masters in case South Carolina comes back to the Union."[25] Once Philbrick read the proclamation, however, he wrote, "I now feel more than ever the importance of our mission here, not so much for the sake of the few hundreds under my own eyes as for the sake of the success of the experiment we are now trying … I don't think the old masters will ever be successful in employing the blacks, but I do believe that Yankees can be."[26] He was right. Saxton immediately asked for, and received, permission to recruit black soldiers.[27] Saxton thus would eventually accomplish what Hunter had been unable to do; he established black regiments of soldiers to their benefit and to the benefit of the Union army.

The Confederate officers who fought at Secessionville fared no better than did their Union counterparts. Colonel Lamar, commander of the battery and earthworks had the fort named after him, it is true, but that honor did not accrue as the result of the Battle of Secessionville. Lamar recovered from his Secessionville wounds only to fall victim to the ubiquitous regiments of mosquitoes that plagued James Island. He died in 1863 from an intermittent fever contracted there, and the official naming of Fort Lamar marked his death.

General Evans, commander of the Third Military District of South Carolina, had directed much of the defense. He saw further action at Bull Run, Antietam, and Vicksburg, but by late 1863 he too was in disgrace. He was twice court-martialed, charged with drunkenness and disobedience. Although he was acquitted, General Beauregard relieved him of command. In 1864, an inexplicable fall from a horse that was standing still effectively spelled the end of his military career, and he retired to become a high school principal in Alabama.

General Pemberton, commander of the Department of Georgia and South Carolina, never gained the confidence of the citizens of Charleston. During the very days when he was supervising the preparations at Secessionville, William Porcher Miles, a Confederate congressman from Charleston, was petitioning Robert E. Lee for his removal.[28] Shortly after the Battle of Secessionville, Pemberton was transferred to Mississippi. On 4 July 1863, he surrendered to Grant at Vicksburg. After his exchange, he resigned his commission to become a gentleman farmer and inspector of artillery.

The citizens of Charleston failed to credit much importance to the Battle of Secessionville. Ever since the signing of the Ordinance of Secession at Institute Hall on 20 December 1860—ever since the capture of Castle Pinkney and the occupation of Fort Moultrie on 27 December 1860—ever since the guns of Fort Johnson fired the first shot against Fort Sumter, Charlestonians had been expecting an attack on their city. They had been sure that the Expeditionary Force that seized Port Royal Sound meant to move on Charleston Harbor. They had left the city *en masse* after the fall of Fort Pulaski in April 1862. A Confederate soldier who took a furlough in early June to visit the city found it "completely deserted … all the houses seemed to be closed. Stores closed and those with their doors open have no goods in them."[29]

Reports that Union gunboats had entered the Stono River and that federal troops had landed on James Island caught the attention of those who remained in Charleston at the beginning of June, but when no real attack materialized, most people relaxed once more. The local papers even reprinted a quip from the New York *Tribune*, hoping to stir up the complacency of the local citizenry: "'Doom' hangs over wicked Charleston. That viper's nest and breeding place of rebellion is, ere

this time, invested by Union Arms—perhaps already in our hands. If there is any city deserving of holocaustic infamy, it is Charleston. Should its inhabitants choose to make its site a desert, blasted by fire, we do not think many tears would be shed."[30] But Charleston had already been devastated by fire, and few thought the Union army could do more damage than had already been done.

The Rev. Thomas Smyth and his family were still in residence in their comfortable home on Meeting Street. They had packed up their most valued books and art works for storage in Columbia, but the good Presbyterian minister refused to budge from his home until it became imperative to do so. Even Mrs. Smyth, who had spent the beginning of the war dithering about the fate of her sons, was not frightened by this most recent battle. Once assured of the safety of her sons Adger and Augustine, both of whom had been in the fight, she spent the days after the battle helping with the wounded who were brought to Charleston for care. She saw to it that those who were not injured too badly were made comfortable in local houses and made frequent trips to the hospital to care for one of Gus's close friends, James Tavernor. She arranged for Taverner's fiancée, Miss Clifford, to come down from Columbia to be with him. And when he died from the wounds he suffered at Secessionville, she helped make the arrangements, and held his funeral in her own front room.[31] Margaret Adger Smyth came into her own as a result of the battle, able now to rise above her own fears and cope with whatever life had in store for her. The Smyths remained in Charleston until September 1863, when they were literally driven out by Union guns shelling the town. They moved north to Summerton, where they remained until the summer of 1865.[32]

Those who had already moved out of Charleston awaited news of the battle with some curiosity but not with a great deal of fear. On 11 June, Mary Chesnut wrote in her diary: "Sixteen more Yankee regiments have landed on James Island. Eason writes: 'They have twice the energy and enterprise of our people.' I answered: 'Wait awhile. Let them alone until climate and mosquitoes and sand flies and dealing with Negroes takes it all out of them'." She was not quite so complacent about the qualifications of Gen. Pemberton, however:

> It is told of Pemberton, probably because he is a Yankee born, that he has stopped the work of obstruction in the Harbor, and that he has them busy making rat holes in the middle of the city for men to hide in. Why? No one knows. All the cannon is on the Battery, but there are no casements for men to retire into. It is all crimination and recrimination, everybody's hand against everybody else. Pemberton is said to have no heart in this business, so the city cannot be defended.[33]

When she received news of the battle itself, she gave a small cheer: "At Secessionville, we went to drive the Yankees out, and we were surprised ourselves. We lost one hundred, the Yankees four hundred. They lost more men than we had in the engagement. Fair shooting that! As they say in the West, 'We whipped our weight in wildcats' and some to spare." She followed that comment with a rumor: "Scotchmen in a regiment of Federals at Secessionville were madly intoxicated. They had poured out whiskey for them like water." The impact of her enthusiasm is blunted, however, when one realizes that these two comments were sandwiched between a description of a flower garden and her opinion of *Fanny*, the latest book she had read.[34] The Battle of Secessionville was merely a small cloud on her horizon. Mary Chesnut and her husband survived the war but did not return to Charleston. They retired to a new home, "Sarsfield," near the plantation that belonged to General Chesnut's parents.

Susan Middleton, safely, if not too comfortably, housed in Columbia, continued to correspond with her cousin Harriott Middleton, who had moved with her family to her sister-in-law's home in Flat Rock, North Carolina. Since Harriott had been forced to leave Charleston, Susan was now the one to pass on rumors of what was happening at home. Susan learned about the initial landing of Union troops on James Island from a visitor who had told her, "All agree that in spite of the newspapers we were 'badly whipped' on James Island last Tuesday." Her major concern, however, was that Gen. Pemberton was "much censured" in Charleston. She reported, "Our poor Pemberton goes about wringing his hands and declaring he has not a friend in Charleston, but Evans told him that unless he c[ou]ld be allowed to attack the Yankees on James Island, he w[ou]ld break his sword and leave the service … God grant him success, for they say driving them from James Island is our only hope of saving Charleston… ."[35]

News of the Battle of Secessionville seems to have reached the Middleton cousins almost simultaneously, for their comments crossed in the mails. Susan wrote: "Does not this gallant fight on James Island make you hope still for our dear old town? It is said that Gen Pemberton has turned over the defenses of it to Evans, who says, 'that island is too small for two armies—one or the other must give way'." Harriott was equally pleased, though still worried about the incompetence of the Confederate general: "Is not the success on James Island delightful? I hear that we have 10 or 12,000 troops there—and if Evans is to be in command there I shall fear nothing. I am only afraid that it may be some mistake, as I do not see his name mentioned in the Charleston papers. Why can't they get rid of Pemberton?"[36]

For the rest of the summer, the cousins were more concerned with what was happening in Virginia than they were with activity closer to home. Their correspondence was full of sad news of deaths among their friends and family, of illness and the plights of the elderly, of widows dying from grief, and of the horrid behavior of Yankees. Occasionally, however, a rumor about Secessionville emerged and Susan was happy to pass it on. One neighbor had talked to a New Hampshire prisoner, who passed on this story echoing the rumors heard by Mary Chesnut: "The evening before the Secessionville fight, the men were told by their General that in six hours after that battery was attacked, they would be in Charleston, liquor was freely distributed among them, every officer was more or less drunk, and the canteens were filled with whiskey just before going into action."[37] This emphasis on whiskey in the Union lines is curious. It seems to suggest that the victory was more attributable to drunken Yankee soldiers than to Confederate skill. It may have been true; the Scotch-Irish never objected to the restorative effects of good whiskey. But it might also have been an attempt to demonize the enemy as rationale for killing so many of them.

The extended family of the Middletons suffered greatly from the war. Both of Harriott's brothers died in battle, Henry in 1861 and Frank in 1864; Susan's brother Oliver also died in battle. Mary Chesnut described the troubles visited on Susan's mother: "Poor Mrs. Middleton has paralysis. Has she not trouble enough? … Their plantation and house at Edisto destroyed, their house in Charleston burned, her children scattered, starvation in Lincolnton, and all as nothing to the one dreadful blow—her only son killed in Virginia. Their lives are washed away in a tide of blood. There is nothing to show they were ever on earth."[38] On 22 February 1865, Union troops burned Middleton Place, home to generations of Middletons since 1741; only one wing could be restored some years later. For the Middletons, too, the Battle of Secessionville mattered little in the face of much larger disasters.

Emma Holmes continued to keep her diary throughout the course of the war, and her basic views never changed. She was a devoted citizen of the Confederacy and hated the Union. On 22 April 1865, she wrote: "To go back into the Union!!! No words can describe all the horrors contained in these few words. Our souls recoiled shuddering at the bare idea … Our southern blood rose in stronger rebellion than ever and we all determined that, if obliged to submit, never could they *subdue* us."[39] Her descriptions of battle outcomes cannot be trusted—perhaps because the Charleston papers were so badly informed, but more likely because she refused to admit the Confederacy could lose. Her report about James Island on 9 June was completely off the mark. She claimed that the Confederates had eight or nine thousand men there along with two classes from the Citadel, while "Saturday evening the telegraph announced that all the Yankees had left James I. so that we could now continue our work on the obstructions in the Stono."[40] She, too, was suspicious of Gen. Pemberton. On 13 June, she noted that he had stopped fortifying the streets of Charleston and commented, "This is certainly very singular behavior on Pemberton's part and, as he is a Pennsylvanian, engenders suspicion about him."[41] Miss Holmes did not, however, discuss the Confederate victory at Secessionville. To her, this was simply the sort of victory one expected to happen. During the rest of the war, Emma Holmes supported herself as a private tutor in Camden. She returned to Charleston in 1865, where she spend the rest of her life as a teacher.

Back in Silver Spring, Maryland, Elizabeth Blair Lee heard almost nothing about Secessionville. One letter, written on 25 June, mentions that the papers were reporting that Charleston had been reinforced, but that Beauregard's army was "scattered & demoralized."[42] She was much more concerned about the fate of Richmond, the Seven Days' Campaign, and the Battle of Malvern Hill, when McClellan gave up the effort to take the confederate capital.[43] Nor did she hear anything about the slavery problems in South Carolina; throughout the war, she was more interested in preserving the Union than in freeing the slaves.[44] On 23 September 1862, she wrote about emancipation: "The Presidents proclamation took the breath out of me this morning. He is in the hands of the Phillistines—but God will help us—& I do not despair ... I still hope for successful end of the war & our Governments preservation—in spite of *all* its enemies." The next day, she wrote: "There is no excitement about the Presidents proclamation but the papers which speak here indicate that is a mistake ... the Southern people are not going to free the Blacks & the Govt cant enforce such a proceeding."[45] After the war, her husband remained on active naval duty, retiring as rear admiral in 1873. He died in 1897. She continued working with the Washington City Orphan Asylum until her eightieth birthday and died in 1906 at the age of eighty-eight

The Leveretts, who had been displaced so early by the invasion of the Southern Expeditionary Force, took some notice of the Battle of Secessionville. Mrs. Leverett was not particularly impressed by the Confederate victory because she believed that Gen. Pemberton had mishandled the whole affair. In one letter she wrote, "Where was Gen. Pem's head? He must nervously be afraid of everything. Oh, that we had a general that was afraid of nothing ... that did know the country & the people too! The Governor telegraphed to him by no means to let the Yankees land on James Island, but he would, & I'm told that after they landed, he burst into tears ..."[46] Mary Leverett lost two sons to disease during the war, and her husband, Rev. Charles Leverett, died in 1868. Young Milton Leverett, however, was able to reclaim Canaan, the family plantation near Beaufort, after the Union troops departed. He devoted his life to restoring the family lands and taking care of his mother and five sisters. In 1875, the family home at 1301 Bay Street in Beaufort,

where the Roundheads had once established their headquarters, was also restored to the possession of Mrs. Leverett.

The Confederate troops stationed on James Island had some difficulty in assimilating the results of the Battle of Secessionville. The commanding officers stressed their amazing success in fending off an attack in which they were greatly outnumbered. It was with pride that they reported what Pemberton called the "dangers and glory of this admirable repulse."[47] The men, however, remained convinced that the Battle at Secessionville had been only the first phase of an ongoing attack. Charles Webb, stationed at Fort Pemberton, wrote to his brother Lockwood on 19 June, predicting that "the great fight will come off very soon as the Yankees are making a regular fort on James Island on Legare's place to bear on our batteries at Secessionville which is about 1000 yards distant."[48] His description of the actual battle that had taken place on 16 June praised the outcome but downplayed the action:

The Batteries at Secessionville have been at work shelling and being shelled by 5 gun boats and a land battery about 1000 yards distant two days steady before the Yankees attempted to take it by storm which proved a perfect failure to them and a great victory for us. Out of about 1000 shells that came in and hit the place, there was one man killed and he lying down in his tent. The Battle of Secessionville was quite a hotly contested one which the fight lasted ... Some of the prisoners said they expected to meet with but little resistance in this "on to Charleston," but found it was not as easy a road to travel as they anticipated.[49]

2nd Lt. R. Y Dwight, Company D, 1st South Carolina Infantry, wrote to his friend Ellison Capers after the battle to congratulate him on his role in the defense of Tower Fort: "I am perfectly satisfied with the result of that affair. I don't think the enemy have suffered nearly as much in any battle of the war in proportion to the numbers engaged as in this Battle of Secessionville. It was a terrible slaughter of them." He, too, however, focused on the continuing need to fend off an attack on the city of Charleston:

> I am very hopeful of the successful defence of our noble old city. If the Generals are reliable I believe it will be accomplished. Certainly the men are brave, and ready to stand to the last for the city's defence ... I believe that we will be able to repel them at every point around Charleston, and that even our weak point the harbour defence will be successfully held and defended ... We have vindicated our prowess in battles where the superiority of men, and not the perfection of machinery, has decided the day. These Yankees are pretty well convinced that we can whip them, or at least that they cant whip us ...[50]

Those who had been expecting an attack on Charleston ever since November found it hard to believe that with just one battle at Secessionville, the Confederate forces had managed to drive off the Union army. But as the days passed, and the Yankees made only half-hearted attempts to re-organize themselves, it became more and more apparent that there would not be another attack. The *Charleston Daily Courier* could not help but gloat: "The deluded tools and victims of Lincolnism ... who thus expected to reach Charleston are actually in Charleston, but wounded and prisoners, while many others have found burial in the soil of James' Island, and others, unburied, are feeding the fish of our waters."[51]

For some Confederate soldiers, the victory had come at the expense of their idealism. Gus Smythe, who had been anxious to share in the glories of war, found that the horrors of battle had become all too real. He had once been a prolific letter-writer, but he had little to say in the weeks following the battle. When he received an offer to apply for a position with the Signal Corps in August, he leaped at the opportunity to distance himself from dusty drills, ever-present insects, and the bloody memories of the infantry. It was an offer made possible through his family connections and his school ties to the commander of the unit, Captain Joseph Manigault. Gus described his new position to his aunt, Janey Adger: "My business hours now are from 9 A.M. to 1 ½ P.M. & from 4 to 6 P.M. The manual labor is quite hard as the flag & staff are pretty heavy, but then there is not very much of it, & besides there is more interest in it than drilling. As to the accommodations, they are MUCH better than in camp, as we (in town) all stay in houses ..."[52] In fact, Gus was living at home at No. 12 Meeting Street. When his parents finally agreed to leave Charleston, he stayed on in the house with the family dog, where he could keep an eye on the family possessions and then stroll to work just a few blocks away. He shared his comfortable accommodations with Benti Middleton, son of Arthur Middleton and his wife, the Countess Bentivoglio. Benti's uncle, Williams Middleton, owned a townhouse on the corner of Meeting and Battery, but it had been taken over by the military. When Benti could not stay there, Gus welcomed his company.

Gus's first posting in the Signal Corps was to the Bathing House, on the Battery, just at the foot of Meeting Street. In late March, 1865, Gus moved to the steeple of St. Michael's Church on Meeting Street, where he could use a telescope to observe the Yankees on Morris Island and the ships blockading the harbor. He complained, as usual; his duty hours had been extended and he had to work every other night. There were 170 steps to climb to reach the platform, where the wind always seemed to blow. Still, he was comfortable, and a long way from combat: "Our place is in the upper piazza, above the clock. We have it boarded in, & bunks put in for us to sleep in ... I still eat at home & shall try to fix it to sleep there every other night, when I am not on duty."[53] He even had another small dog to keep him company and occasional visits from young women who wanted to see the view from the steeple.[54]

When Charleston finally fell, Gus left the city to join the 5th South Carolina Cavalry. He was reported missing after the Battle of Bentonville, and his family presumed him dead. But Gus was a survivor, if not a dedicated military man. According to one admirer, "a very skinny Gus rode into his fiancée's yard in Columbia with two horses, and a pair of mules that he had exchanged for his watch." He and Louisa McCord were married on 25 July 1865. In his later years, he became a prominent Charleston lawyer, a state senator, and the owner of a cotton-milling firm.[55] For Gus, the Battle of Secessionville faded into the background of his memory. If it changed his life in any way, he himself was not aware of it.

The Roundheads, on the other hand, had suffered greatly during the fighting, and the effects of the Battle of Secessionville remained with them for a long time. Col. Daniel Leasure noticed the difference almost immediately, although he tried to put the best possible interpretation on it. "Since our Roundheads have had their baptismal blood pounded into the bosom of this rebellious state," he wrote to his wife, "they never feel so contented and happy as when near the enemy. The whole nature of the men seems changed and they have the look and bearing of veterans. The regiment now shows its blood and its intellectual superiority in all critical and dangerous positions." He also noticed that he was receiving much more respect because his brigade had performed so well under difficult circumstances. "Everybody seems to treat me with much consideration, and that is a thing I have not been accustomed to in my former experience with Stevens."[56]

But not all was well in the Roundhead camp. A small party of Roundheads was al-most immediately sent off to western Pennsylvania to recruit new members, but Col. Leasure acknowledged to his wife that the news of the battle would surely discourage others from enlisting: "I don't suppose they can do much by way of recruiting, as the people out West have such a horror of South Carolina."[57] The Battle of Secessionville was followed by a flurry of departures. Adjutant William Powers resigned on 3 July, and Lt. Col James Armstrong followed him, pleading "feeble health" on 12 July. Three young lieutenants also resigned during the next weeks, and two privates deserted. The regimental band might have continued to be an integral part of the Roundhead experience, but the expense of maintaining individual musicians' units in each regiment became an issue. On 17 July 1862, Congress issued Public Law 165, which abolished the regimental bands and gave the musicians thirty days to enlist as regular soldiers or accept a discharge. John Nicklin and William Gordon, the two primary musicians, transferred to Company K, but the other nine members accepted their discharges.[58] The loss of the band, of course, also meant the end of the regimental newspaper, for the musicians were the writers and printers of *The Camp Kettle*. The regiment might have been behaving more like professional soldiers after their first battlefield experience, but much of the music and humor had gone out of their lives.

Even those who had not participated in the actual attack were finding it hard to deal with the aftermath. Capt. D. M. Cubbison, a band member who had been in Beaufort on 16 June, tried to describe the battle to his father:

> The whole affair was a terrible thing. I don't know what ought to be done with old Benham; he made fun of the fight after it was over; it is a pity he was not hung in Virginia. General Stevens, (God bless him, if there ever was a soldier, he is one) done all he could to get Benham not to attack the fort in that way, but it was

of no use. Stevens wanted to shell the fort for four hours and then charge on it, but Benham would not listen to it. All the other generals agreed with Stevens. That night on going out with his men, Stevens wept like a child; he told Col. Leasure that it was awful to take men out to be cut to pieces as they would be, he said they were bound to be cut to pieces. The night after the battle, Stevens did not sleep a wink; one of his clerks told me so …You still seem to think that the war will be over soon, and that we will be home in one year from the time we started, but I think differently. I do not expect to be home for six or nine months yet. I do not want to discourage you, but it looks so to me.[59]

The Union forces remained on James Island for the rest of the month. Col. Leasure described his men as "very busy fortifying ourselves and erecting batteries against the fort we had once fairly won and foolishly abandoned."[60] They were never to get a chance to use them. Deciding that there was no more to be gained, Gen. Hunter ordered the troops to abandon James Island. The Roundheads boarded a steamer on 4 July, sailed to Hilton Head, and then returned to Beaufort, where they camped outside of town. On 10 July, they embarked on the *Merrimac* for Virginia. Rev. Brown wrote: "Our departure at this juncture is wonderfully unexpected. Most of the men are pleased. They think it is getting so much nearer home. Poor fellows, many of them will see the other side of the Jordan before the regiment returns to Western Pennsylvania and not all of them contemplate the possibility of such a fact not withstanding the month of June reduced our number 22 or 23."[61]

Such pessimism was uncharacteristic of the regiment's enthusiastic chaplain; he too had been somewhat changed by the events of 16 June. Rev. Browne stayed with the regiment for the promised "two years and four months leave" granted by his church back home, a period that corresponded with the regiment's first term of enlistment. One account has preserved his fine reputation as regimental chaplain:

> Officers and men recognized his steady discharge of duty on the battle-field, or in the services of religion each evening, when the regimental psalm of praise rose over camp or bivouac, and as was frequently the case floated into the rebel lines. They had jokes pointed with reference to the chaplain's bravery, and reminiscences of his coolness. Some of them remembered, for instance, how brave it made them feel to hear him say, "Boys, trust God, and keep your powder dry!" amidst the heavy fall of rain, with thunder and lightning, and rebel bullets whizzing above their heads … .[62]

He returned to New Castle and resumed his pastoral responsibilities in January 1864. His subsequent career included terms as a member of the Pennsylvania senate, the president of Westminster College, a candidate for governor for the Prohibition Party, and a moderator of the General Assembly of the United Presbyterian Church.[63]

Nurse Nellie Leath's association with the Roundheads also ended shortly after Secessionville. She traveled with the regiment to Newport News, but her behavior on board the ship, although never described in detail, seems to have sealed the official decision to leave her behind when the Roundheads moved on. In a letter to his wife, Rev. Browne reported: "I wrote you that Nelly is not to accompany us from here. —White has just been in, & I have heard the camp gossip. I did not before know that the thing was known. But it is & to shew what vile gossips men in camp are—the camp version is that the Col. Has to leave her—is not permitted to take her in." But although the chaplain was willing to dismiss the camp rumors swirling around her name, he freely expressed his own opinion of her character: "I look upon her as a vain and empty fool … She has been the means of injuring the Colonel's name most wonderfully. He deserves it, of course, for his exceeding impudence … As to his poor family, it chafes me to think how much they are injured by the acting of this silly drama …" He concluded by quoting the morality lecture he had given the colonel when he learned that Nellie was to be left behind: "This did not prevent my going on to tell him how she had paraded him and her relations to him with a foolish vanity that had done him an immense amount of harm on the 'Ocean Queen' and ever since."[64]

Nellie fell ill shortly after she was told of her dismissal, and those around her felt sure she was dying. On 1 August, Browne told his wife, "Nellie is very low. She can hardly by any possibility live." Two days later he followed up on this report, "As we commenced our prayer meeting, I noticed the liter bearers carrying Nellie away to the General Hospital at Newport News and since I commenced writing the wagon has gone past with her baggage. Poor Nellie!" But "Poor Nellie" was more resilient than everyone thought. One eyewitness account proved that she was working under her maiden name, Nellie M. Chase, in a military hospital run by the 79th New York outside of Fredericksburg by December 1862.[65] Frank Moore wrote a book about the nurses of the Civil War to honor his mother. The stories he told came from first-hand accounts, and Nellie's chapter relied on the testimony of a man whose life she had saved. According to his narrative, she discovered that what appeared to be a bloody mangled head was only the result of a minor scalp wound that bled profusely. In the eyes of this unnamed soldier, Nellie was "a noble girl … an angel of mercy … a woman with the soul to dare danger; the heart to sympathize with the battle-stricken; sense, skill, and

experience to make her a treasure beyond all price."[66]

After that incident, however, all records of Nellie's existence disappeared. As a recent book about army nurses has pointed out, "A woman who was talked about, regardless of her testimony, did not pass the litmus test of virtue … What separated 'bad' women from 'good' was a matter of reputation …"[67] After the publication of his book, Frank Moore received an anonymous letter that suggested: "If you intend issuing another edition of The Women of the War, that you had better make some inquiries about Miss Chase's character before you put her along with truehearted girls like Georgy Willets, Mary Shelton, or Maria Hall. Most any one of an old Roundhead Regiment except the Col. can give you a great deal of information."[68] Nellie Chase Leath may well have been a victim of her own reputation. The handwriting of the anonymous letter, however, suggests that she was also the victim of Rev. Browne, whose attacks on Nellie's behavior pursued her throughout her military career.

Col. Daniel Leasure was delighted to give up his brigade responsibilities and return to command of his beloved Roundheads when the men of the South Carolina Expeditionary Corps were quietly dispersed to other theaters of operation. The 100th Pennsylvania Roundheads saw action at the Second Battle of Bull Run, where they lost twenty-seven men, and where Col. Leasure was seriously wounded. They saw minor action at Chantilly, South Mountain, and Antietam before Leasure was able to return to the front. They also served at Fredericksburg and Vicksburg and with Sherman at Jackson, Mississippi, during their first term of enlistment. Almost the entire regiment reenlisted on 1 January 1864. Major James H. Cline remembered: "On the first of January, 1864, while subsisting on less than two ears of corn a day per man, the entire regiment, with the exception of twenty seven, re-enlisted to the number of three hundred and sixty-six, for a term of three years and immediately started home on a veteran furlough." While there they recruited enough new men to raise numbers to total of 927.[69] The Roundheads saw heavy duty at Wilderness, where Leasure was wounded again; at Spottsylvania, where they lost forty-four men; at Cold Harbor, with a loss of eighteen; and in the several battles of the Siege of Petersburg, with a combined loss of eighty-eight.[70] They were mustered out on 24 July 1865.

Of the seventy original volunteers of Company C, over forty percent became casualties of war. Nine men were killed in battle; six died of disease or of complications from their wounds; fourteen were so seriously ill or injured that they were discharged before the end of their term of enlistment.[71] During the course of the war, the regiment had enlisted some 2,014 men; their casualty rate exceeded fifty percent. Of those, 195 were killed in action or died of wounds; 29 died in prison camps; 663 suffered non-fatal wounds; another 185 died of disease or accident during their terms of enlistment. Col. Leasure himself mustered out of the regiment on 30 August 1864, just a month after learning that his son Geordy had been killed in the Battle of the Crater during the Siege of Petersburg. He returned to private medical practice in Pittsburgh, although he never fully recovered from his wounds. In the late 1870s, he moved to St. Paul, Minnesota, where he died in 1884.[72]

There were no national heroes created by the Engagement of Secessionville, but heroic behavior was not lacking. The real accolades must go to the volunteer soldiers such as James McCaskey and his friends. These were the men who answered their country's call out of a sense of duty, —men who could be content to sleep on the ground so long as they were "turnover comfortable,"—men who could dismiss 100 degree temperatures as "pretty warm,"—men who would march

James McCaskey Memorial Headstone, North Sewickley Cemetery
Photo by Floyd Schriber

into their first real battle to face cannon fire with unloaded muskets because they had been so ordered.

Sgt. James McCaskey, along with many others who died on the battlefield at Secessionville, was buried in a mass grave pit in front of the fortifications at Secessionville. His parents received no further word of his fate. In some despair, the Mc-Caskey family decided to leave Pennsylvania, where they were constantly reminded of his death by seeing James's friends and comrades return from the war. Leaving the family farm in the hands of their oldest daughter and her husband, the McCaskeys set out in their ox-drawn wagon for Kansas, joining that large migration inspired by the Homestead Act of 1862. Their journey, however, was short-lived, for John McCaskey fell victim to consumption, and the family returned home. John McCaskey died in 1875, and his widow ordered three tombstones for the family plot in North Sewickley Cemetery: one for John, one to be saved for her own death, and one to mark an empty grave for James Mc-Caskey. The marker still stands, along with a G.A.R marker to commemorate his service. Below the details of his death, an inscription has worn into illegibility. For a memorial, however, one can turn to an editorial in the *New York Times*, July 15, 1862, about what it had started to call "the James Island Fiasco." Its concluding sentence was a fitting epitaph for those who fought and

New Monument at Secessionville – Legend
Photo by Floyd Schriber

died on that day in June 1862: "It is enough to know the affair at Secessionville was in the highest degree disgraceful; and that none of the disgrace attaches to the men, who fought with peculiar daring and persistency." More recently, restorers of Fort Lamar have erected a four-sided monument to commemorate the casualties on both sides. It reads:

The Battle of Secessionville fought here on 16 June 1862 broke the Union advance through James Island against Charleston and was the most significant battle of the Civil War in South Carolina. Confederate troops under Col. Thomas G. Lamar defended simple unfinished earthwork. Later enlarged and named Fort Lamar, which sat in the narrow end of a funnel-shaped strip of ground flanked by tidal creeks and marsh. Union troops under Gen. Henry W. Benham launched several assaults against the earthwork which anchored the eastern end of the Confederate line, but were repulsed with heavy casualties and soon evacuated James Island altogether a few days later.

A total of 693 Federals and 204 Confederates were killed, wounded, or captured. Of these totals, 107 Federals and 52 Confederates lost their lives on this battlefield. Walk softly on this hallowed ground.

APPENDIX A

THE ROUNDHEAD REGIMENT
REGIMENTAL ROSTER
AUGUST 31, 1861

FIELD AND STAFF OFFICERS:
Col. Daniel Leasure, Regimental Commander.
William H. Powers, Adjutant.
Alva H. Leslie, Quartermaster.
Ferdinand H. Gross, Surgeon.
Robert Audley Brown, Chaplain.
John B. Nicklin, Leader of Regimental Band (with nine musicians).

COMPANY A, Washington County, Captain James Armstrong. 12 officers; 73 enlisted.

COMPANY B, Lawrence County, Captain Matthew M. Dawson. 12 officers; 92 enlisted.

COMPANY C, Butler County, Captain James E. Cornelius. 11 officers; 58 enlisted.

COMPANY D, Beaver County, Captain William C. Shurlock. 7 officers; 49 enlisted.

COMPANY E, Lawrence County, Captain Samuel Bentley. 12 officers; 94 enlisted.

COMPANY F, Lawrence County, Captain James H. Cline. 15 officers; 73 enlisted.

COMPANY G, Mercer County, Captain Simeon H. Brown. 16 officers; 79 enlisted.

COMPANY H, Lawrence County, Captain Adam Moore. 11 officers; 50 enlisted.

COMPANY I, Lawrence County, Captain Hillery W. Squier. 18 officers; 49 enlisted.

COMPANY K, Lawrence County, Captain James S. Van Gorder. 11 officers; 53 enlisted.

COMPANY L, Westmoreland County, Captain Mungo M. Dick. 8 officers; 92 enlisted. (This company transferred to the 105th Pennsylvania Regiment, known as the "Wildcats," on 4 September 1861. They had no further identification with the Roundheads.)

COMPANY M, Westmoreland County, Captain David A. Leckey. 14 officers; 76 enlisted.

APPENDIX B

THE SOUTH CAROLINA EXPEDITION
THE ASSEMBLED FLEET
OCTOBER 29—NOVEMBER 7, 1861

A final accounting of the fleet appeared in the Washington Intelligencer on 29 October. The Richmond Examiner reprinted it on 4 November, and the Charleston Daily Courier published the reprint on 6 November. This account lists over eighty vessels. They carried some thirty thousand soldiers, fifteen hundred horses, infantry weapons for ten thousand men, food and water supplies to last three and a half months, entrenching tools, prepared frames of barracks, two hundred extra wagons and civilian wagon drivers, carpenters, and masons, Parrot guns, and thousands of shells, shot, grape, and canister for each battery. Starred ships took part in the actual bombardment at Port Royal Sound.

Steamers:
>   *Flagship Wabash, (Commander C. R .P. Rodgers and Lieutenant John S.
>   Barnes), twenty-eight 9-inch guns, fourteen 8-inch guns, two 10-inch pivots.
>   *Bienville, (Commander Charles Steedman), eight 32-pounders
>   Minnesota, 57 guns.
>   Roanoke, 54 guns.
>   *Susquehanna, (Captain J. L. Lardner), fifteen 8-inch guns.

Sailing Vessels:
>   Frigate St. Louis, 50 guns.
>   *Sloop Vandalia, (Commander F. L. Haggerty), four 8-inch guns, sixteen 32-
>   pounders.
>   Sloop Jamestown, 22 guns.
>   Sloop Cumberland, 24 guns.
>   Sloop Savannah, 24 guns.
>   Sloop Dale, 16 guns.

Gun Boats, most armed with an 11-inch Dahlgren, a rifled gun, and a few 24-pounders:
>   Albatross.
>   Alabama.
>   *Augusta, (Commander E. G. Parrott), eight 32-pounders.
>   *Curlew, (Lt-Commanding P. G. Watmough), six 32-pounders, one 30-pounder.
>   Dale.
>   Florida.
>   Harriet Lane.
>   Iroquois.
>   *Isaac Smith, ((Lt-Commanding J. W .A. Nicholson), one 30-pounder rifle.
>   James Adger.
>   *Mohican, (Commander S. W. Godon), two 11-inch pivots, four 32-pounders.
>   Monticello.
>   Mount Vernon.

New London.

Ottawa, (Lt-Commanding T. H. Stevens), one 11-inch pivot, one 20-pounder rifle, two 24-pounder howitzers.

Pawnee, (Lt-Commanding B. H. Wyman), eight 9-inch pivots, two 12-pounder rifles.

Pembina, (Lt-Commanding J. P. Bankhead), one 11-inch pivot, one 20-pounder rifle, two 24-pounder howitzers.

Penguin, (Lt-Commanding T. A. Budd), four 32-pounders.

Pocahontas, (Commander Percival Drayton), one 11-inch pivot, four 32-pounders.

Quaker City.

R. B. Forbes, (Lt-Commanding H. S. Newcomb), two 32-pounders.

Seminole, (Commander John P. Gillis), one 11-inch pivot, four 32-pounders.

Seneca, (Lt-Commanding Daniel Ammen), one 11-inch pivot, one 20-pounder rifle, two 24-pounder howitzers.

Unadilla, (Lt-Commanding Napoleon Collins), one 11-inch pivot, one 20-pounder rifle, two 24-pounder howitzers.

Yankee.

Young America.

Steamer Transports:

Ariel.

Atlantic.

Alabama.

Baltic.

Belvidere.

Ben Deford.

Champion.

Cahawbet.

Contzacoaleos.

Daniel Webster.

DeSoto.

Empire City.

Ericsson.

Florida.

Illinois.

Locust Point.

Marion.

Matanzas.

Mercedia.

Ocean Queen.

Oriental.

Parkersburg.

Philadelphia.

Potomac.

Roanoke.

Santiago de Cuba.
Spalding.
Star of the South.
Vanderbilt.
Winfield Scott.

Sailing Vessels:
Great Republic.
Ocean Express.
Courier.
Zenos Coffin.
Golden Eagle.
Gem of the Seas.

APPENDIX C

ROUNDHEAD CASUALTY LISTS

These lists have been compiled from a number of sources, including newspaper accounts, official records, and private letters.

NON-BATTLE DEATHS, AUGUST 1861—MAY 1862

DISEASE AND ACCIDENT:
 Peter Bloieberg, Company A.
 Jacob Hartsein, Company A.
 James Lowrie, Company A.
 Benjamin Scott Stuart, Company A.
 William S. Sample, Company B.
 Aaron Angle, Company B.
 James Davidson, Company B.
 Andrew McComb, Company B.
 William M. Ramsey, Company B.
 Solomon W. Smith, Company C.
 Lt. David S. McCreary, Company F.
 Lt. James L. Banks, Company F.
 John Thompson, Company F.
 Mathias Crowl, Company F.
 John Gates, Company F.
 John D. Kirk, Company G.
 Edward Corben, Company I.
 George M. Hammond, Company I.

BATTLE OF 2 JUNE 1862

KILLED:
 William S. McKnight, Company F.
 Solomon W. Fisher, Company F.

MORTALLY WOUNDED:
 Harrison White, Company D, shot through the abdomen.
 James Bell, Company I, shot through the head.

BADLY WOUNDED:
 Thomas McKeever, Company A, shot through the upper part of the left lung.

PRISONERS:
 Corporal James W. Bard, Company A.
 John Klotzbaiker, Company A.
 James Kerr, Company A.

Capt Samuel S. McClure, Company D.

Lt. Robert J. Douthitt, Company D.

Joseph C. Finkhouser, Company D.

George R. Watt, Company D.

Corp. Joseph F. Herron, Company D.

Thomas Cook, Company D.

Daniel Kenard, Company D.

Joseph Wible, Company D.

James H. Cline, Company F.

Sgt. David J. Gilfillan, Company F.

Robert F. Moffatt, Company F.

Corporal Robert A. Forbes, Company F.

James W. Aiken, Company F.

Robert Duke, Company F.

John Irwin, Company F.

John H. McMasters, Company F.

Sgt. Conrad Shaffer, Company F.

John Calvin Sampson, Company F, died in captivity.

James Smith, Company F.

BATTLE OF SECESSIONVILLE, 16 JUNE 1862

KILLED:

William A. Anderson, Company C.

Sgt. Jacob Leary, Company C.

Sgt. James McCaskey, Company C.

Corp. John S. Watson, Company C.

John. T. McCaslin, Company E.

James. A. Parker, Company E.

Augustus Reed, Company E.

James S. Patterson, Company F.

George Whetstone, Company H.

2nd Lt. Samuel J. Morrow, Company I.

Thomas Gorman, Company K.

Thomas Eba, musician, Company M.

Peter Harrison, Company M.

David Merideth, Company M.

Sgt. John H. Merrick, Company M.

SERIOUSLY WOUNDED:

Caleb Joseph, Company B, leg amputated below the knee.

Robert E. Reed, Company B, bullet wound through calf.

John N. Moore, Company C, flesh wound, cut in shoulder, slight.

Hugh Wilson, Company C, lost one eye.

William Harlan, Company E, a bullet through the knee.

John S. Barber, Company E, flesh wound, bullet through the leg.

John S. Dick, Company E, flesh wound, bullet through the leg.

Daniel Harpst, Company F, flesh wound in arm.

George W. Washbaugh, Company G, slight wound in the top of head.

C. T. Stansberry, Company H, dangerously.

Henry H. Robison, Company I, bruise from bomb-shell, left side, severe.

Thomas Williams, Company M, severe bruise and lacerated wound, side and hand.

PRISONERS:

William R. Somers, Company H

SLIGHTLY WOUNDED:

William Claffey, Company A.

Sgt. John Elliot, Company B.

Noah A. Sewall, Company B.

Corp. Addison Cleland, Company C.

Thomas N. Miles, Company C.

Henry Dillaman, Company C.

Frederick Baudler, Company C.

John E. Walton, Company C.

Corp. Harlin Book, Company E.

Sgt. Samuel B. George, Company E.

Jesse B. Shaner, Company E.

Corp. Nathan Offutt, Company E.

George Montgomery, Company E.

Sgt. George Maxwell, Company E.

Samuel B. Campbell, Company G.

1st Lt. John P. Blair, Company I.

Robert Davis, Company I.

1st Lt. Joseph H. Gilliland, Company K.

Corp. Evan Morris, Company K.

LIST OF ABBREVIATIONS

BCGS   Beaver County Genealogical Society, Research Center for Beaver County, Beaver Falls, PA.

CK   *The Camp Kettle*, regimental newspaper for the 100th Pennsylvania Volunteer Infantry Regiment.

DU   Manuscript Department, Perkins Library, Duke University, Durham, NC.

HSWP   Library and Archives Division, Historical Society of Western Pennsylvania, Pittsburgh, PA.

HCLA   Historical Collections and Labor Archives, Pattee Library, Pennsylvania State University, University Park, PA.

HW   *Harper's Weekly*.

LC-AM   Civil War Collections, American Memory, Library of Congress, Washington, DC.

LC-P&P   Prints & Photographs Division, Library of Congress, Washington, DC.

LCHS   Civil War Collections, Lawrence County Historical Society, Joseph A. Clavelli History Center, New Castle, PA.

NARA   National Archives and Records Administration, Washington, DC.

NYHS   Gilder Lehrman Institute of American History, New York Historical Society, New York, NY.

ORA   Scott, Robert N., Jr., comp. *The War of the Rebellion: A Compilation of the Official Records of the Union and Confederate Armies, Series I*. Reprint. Harrisburg, PA: National Historical Society, 1985.

ORN   Rawson, Edward K., George P. Colvocoresses, and Charles W. Stewart, comps. *Official Records of the Union and Confederate Navies in the War of the Rebellion, Series I*. Washington, DC: Government Printing Office, 1901.

SCHS   Archives, South Carolina Historical Society, Charleston, SC.

SCL-USC   South Caroliniana Library, University of South Carolina, Columbia, SC

USAMHI   U. S. Army Military History Institute, U. S. Army Heritage and Education Center, Carlisle, PA.

ENDNOTES

CHAPTER 1: SIX HOUSES AND A TAVERN

[1] For a fuller discussion of the linen industry in Ulster, see Griffin, *People with No Name*, 27-32.

[2] Griffin, *People with No Name,* 60-66.

[3] A famous painting by William Allan commemorates the event. It is, however, somewhat misleading in its portrayal and has caused some confusion about the details. The painting is called "The Signing of the National Covenant in Greyfriars Kirkyard," and shows a large crowd, dressed in spring-like finery, assembled around a large flat tombstone. The huge document is spread out on the length of the tomb so that all could sign. Since we are talking here about February in Scotland, and since the signing went on long into the night, it is unlikely that the events actually took place outdoors, no matter what the picture shows!

[4] One of these copies, perhaps the original, is on display in the Huntley House Museum in Edinburgh. Anyone familiar with the Declaration of Independence will recognize the size and flourishes of the signatures.

[5] The story of their settlements is told by Klett, *Scotch-Irish in Pennsylvania.*

[6] Bausman, *History of Beaver County,* 150. This text is also available at *Historic Pittsburgh Full-Text Collection,* http://digital.library.pitt.edu.

[7] Walton, "Savages and Settlers,"; Bausman, *History of Beaver County*, 149.

[8] Bausman, *History of Beaver County*, 166.

[9] Bausman, *History of Beaver County*, 957.

[10] Today this land lies approximately at the intersection of state highways 65 and 288.

[11] Webb, *Born Fighting*, 118.

[12] These colorful phrases come from Bausman, *History of Beaver County,* 441.

[13] Perry, *Scotch-Irish in New England*, 41; quoted by Leyburn, *The Scotch-Irish*, 152.

[14] J. C. Stevenson, "The Roundheads," M. Gyla McDowell Collection, HCLA, 1.

[15] Bausman, *History of Beaver County,* 147.

[16] Bausman, *History of Beaver County,* 482-483.

[17] Bausman, *History of Beaver County,* 485-486.

[18] The original documents are in the possession of the Prothonotary's Office, Beaver County, PA.

[19] These details have been extracted from family letters in the author's possession.

[20] Bausman, *History of Beaver County*, 275.

[21] All the following dates have been taken from the chronology and history provided on the Beaver County Historical Society website, *Beaver County [Pennsylvania] History Online.* Available at http://www.bchistory.org.

[22] Beveridge, *Cups of Valor*, 67.

[23] Available at: http://www.bchistory.org/beavercounty/BeaverTown/.

[24] Ibid.

[25] Welchley, "Statistics of Beaver Co.," *Western Argus*, March 3, 1841; reprinted in *Milestones,* 10-2 (Spring 1985).

[26] Available at: http://www.bchistory.org/beavercounty/BeaverTown/.

[27] Yargates, "Steamboat Building in Beaver County," *Milestones* 7-2 (Spring 1982).

[28] *Western Argus* (Beaver, Penna.), 15 December 1841.

[29] *Census, 1850.* Beaver County, Pennsylvania. NARA.

[30] Bausman, *History of Beaver County*, 251-256, traces the development of these railroads. Today the Pittsburgh & Lake Erie runs on the rail beds of the Conneaut & Beaver west of the river; the Penn Central follows the Cleveland & Pittsburgh line on the east; the Connoquenessing Creek branch line has become the B & O.

[31] Pictures of some of these nineteenth-century homes may be found on the web at: http://www.bchistory.org/beavercounty/BeaverCountyCommunities/Beaverfolder/Tour/tourofBeaver.html.

[32] *Milo Adams Townsend and Social Movements of the Nineteenth Century*, available at: http://www.bchistory.org/beavercounty/booklengthdocuments/AMilobook/title.html.

[33] Switala, *Underground Railroad in Pennsylvania*, 60-65.

[34] Weyand, "The Anti-Slavery Movement in Beaver County," reprinted in Bausman, *History of Beaver County*, 1141-1146.

[35] Bonzo, "Brief History of North Sewickley Presbyterian Church," typed copy dated March 10, 1980, BCGS.

[36] Bausman, *History of Beaver County*, 1146.

[37] Bausman, *History of Beaver County*, 1149.

CHAPTER 2: WE KNOW ONLY OUR COUNTRY

[1] Henry Steele Commager noted this fundamental truth about the similarities of the opposing sides in the introduction to his *The Blue and the Gray*, xxxiii-xxxviii.

[2] McPherson made this point clearly by giving the title of "Amateurs Go to War" to a chapter of his prize-winning study of the Civil War, *Battle Cry of Freedom*.

[3] McPherson, *Battle Cry of Freedom*, 313. Eicher, *The Longest Night*, 58, provides specific figures on Union manpower.

[4] Wilcox and Ripley, "The Civil War at Charleston," 3.

[5] Ibid.

[6] The difference in spelling here is not an error. According to Thomson, *Charleston at War*, 3, Gus added the final "e" to his last name when he entered college to avoid being confused with another young man with the same name. His father had made a similar move, changing Smith to Smyth to avid confusion with another Rev. Thomas Smith.

[7] "Thomas Smyth," *The Southern Presbyterian Review*, Digitization Project found at http://www.pcanet.org/history/periodicals/spr/bios/smyth.html.

[8] Erskine, "Smyth, Thomas," *American National Biography*.

[9] T. Smythe, Letter of 7 February 1860, Augustine Thomas Smythe Collection (1209.03.02.04), SCHS.

[10] Harrison, *College Cadets,* 32-45.

[11] Harrison, *College Cadets*, 48.

[12] Harrison, *College Cadets*, 50.

[13] Harrison, *College Cadets*, 53.

[14] South Carolina College, Cadet Company Committee, circular letter, dated 18 October 1861, SCL-USC. The letter, signed by Gus Smythe and five others, sought to repay this debt by assessing each member of the corps $1.00.

[15] Iredell Jones, Letter to parents, 11 April 1861, Iredell Jones Collection, SCL-USC.

[16] Harrison, *College Cadets*, 60.

[17] Chesnut, *A Diary from Dixie*, 39.

[18] L. M. Smythe, "Recollections of Louisa McCord Smythe," (1209.03.02.05), SCHS.

[19] This and other official documents from the Civil War can be accessed at: http://members. home.net/civilwarcsa/history/linpro1.html.

[20] Leasure, "A Brief History of the Lawrence Guards," in a letter to E. C. Durban, 27 January 1885; quoted by S. Stevenson, Manuscript, LCHS.

[21] The following details are summarized from nearly identical accounts in these works: *History of Lawrence County* ; Hazen, ed., *The 20th-Century History of New Castle and Lawrence County*; Fox, Regimental Losses; Gavin, ed., *The Civil War Letters of Corporal Frederick Pettit*; Gavin, *History of the 100th Pennsylvania Volunteer Regiment*; and J. Leasure, "Exploits of Dr. Leasure and the Roundheads," *Washington Times*, 19 June 1993.

[22] Gen. James S. Negley, a Pittsburgh native, was commissioned in April 1861. Andrew G. Curtin was the governor of Pennsylvania. This, and the following quotes, are taken from a newspaper clipping found in a scrapbook that originated from the New Castle area in Lawrence County, PA. The original owner of the scrapbook is unknown. Roundhead descendant Tami McConahy has transcribed articles pertinent to the 100th PVI, for inclusion into the 100th Pennsylvania Website, available at: http://www.100thpenn.com/scrapnewspaper.htm.

[23] Leasure, Letter, M. Gyla McDowell Collection, HCLA; quoted by Gavin, *Campaigning with the Roundheads*, 4.

[24] McConahy, ed. newspaper clippings at: http://www.100thpenn.com/scrapnewspaper.htm.

[25] Ibid.

[26] Ibid.

[27] "The Guards at Home," *Lawrence Journal* (New Castle, 10 August 1861).

[28] S. Stevenson, Manuscript, LCHS.

[29] Passage from newspaper article titled, "Odd War Nicknames: Crack Regiments with High Sounding Adopted Titles," in Col. N.J. Maxwell Scrapbook, David L. Welch Collection. The regimental website at http://www.100thpenn.com/100TH_PVI_MAIN.htm includes several items from this scrapbook.

[30] Bates, *Pennsylvania Volunteers,* 3:553.

[31] "Lawrence's Regiment," *Lawrence Journal* (New Castle, 10 August 1861).

[32] Bates, *Pennsylvania Volunteers*, 552.

[33] *CK*, Vol. 1, No. 3 (5 October 1861). On the front page of this little regimental broadsheet, the editor announced that "Our friends, as well as the soldiers, will be gratified by a perusal of Gov. Curtin's note … It sets a vexed question at rest, and will relieve much anxiety."

[34] *Census, 1860*. Beaver County, Pennsylvania, NARA.

[35] Moffatt, Diary, M. Gyla McDowell Collection, HCLA.

[36] J. C. Stevenson, Typescript of Diary, LCHS.

[37] Ibid.

[38] Ibid.

[39] Bates, *Pennsylvania Volunteers*. For details, see Appendix A.

[40] J. H. Stevenson, "Company K, Leasure Guards," LCHS.

[41] Census, 1860. Beaver County, Pennsylvania, NARA.

[42] J. C. Stevenson, Typescript of Diary, LCHS.

[43] Matviya , "Basic Training at Camp Wilkins." Available at http://www.contrib.andrew.cmu.edu/~jw3u/Library09.htm.

[44] Ibid.

[45] According to Hazen, *History of Lawrence County*, 705, the Roundheads adopted the little boy and made him their official drummer when they returned from the war.

[46] Quoted in Holland, *Our Army Nurses;* edited and reissued by Hoisington, iii.

[47] Over the course of her enlistment, Nellie shared these details with Col. Leasure and Rev. Browne. Browne reported them to his wife in a letter dated 27 February 1862. Transcript in M. Gyla McDowell Collection, HCLA.

[48] Moffatt, Diary, M. Gyla McDowell Collection, HCLA.

[49] J. C. Stevenson, Diary, LCHS.

[50] McPherson, *Battle Cry of Freedom*, 284-285.

[51] Archives of Maryland, Volume 0430, Page 0155—Proceedings of the House, April, June and July Special Sessions, 1861.

[52] Cline, *The Major,* 11. HSWP.

[53] Bates, *Pennsylvania Volunteers*, 3:553. Today the area is a public park located at the corner of S Street and 23rd Street.

[54] Leech, *Reveille in Washington*, 205.

[55] "Sights and Sounds," *Camp Kettle*, Vol. 1, No. 3 (5 October 1861), 3.

[56] Hazen, *History of Lawrence County*, 203.

[57] Miller, "'A Perfect Institution Belonging to the Regiment."

[58] "Our Bow," *CK*, Vol. 1, No. 1 (21 September 1861).

[59] In editing James's letters, I have reproduced his eccentric spelling and punctuation exactly as he wrote. To do otherwise would give a false impression of his level of education.

[60] Ibid. Several issues of *CK* are extant in Civil War Miscellaneous, Pennsylvania Infantry—100th Rgt., 12 September 1861-15 May 1862, USAMHI.

[61] Ibid.

[62] "Bully," *CK*, Vol. 1, No. 3 (5 October 1861), 4.

[63] "Be Patient," *CK*, Vol. 1, No. 7 (5 December 1861), 3.

[64] "Sutler," *CK*, Vol. 1, No. 2 (28 September 1861), 3.

[65] "Rations," *CK*, Vol. 1, No. 3 (5 October 1861), 2.

[66] McGranahan, "The American Civil War," at http://americanrevwar.homestead.com/files/civwar/bands.html.

[67] "Where We Are," *CK*, Vol. 1, No. 1 (21 September 1861), 4.

[68] "Band," *CK*, Vol. 1, No. 3 (5 October 1861), 1.

[69] *Book of Biographies, Lawrence County*, 21-22.

[70] Gen. 28:20-21, KJV.

[71] Psalms 188: 6, KJV.

[72] Browne, Letter to his father on 26 September 1861, M. Gyla McDowell Collection, HCLA. The biblical text reads: "My son, despise not thou the chastening of the Lord, nor faint when thou art rebuked of him; For whom the Lord loveth he chasteneth, and scourgeth every son whom he receiveth."

[73] "The Roundheads," *CK*, Vol. 1, No. 3 (28 September 1861), 3.

[74] He described the scene in a letter to his wife dated 26 September 1861. M. Gyla McDowell Collection, HCLA.

[75] "Still They Come," *CK*, Vol. 1, No. 3 (5 October 1861), 1.

CHAPTER 3: A WONDERFUL SHEET OF WATER

[1] *ORA* 6:168.

[2] Dyer, *Compendium of the War of Rebellion*, 1:362-63.

[3] Marchand, *Charleston Blockade*, 6-9.

[4] See Appendix B for a complete listing.

[5] DuPont, *Civil War Letters*, 181.

[6] Dyer, *Compendium*, 3:1436.

[7] Webb, *Born Fighting*, 158.

[8] Lord, *Civil War Collector's Encyclopedia*, 297-311.

[9] J. C. Stevenson. Diary, 6 October 1861.

[10] Bates, *Pennsylvania Volunteers*, 3:572-75.

[11] See letter dated 18 June 1862, Author's Collection.

[12] Bates, *Pennsylvania Volunteers*, 3:553.

[13] J. C. Stevenson, Diary, 12 October 1861, HSLC.

[14] Browne, Letter of 12 October 1861, M. Gyla McDowell Collection, HCLA

[15] Browne, Letter of 14 October 1861, M. Gyla McDowell Collection, HCLA.

[16] Moffatt, Diary, 14-15 October 1861, in M. Gyla McDowell Collection, HCLA.

[17] J. H. Stevenson, "Company K, Leasure Guards," LCHS.

[18] Browne, Letter dated 18 October 1861, M. Gyla McDowell Collection, HCLA.

[19] From the scrapbook collection of Tami McConahy, 100th Pennsylvania Website, found at http://www.100thpenn.com/scrapnewspaper.htm.

[20] *ORA* 6:180.

[21] Penney, "Diary," HSWP.

[22] Browne, Letter to his father, 21 October 1861; J. H. Stevenson, "Company K, Leasure Guards," LCHS.

[23] Details come from letters written by Rev. Browne and two privates from Company F, William McKnight and M. K. McDowell, in the M. Gyla McDowell collection, HCLA. *The Charleston Daily Courier* for 6 November 1861 added accounts of what the ships carried.

[24] J. C. Stevenson, *Scrapbook*, LCHS, 30.

[25] Browne, Letter of 6 November 1861, M. Gyla McDowell Collection, HCLA.

[26] Holmes, *Diary*, 45.

[27] Holmes, *Diary*, 46.

[28] Wilcox, "Blockade Strangled the South," 28.

[29] Marchand, *Charleston Blockade*, xi.

[30] *HW,* 26 October 1861, 690.

[31] See report of conference presided over by DuPont, *ORA*, 53:67-73.

[32] "DuPont and the Port Royal Expedition," *Battles and Leaders*, 1:673.

[33] *ORA* 6:181.

[34] DuPont, *Civil War Letters*, 171.

[35] *ORA* 6:184.

[36] Cline, *The Major*, 14-15.

[37] Osbon's story is told by Perry, *A Bohemian Brigade*, 86-109.

[38] "The Capture of Beaufort, South Carolina," *HW*, Vol. 5 (November 30, 1861), 760-765.

[39] *CK*, Vol. 1, No. 5, aboard the Steamer Ocean Queen (4 November 1861), 4.

[40] Browne, Letter to wife, 5 November 1861, M. Gyla McDowell Collections, HCLA.

[41] Hamilton, Letter to his wife, 5 November 1861, aboard the *Ocean Queen*, M. Gyla McDowell Collections, HCLA.

[42] DuPont, *Civil War Letters*, 205.

[43] *HW*, 30 November 1861, 763.

[44] Browne, Letter to wife, 5 November 1861, M. Gyla McDowell Collections, HCLA.

[45] For a complete description of the battle, see Dupont, *Civil War Letters*, 205, 222-32.

[46] Simons, "Special Order #1," Military papers, 1835-1877 (bulk 1860-1862). (227.01.0), SCHS. Also see *ORA* 1:7.

[47] Burton, *The Siege of Charleston*, 67-68.

[48] *Charleston Mercury*, Monday, 11 November 1861.

[49] Burton, *Siege of Charleston*, 70.

[50] L. M. Smythe, "Recollections of Louisa McCord Smythe" (1209.03.02.05), SCHS.

[51] Augustine Thomas Smythe Collection (1209 *Charleston Courier*. 03.02.04), SCHS.

[52] Ibid.

[53] Harrison, *College Cadets*, 80-81.

[54] Quoted by Rosen, *Confederate Charleston*, 83.

[55] Jones, *Port Royal*, 230.

[56] "The Bombardment," *HW*, Vol. 5 (Nov. 30, 1861), 762.

[57] Survivors' Association of the State of South Carolin, Records, 1861-1878. (1122.00), SCHS.

[58] "The Bombardment of Port Royal," *Charleston Daily Courier*, 11 November 1861.

[59] *HW*, 30 November 1861, 763.

[60] Hayes, "The Battle of Port Royal, 392; quoted by Burton, *Siege of Charleston*, 74.

[61] *ORA* 6:4.

[62] Lattimore, *Fort Pulaski*, 20; *ORA* 6:23-27.

[63] *ORA*, 6:367.

[64] Burton (*Siege of Charleston*, 80) has speculated that, if that rail line had been cut soon after the Battle of Port Royal, the Confederates might have suffered a death blow.

[65] See Gavin, *Campaigning with the Roundheads*, 55-59, for some other colorful details.

[66] *Charleston Daily Courier*, 6-8 November 1861.

[67] Report to Headquarters, 3rd Military District, 24 November 1861, (1122.00), SCHS.

[68] Chesnut, *Unpublished Diaries*, 196-197.

[69] Elmore, *The Heritage of Woe*, 12.

[70] *ORA* 6:14-16. The general referred to in this quotation was probably Robert E. Lee, who had recently taken command of the Confederate forces in the area.

[71] DuPont, *Civil War Letters*, 1:226.

CHAPTER 4: THE SINKING OF A STONE FLEET

[1] Steiner, *Disease in the Civil War*, 67.

[2] Wiley, *The Common Soldier*, 110.

[3] Browne, Letters, 12-17 November 1861, M. Gyla McDowell Collection, HCLA.

[4] Ibid.

[5] Lord, *Civil War Encyclopedia*, 206.

[6] Bates, *Pennsylvania Volunteers*, 3:572-75.

[7] Dupont, *Civil War Letters*, 1:264.

[8] Dupont, *Civil War Letters*, 1:293.

[9] McDowell, "Reminiscences," M. Gyla McDowell Collection, HCLA.

[10] *ORA* 16:4-6.

[11] *Voices of the Civil War: Charleston*, 19.

[12] *Voices of the Civil War: Charleston*, 23.

[13] Book, Letter of 28 December 1861, at http://www.100thpenn.com/scrapnewspaper.htm.

[14] Browne, Letter, 30 November 1861, Scrapbook.

[15] Walkley, quoted by Gavin, *Campaigning with the Roundheads*, 60.

[16] Browne, Letter, 30 November 1861, Scrapbook.

[17] Ibid.

[18] Cawley, *Leaves from a Lawyer's Life*, 47.

[19] "Beaufort," *CK,* 30 December 1861.

[20] H. Stevens, quoted by Jones, *Port Royal*, 246.

[21] DuPont, *Civil War Letters*, 229.

[22] "Confiscated," *CK,* 30 December 1861.

[23] Book, Letter of 18 December 1861, Scrapbook.

[24] Moffatt, Diary, 10-12 December 1861, M. Gyla McDowell Collection, HCLA. *CK* also reported the confiscation.

[25] Browne, Letter of 12 November 1861, M. Gyla McDowell Collection, HCLA.

[26] McDowell, "Reminiscences," M. Gyla McDowell Collection, HCLA.

[27] McDowell, M. Gyla McDowell Collection, HCLA.

[28] "Free Speech in Beaufort," *CK*, 30 December 1861, 1.

[29] Chesnut, *Unpublished Diaries,* 199-202.

[30] Chesnut, *Unpublished Diaries*, 204-205.

[31] Elmore, *Diary*, 23.

[32] Elmore, *Diary*, 21.

[33] Holmes, *Diary*, 98.

[34] F. K. Middleton, Family Letters in Cheves-Middleton collection, folder #12/164/11, SCHS.

[35] Ibid.

[36] A. T. Smythe, (1209.03.02.04), SCHS.

[37] L. M. Smythe, "Recollections of Louisa McCord Smythe," (1209.03.02.05), SCHS, 50-51.

[38] *The Leverett Letters*, 146.

[39] Rosen, *Confederate Charleston*, 89.

[40] Holmes, *Diary*, 105-111.

[41] Holmes, *Diary*, 111.

[42] Wilcox, *Civil War at Charleston*, 28.

[43] Dyer, *Compendium*, 2:831.

[44] *ORN*, 12:522.

[45] Marchand, *Charleston Blockade*, 89.

[46] Ripley, "Stone Fleet Sunk Off Charleston," *Civil War at Charleston*, 29-30.

[47] *HW*, 11 January 1862.

[48] Cawley, *Leaves from a Lawyer's Life*, 53.

[49] Marchand, *Charleston Blockade*, 63-64.

[50] *ORA* 6:42-43.

[51] Marchand, *Charleston Blockade*, 112-30.

[52] *ORA* 6:393.

CHAPTER 5: GRINDING THE SEED CORN

[1] See Stone, *Causes of the English Revolution*, for a prime example.

[2] John Hart of the Irish Jasper Greens; quoted by Lattimore, "Fort Pulaski," 21.

[3] Harrison M. Beardsley, Letter of 24 December 1862, SCL-USC.

[4] Charles Lafferty, quoted by Lattimore, *Fort Pulaski*, 21.

[5] *CK*, Vol. 1, No. 9 (7 January 1862), gives a complete account, although the pagination is a bit confusing. Rev. Brown, in a letter written to his father on 11 January 1862: "Having some acquaintance with the vagaries of types, you will soon see the 'Imp' has put the first page inside, and the whole paper reminds one of a cat chasing her tail."

[6] "Speedily Avenged, " *CK*, Vol. 1, No. 9 (7 January 1862).

[7] Dyer, *Compendium*, 1:831; *ORA*, 6:56-7.

[8] Daniel Leasure, Letter of 3 January 1862, M. Gyla McDowell Collection, HCLA.

[9] "Cui Bono," *CK,* Vol. 1, No. 9 (7 January 1862).

[10] Couper, *One Hundred Years at VMI*, 2:107; quoted by J. Conrad, *The Young Lions*, 38.

[11] Hull, *Boy Soldiers of the Confederacy*, 150-151; quoted by Couper, *One Hundred Years at VMI*, 2:44.

[12] *Natchez Daily Courier*, 27 September 1861.

[13] *ORA* 6:209.

[14] *ORA* 6:213.

[15] Hagood, *Memoirs*, 52.

[16] Ibid., 53.

[17] Ibid., 60.

[18] *ORA* 6:214-20.

[19] *ORA* 6:225.

[20] F. K. Middleton, Cheves-Middleton Collection, folder #12/164/12, SCHS.

[21] Harriott Middleton, Cheves-Middleton Collection, folder #12/166/2, SCHS.

[22] Ibid.

[23] *Best Companions*, 89-91.

[24] Browne, Letter, 7 January 1862, M. Gyla McDowell Collection, HCLA.

[25] "Strange," *CK*, 30 December 1862, 4.

[26] Browne, Letter, 14 April 1862, M. Gyla McDowell Collection, HCLA.

[27] Holmes, *Diary*, 147.

[28] Moffatt, *Diary*, M. Gyla McDowell Collection, HCLA.

[29] Holmes, *Diary*, 144.

[30] Holmes, *Diary*, 135.

[31] Holmes, *Diary*, 140-142.

[32] Browne, Letter, 10 January 1862, McDowell Collection, HCLA.

[33] Browne, Letter, 9 January 1862, McDowell Collection, HCLA.

[34] Browne, Letter, 25 January 1862, McDowell Collection, HCLA.

[35] Browne, Letter, 14 April 1862, McDowell Collection, HCLA.

[36] Ibid.

[37] It is difficult to identify these soldiers more specifically because Company E listed four soldiers named Lock (David, John, William, and James) and three named Hanna (Abraham, Alexander, and John). This difficulty, however, points up the familial nature of the Round-heads' troops.

[38] "Correction," *CK*, 25 January 1862, 3.

[39] Henry Applegate, Letter, 7 March 1862, USAMHI.

[40] Ibid.

[41] Browne, Letter, 14 April 1862, M. Gyla McDowell Collection, HCLA.

[42] *ORA* 14:345.

[43] Chesnut, *Diary from Dixie, passim.*

[44] Figures tend to vary, depending on those who are counting. Several websites, however, give a sense of the losses. See http://www.civilwarhome.com/c1862.htm.

[45] *Charleston Mercury*, 24 February 1862.

[46] Phelps, *Charlestonians in War*, 48-50.

[47] *Leverett Letters*, 110.

[48] Lee, *Wartime Washington*, 114.

[49] The complete text of the resolution may be found in *ORA* 1:973.

[50] Chesnut, *Diary from Dixie,* 199, 204.

[51] Chesnut, *Diary from Dixie,* 198.

[52] Chesnut, *Diary from Dixie,* 199.

[53] Chesnut, *Diary from Dixie,* 197. This Mrs. McCord was the mother of Louisa McCord, the young woman being courted by Gus Smythe.

[54] Margaret Adger Smyth, Letter of 9 March 1862 (1209.03.02.04), SCHS.

[55] "Thomas Smyth," *Southern Presbyterian Review*, at http://www.pcanet.org/history/periodicals/spr/bios/smyth.html.

[56] This is Woodburn Plantation near Pendleton, home of Dr. John Bailey Adger.

[57] Margaret Adger Smyth, Letter of 9 March 1862. (1209.03.02.04). SCHS.

[58] A. T. Smythe, Letter of 11 March 1862 (1209.03.02.04), SCHS.

[59] A. T. Smythe, Letter of 21 March 1862 (1209.03.02.04), SCHS.

[60] Ibid.

[61] Browne, Letter, 6 March 1862, M. Gyla McDowell Collection, HCLA.

[62] Browne, Letter, 13 January 1862, M. Gyla McDowell Collection, HCLA

[63] Browne, Letter, 10 March 186,. M. Gyla McDowell Collection, HCLA.

[64] *ORA* 6:218.

[65] Rose, *Rehearsal for Reconstruction*, 33-35.

[66] *Charleston Mercury*, 26 April 1862.

[67] *ORA* 6:222.

[68] *Ibid.*

[69] Rose, *Rehearsal for Reconstruction*, 25.

[70] Ibid, 35; quoting from the "First Annual Report of the Boston Educational Commission for Freedmen, May, 1863", 4, 7.

[71] Quoted in Rose, *Rehearsal for Reconstruction*, 45-47.

[72] Rose, *Rehearsal for Reconstruction*, 28-29.

[73] Browne, Letter, 13 March 1862. M. Gyla McDowell Collection, HCLA.

[74] Rose, *Rehearsal for Reconstruction*, 65-66.

[75] *ORA* 6:247.

[76] *ORA* 6:248.

[77] Boatner, *Civil War Dictionary*, 58-59.

[78] DuPont, *Civil War Letters*, 1:396-97.

[79] Ibid.

[80] Ibid.

[81] Steiner, *Disease in the Civil War*, 70.

[82] Moffatt, *Diary,* M. Gyla McDowell Collection, HCLA.

[83] Steiner, *Disease in the Civil War*, 75.

CHAPTER 6: THIS CURSED SOIL OF SOUTH CAROLINA

[1] *ORA* 6:263.

[2] Boatner, *Civil War Dictionary*, 797.

[3] McClellan (Ship), *Logs* (34/219), SCHS.

[4] Lattimore, *Fort Pulaski*, 28.

[5] A summary of the Union armament appears in Lattimore, *Fort Pulaski*, 29.

[6] Browne, Letter of 9-10 April 1862, M. Gyla McDowell Collection, HCLA.

[7] Browne, Letter of 13 April 1862, M. Gyla McDowell Collection, HCLA.

[8] Lattimore, *Fort Pulaski*, 36.

[9] J. H. Stevenson, Letter to E. S. Durban dated 13 April 1862, at http://www.100thpenn.com/letters.htm.

[10] McKee, Letter, at http://www.100thpenn.com/scrapnewspaper.htm.

[11] Gavin, *Campaigning with the Roundheads*, 73-74.

[12] Browne, Letter of 14 April 1862, M. Gyla McDowell Collection, HCLA.

[13] Browne, Letter of 26 February 1862, M. Gyla McDowell Collection, HCLA.

[14] Lee, *Wartime Washington*, 128.

[15] Jones, *Port Royal Under Six Flags*, 250.

[16] Chesnut, *Diary from Dixie*, 211.

[17] Holmes, Diary, 144.

[18] Holmes, *Diary*, 154-15.

[19] A. T. Smythe, Letter dated 14 April 1862 (1209.03.02.04), SCHS.

[20] *Leverett Letters,*117-118.

[21] *ORA* 6:134.

[22] DuPont, *Civil War Letters*, 418.

[23] *New York Times*, 28 April 1862.

[24] *Charleston Mercury*, 30 April 1862.

[25] *New York Times*, 10 April 1862.

[26] *ORA* 6:30-1.

[27] *New York Times*, 9 April 1862.

[28] *ORA* 6:201-202.

[29] *ORA* 14:346.

[30] Steiner, *Disease in the Civil War*, 80.

[31] See similar comments in Wiley, *The Common Soldier*, 63, 87, and 88.

[32] Philbrick, *Letters from Port Royal*, 55.

[33] Susan Walker, Letter of 25 March 1862, quoted by Jones, *Port Royal Under Six Flags*, 249.

[34] Ibid., 248.

[35] Ibid., 249.

[36] Philbrick, Letter of 17 March 1862, in *Letters from Port Royal*, 10-11.

[37] Ibid. (One wonders what the Roundheads would have made of that statement!)

[38] *The Nation*, 30 May 1867, quoted in *Letters from Port Royal* 26-27, n. 1.

[39] Rose, *Rehearsal for Reconstruction*, 91.

[40] Ibid., 85-86.

[41] Ibid., 68-69.

[42] Ibid., 79.

[43] Ibid., 160.

[44] Jones, *Port Royal Under Six Flags*, 250.

[45] *ORA* 14:341.

[46] *New York Times*, Editorial, 17 May 1862.

[47] Quoted in *Letters from Port Royal*, 62-63.

[48] Ibid., 52.

[49] Jones, *Port Royal Under Six Flags*, 251.

[50] Ibid., 252.

[51] Ibid.

[52] Quoted in *Letters from Port Royal*, 39.

[53] Ibid., 40.

[54] Ibid., 42.

[55] Ibid., 43.

[56] J. H. Stevenson, "Leasure Guards," LCHS.

[57] "Proclamation Revoking General Hunter's Order of Military Emancipation of May 9, 1862," *Collected Works of Abraham Lincoln*, 5:222. Available at http://www.hti.umich.edu/l/lincoln/.

[58] Jones, *Port Royal Under Six Flags*, 262, notes that although Hunter began the recruitment in May, "the first slave regiment of Freed slaves mustered into the service of the United States in the Civil War was the First Regiment of South Carolina Volunteers, organized at Port Royal on November 7, 1862."

[59] Quoted by Bennett, "Chronicles of Black Courage."

[60] Steinmeyer, "Marion Rifles," SCHS.

[61] Marchand, *Charleston Blockade*, 169; S. Jones, The Siege of Charleston, 93.

[62] Marchand, *Charleston Blockade*, 169.

[63] Holmes, *Diary*, 123.

[64] Ibid., 161.

[65] *Leverett Letters*, 120.

[66] Claudia Smith Brinson recently explored the full story of the Chisholm family and their plantation at Coosaw during the Civil War. See "Coosaw Holds Rich S.C. History," *The State*, Oct. 27, 2002.

[67] "Middleton Correspondence, 1861-1865," 62-63. The tradition of turning enemy skulls into drinking cups, of course, was nothing new. Livy mentions the Boii making a drinking cup of the skull of the Roman consul Postumus. Similar tales are told of other peoples from Tibet to Scandinavia, from the beginnings of the Christian Era to the nineteenth century.

[68] Holmes, *Diary*, 158.

[69] Ibid., 65.

[70] Ibid.

[71] Margaret Adger Smyth, Letter dated 7 June 1862 (1209.03.02.04), SCHS.

[72] Ibid.

[73] Chesnut, *Diary from Dixie*, 222.

[74] Ibid., 216.

[75] Ibid., 217.

[76] Hagood, *Memoirs*, 70-71.

[77] Ibid., 75.

[78] *ORA* 6:420.

[79] "Middleton Correspondence, 1861-1865," 68.

[80] Ibid., 41.

[81] For a full discussion of the quarrel between Evans and Pemberton, see Brennan, *Secessionville*, 11-13.

[82] A. T. Smythe, Letter of 28 April 1862 (1209.03.02.04), SCHS

[83] For Lee's instructions, see *ORA* 14:523.

[84] One modern ecological study calls it "soft enough to swallow a dime." Available at http://www.ser.org/content/past_recipients.asp.

CHAPTER 7: ONWARD TO CHARLESTON

[1] Henry J. Hunt to Braxton Bragg, 23 April 1861, GLC 925.02, NYHS.

[2] A. T. Smythe, Letter dated 31 May 1862 (1209.03.02.04), SCHS.

[3] Lusk, *War Letters*, 149.

[4] Marchand, *Charleston Blockade*, 189.

[5] *ORA* 14:348.

[6] *ORA* 14:345.

[7] The First Division comprised the 3rd New Hampshire; Battery I of the 3rd Rhode Island Artillery; the 1st New York Engineers; the 6th Connecticut; the 47th New York; and the 45th, 76th, and 97th Pennsylvania regiments.

[8] The Second Division included the 8th Michigan; the 1st Connecticut Artillery; Company H of the 1st Massachusetts Cavalry; the 79th New York; and the 100th Pennsylvania regiments, all stationed at or near Beaufort. For details of Benham's plan, see Brennan, *Secessionville*, 59-65.

[9] *ORA* 14: 534-536.

[10] In 1863 it was named for Colonel Thomas G. Lamar, who commanded it in June 1862 until he was wounded. See Burton, *Siege of Charleston*, 99 and 109.

[11] *ORA* 14: 535.

[12] Ibid.

[13] Webb , Family papers (259.03.02), SCHS.

[14] *ORA* 14:28.

[15] Simonton, "Eutaw Battalion Order Book 1862" (34/220), SCHS.

[16] A. T. Smythe, Letter dated "Wednesday Morn" (1209.03.02.04), SCHS.

[17] John Sheppard, Sheppard Family Papers, SCL-USC.

[18] Adler, Letter appended to Cline, *The Major*.

[19] *New Castle Courant*, "Extra" for 17 June 1862. The article referred to this Massachusetts regiment as a "green regiment" that "suddenly fell back in a great panic," but the judgment was unfair. This Irish regiment was formed in May 1861, and had more experience and training than did the Roundheads. Transcription at http://www.100thpenn.com/scrapnewspaper.htm.

[20] The Eutaw Battalion included the Charleston Riflemen; the Irish Volunteers; the Beauregard Light Infantry; the Sumter Guards; the Calhoun Guards; and four companies of the 24th South Carolina Volunteers: the Marion Rifles, the Pee Dee Rifles, the Evans Guard, and the Colleton Guard.

[21] *ORA* 14: 29-30.

[22] Browne, Letter of 14 June 1862, M. Gyla McDowell Collection, HCLA.

[23] The names of the captured Roundheads appear in Appendix C.

[24] The full story of the mired artillery pieces appeared in the *Charleston Mercury* on 9 June 1862.

[25] S. G. Leasure, Letter of 4 June 1862, included in S. Stevenson, Manuscript, LCHS.

[26] Brennan, *Secessionville*, 84-87.

[27] D. Leasure, Letter dated 4 June 1862. M. Gyla McDowell Collection, HCLA.

[28] For the details of the Campbell brothers' pre-war experiences, see Johnson, "Introduction," *Him on One Side, Me on the Other.*

[29] A. Campbell, Letter of 10 June 1862, in *Him on One Side, Me on the Other,* 92.

[30] Cline, Letter, 5 June 1862, found at http://www.100thpenn.com/scrapnewspaper.htm.

[31] Cline, Letter of 9 June 1862. The full details of their imprisonment and eventual release were not revealed until much later in the war and can be read in a long description found in Cline's Memoirs, HSWP.

[32] *ORN* 13:54-55.

[33] Quoted by Burton, *Siege of Charleston*, 101.

[34] Metcalf, *Personal Incidents*, 21; quoted in *Voices of the Civil War*, 26.

[35] Metcalf, *Personal Incidents*, 22; quoted in Brennan, *Secessionville*, 67.

[36] For examples, see the many references in Brennan, *Secessionville*, 93-111.

[37] J. C. Stevenson, "Condensed History," M. Gyla McDowell Collection, HCLA.

[38] *ORN* 13: 88.

[39] *ORA* 14:552-553.

[40] *ORA* 14:550.

[41] *ORA* 14:558-559.

[42] Quoted in Schreadley, *Valor and Virtue.*

[43] Hagood, *Memoirs*, 81-82.

[44] *ORA* 14: 552.

[45] *ORA* 14: 555.

[46] *ORA* 14:536-537.

[47] *ORA* 14:551.

[48] S. W. Douglass. Letter of June 10, 1862 (118.03.03), SCHS.

[49] *ORA* 14:561.

[50] Pemberton's repeated requests for more men, money, and armaments can be traced in *ORA* 14:531-558.

[51] *ORA* 14:567.

[52] *ORA* 14:35.

[53] *ORA* 14:351.

[54] Quoted by Brennan, *Secessionville*, 140.

[55] Dupont, *Letters*, 2:114-119.

[56] *ORA* 14:46.

[57] *ORA* 14:48.

[58] *ORA* 14:51.

[59] *The Souldiers Catechisme*, 23.

[60] Browne, Letter of 14 June 1862, M. Gyla McDowell Collection, HCLA.

[61] Hamilton, Letter dated 15 June 1862, M. Gyla McDowell Collection, HCLA.

[62] S. G. Leasure, Undated letter to "Moma," LCHS.

CHAPTER 8: GRAPE, CANISTER, SHOT, AND SHELL

[1] The full texts of the official Union Army reports may be found in *ORA* 14:46-85. The corresponding Confederate reports appear in *ORA* 14: 85-104.

[2] *ORA* 14:49.

[3] *ORA* 14:1007.

[4] Boatner, *Civil War Dictionary*, 821.

[5] *ORA* 14:59.

[6] Brennan, *Secessionville*, 164.

[7] *New Castle Courant*, Clipping at http://www.100thpenn.com/page53and55scrap.htm.

[8] *Charleston Daily Courier*, 17 June 1862, 1.

[9] *New Castle Courant*. Clipping at http://www.100thpenn.com/page53and55scrap.htm.

[10] R. L. Crawford, Letter of 18 June 1862. Crawford Collection, SCL-USC.

[11] Quoted by the *New Castle Courant* at http://www.100thpenn.com/scrapnewspaper.htm.

[12] D. Leasure, Letter of 24 June 1862. M Gyla McDowell Collection, HCLA.

[13] *Charleston Daily Courier*, 18 June 1862, 1.

[14] *Him on One Side, Me on the Other*, 98.

[15] Ibid, 102.

[16] *ORA* 14:76-77.

[17] D. Leasure, Letter of 24 June 1862. M. Gyla McDowell Collection, HCLA.

[18] Ibid.

[19] *ORA* 14:80.

[20] *ORA* 14:101.

[21] *ORA* 14:1014.

[22] A. T. Smythe, Letter of 19 June 1862 (1209.03.02.04), SCHS.

[23] Quoted by the *New Castle Courant*, at http://www.100thpenn.com/scrapnewspaper.htm.

[24] D. Leasure, Letter of 24 June 1862. M. Gyla McDowell Collection, HCLA.

[25] See casualty list, Appendix C.

[26] Browne, Letter of 17 June 1862, M. Gyla McDowell Collection, HCLA.

[27] S. Stevenson, Manuscript, LCHS.

[28] Quoted by the *New Castle Courant,* at http://www.100thpenn.com/scrapnewspaper.htm.

[29] *ORA* 14:63.

[30] *ORA* 14:362.

[31] Long, *Civil War Day by Day*, 229.

[32] *ORA* 14:91.

[33] *ORA* 14:51.

[34] *The New York Times*, 28 June 1862.

[35] *ORA* 14:51.

[36] *The New York Times* 28 June 1862.

[37] A. T. Smythe, Letter, 17 June 1862 (1209.03.02.04), SCHS.

[38] *ORA* 14:92-93.

[39] *ORA* 14:93.

[40] *ORA* 14:101.

[41] *ORA* 14:96.

[42] Faust, "The Civil War Soldier and the Art of Dying," 19.

[43] Ibid.

[44] This letter and the one following it previously appeared in Schriber, ed., "A Scratch With the Rebels," *Civil War Times Illustrated*, February 1994, 49.

[45] Gavin, ed., *The Civil War Letters of Corporal Frederick Pettit*, 2. The letter itself can be examined in Civil War Collection, 100th Pennsylvania, USAMHI.

[46] *ORA* 14:71-74.

[47] *The New York Times*, 28 June 1862.

[48] Ibid.

[49] *ORA* 14:42-43.

CHAPTER 9: A PITY HE WAS NOT HUNG IN VIRGINIA

[1] Charles Cawley, *Leaves from a Lawyer's Life*.

[2] *Battles and Leaders*, 4:21.

[3] Burton, *Siege of Charleston*, 98.

[4] *ORA* 14:357.

[5] *ORA* 14:49-50.

[6] *ORA* 14:981.

[7] Eicher, 14. The complete records of this battle can be found in *ORA* 5:129ff.

[8] *ORA* 5: 259.

[9] Lusk, *War Letters*, 152.

[10] H. Stevens, *The Life of General Isaac I. Stevens*, 2:393.

[11] DuPont, *Civil War Letters*, 2:481.

[12] D. Leasure, Letter of 24 June 1862, M. Gyla McDowell Collection, HCLA.

[13] Lusk, *War Letters*, 153-155.

[14] *ORA* 14:982-83.

[15] *ORA* 14:107.

[16] *ORA* 3, part 2:27-28; quoted by Rose, *Rehearsal for Reconstruction*, 152-153.

[17] Ibid, 154.

[18] Ibid, 170.

[19] Ibid, 179.

[20] *Letters from Port Royal*, 84.

21 Rose, *Rehearsal for Reconstruction,* 155.

22 Rose, *Rehearsal for Reconstruction,* 172-173.

23 Rose, *Rehearsal for Reconstruction,* 212-215 and 434.

24 Copies of these documents can be found in The Abraham Lincoln Papers at the Library of Congress, Series 1. General Correspondence. 1833-1916. Available at: http://memory.loc.gov/ammem/alhtml/alhome.html.

25 *Letters from Port Royal,* 91.

26 *Letters from Port Royal,* 92.

27 Rose, *Rehearsal for Reconstruction,* 191. See *ORA* 14:377-387.

28 *ORA* 14:560.

29 Webb, Letter of 19 June 1862 (259.03.02), SCHS.

30 *New York Tribune,* 9 June 1862; quoted by Burton, *Siege of Charleston,* 99.

31 Margaret Adger Smyth, Letters of June 1862 (1209.03.02.04), SCHS.

32 Thomson, *Charleston at War,* 163 and 210.

33 Chesnut, *Diary from Dixie,* 244.

34 Chesnut, *Diary from Dixie,* 253-254.

35 S. Middleton, Letter of 15 June 1862, "Middleton Correspondence, 1861-1865," 69. The battle mentioned was the skirmish at Grimball's Plantation on 10 June 1862.

36 H. Middleton, Family papers, (1168.02.08), #12/166/1, SCHS.

37 S. Middleton, 12 July 1862, "Middleton Correspondence," 166.

38 Quoted in Chesnut, *A Diary from Dixie,* xvii-xviii.

39 Holmes, *Diary,* xxi.

40 Holmes, *Diary,* 173.

41 Holmes, *Diary,* xx.

42 Lee, *Wartime Washington,* 159.

43 Lee, *Wartime Washington,* 160-161.

44 Lee, *Wartime Washington,* 5.

45 Lee, *Wartime Washington,* 187 and n. 5.

46 *Leverett Letters,* 134.

47 *ORA* 14:87.

48 Webb, Family papers (259.03.02), SCHS.

49 Ibid.

50 R. Y. Dwight, Letter of 26 June 1862, Ellison Capers Papers, SCHS.

51 *Charleston Daily Courier,* 21 June 1862.

52 A. T. Smythe, Letter dated 29 October 1862 (1209.03.02.04), SCHS.

53 A. T. Smythe, Letter dated 31 March 1865 (1209.03.02.04), SCHS.

54 Thomson, *Charleston at War,* 163-164.

55 Ibid., 210.

56 D. Leasure, Letter of 28 June 1862, M. Gyla McDowell Collection, HCLA.

57 Ibid.

58 Bates, "1870 Roster of Regimental Band," at: http://www.100thpenn.com/regtband.htm.

59 D. M. Cubbison, Letter of 25 June 1862, Clipping found at http://www.100thpenn.com/scrapnewspaper.htm.

60 D. Leasure, Letter of 28 June 1862, M. Gyla McDowell Collection, HCLA.

61 Browne, Letter of 11 July 1862, M. Gyla McDowell Collection, HCLA.

62 *History of Lawrence County*, LCHS, 170; reprint, http://www.100thpenn.com/brownebio. htm.

63 *Book of Biographies: Lawrence County*, LCHS, 17-22.

64 Browne, Letter dated 24 July 24, USAMHI.

65 Moore, *Women of the War*, 536-540.

66 Ibid.

67 Schultz, *Women at the Front*, 232-233.

68 Anonymous letter to Frank Moore, dated 9 November 1866, DU; cited in Moore, *Women of the War*, n. 92.

69 Cline, *The Major*, 70.

70 See the breakdown at http://www.100thpenn.com/losses.htm.

71 Bates, *Pennsylvania Volunteers*, 3:572-75.

72 J. Leasure, "Exploits of Dr. Leasure and Roundheads," *Washington Times,* 19 June 1993; reprint, http://www.100thpenn.com/drleasure.htm.

BIBLIOGRAPHY

PRIMARY SOURCES

CORRESPONDENCE AND DIARIES

Beardsley, Harrison M. Letters. SCL-USC.

Best Companions: Letters of Eliza Middleton Fisher and Her Mother, Mary Hering Middleton, from Charleston, Philadelphia, and Newport, 1839-1864. Edited by Eliza Cope Harrison. Columbia: University of South Carolina Press, 2001.

Brown, Robert Audley. Letters. Typescript in M. Gyla McDowell Collection, HCLA; originals at USAMHI.

Campbell, Alexander and Campbell, James. *Him on the One Side and Me on the Other: The Civil War letters of Alexander Campbell, 79th New York Infantry Regiment, and James Campbell, 1st South Carolina Battalion.* Edited by Terry A. Johnston, Jr. Columbia: University of South Carolina Press, 1999.

Capers, Ellison. Papers. SCHS.

Cawley, Charles. *Leaves from a Lawyer's Life Afloat and Ashore.* Lowell, MA: Penhallow Printing Co., 1879.

Chesnut, Mary Boykin. *A Diary from Dixie.* Edited by Ben Ames Williams. Cambridge: Harvard University Press, 1980.

————. *The Private Mary Chesnut: The Unpublished Civil War Diaries.* Edited by C. Vann Woodward and Elizabeth Muhlenfeld. New York: Oxford University Press, 1984.

Cline, James Harvey. *The Major: Being a collection of letters and notes …* Privately printed, Victor Vescelius Young, 1935.

Crawford, R. L. Papers. SCL-USC.

Douglass, S. W. Douglass family papers, 1860-1912 (118.03.03), SCHS.

DuPont, Samuel F. *Civil War Letters.* Edited by J. D. Hayes. 3 vols. Ithaca, NY: Cornell University Press, 1969.

Elmore, Grace Brown. *The Heritage of Woe: The Civil War Diary of Grace Brown Elmore, 1861-1868.* Edited by Marli F. Weiner. Athens: University of Georgia Press, 1997.

Hagood, Johnson. *Memoirs of the War of Secession: From the Original Manuscripts of Johnson Hagood, Brigadier-General, C.S.A.* Edited by Butler Hagood. Vol. 1: *Hagood's 1st 12 Months S.C.V.* Columbia, SC: The State Co., 1910; repr. Camden, SC, 1989.

Holmes, Emma. *The Diary of Miss Emma Holmes: 1861-1866.* Edited by John F. Marszalek. Baton Rouge: Louisiana State University Press, 1979.

Johnson, William H. Papers. SCL-USC.

Jones, Iredell. Letters. SCL-USC.

The Leverett Letters: Correspondence of a South Carolina Family, 1851-1868. Edited by Francis Wallace Taylor, Catherine Taylor Matthews, and J. Tracy Power. Columbia: University of South Carolina Press, 2000.

Lusk, William Thompson. *War Letters of William Thompson Lusk.* Edited by William Chittenden Lusk. New York: Privately Printed, 1911.

Marchand, John B. *Charleston Blockade: The Journals of John B. Marchand, U. S. Navy, 1861-1862.* Edited by Craig L. Symonds. Newport, RI: Naval War College Press, 1976.

McCaskey Family. Letters. Author's Collection.

"Middleton Correspondence, 1861-1865." Edited by Isabella Middleton Leland, *South Carolina Historical Magazine*, vol. 63 (1962).

Middleton Family papers, 1861-1905 (1168.02.08), #12/166/ 1, SCHS.

Middleton, Francis K. Cheves-Middleton collection, folder #12/164/11, SCHS.

Middleton, Harriott. Cheves-Middleton Collection, folder # 12/166/2, SCHS.

Moffatt, Robert F. Diary. M. Gyla McDowell Collection, HCLA.

Moore Papers. Manuscript Department, Perkins Library, DU

Penney, James. Diary. HSWP.

Pettit, Frederick. *The Civil War Letters of Corporal Frederick Pettit*. Edited by William Gilfillan Gavin. Shippensburg, PA: White Mane Publishing Company, 1990.

Sheppard Family. Papers. SCL-USC.

Smyth, Margaret Adger. Letters. Augustine Thomas Smythe papers, 1853-1938 (1209.03.02.04), SCHS.

Smythe, Augustine Thomas. Papers, 1853-1938 (1209.03.02.04), SCHS.

Smythe, Louisa McCord. "Recollections of Louisa McCord Smythe." Typescript, Louisa McCord Smythe papers, 1862-ca. 1920 (1209.03.02.05), SCHS.

South Carolina College, Cadet Company Committee, circular letter, dated 18 October 1861, SCL-USC.

Stevenson, James C. "The Roundheads, A Condensed history of this Noted Regiment." LCHS.

————. Typescript of Diary, LCHS.

Stevenson, John H. "Company K, Leasure Guards." LCHS.

Stevenson, Silas. Typescript of "The Epitomized History of the Roundheads." LCHS.

Steinmeyer, John Henry. "Marion Rifles of Charleston, S.C., 1860-1865." Typescript, ca. 1890 (43/889), SCHS.

Wartime Washington: The Civil War Letters of Elizabeth Blair Lee. Edited by Virginia Jeans Laas. Urbana: University of Illinois Press, 1991.

Webb family. Papers, 1818-1930 (259.03.02), SCHS.

NEWSPAPERS

Camp Kettle. Regimental newspaper of the 100th Pennsylvania Regiment.

The Charleston Daily Courier. Charleston, South Carolina.

The Charleston Mercury. Charleston, South Carolina.

The Civil War Extra: From the Pages of "The Charleston Mercury" and "The New York Times". Edited by Eugene P. Moehring and Arleen Keylin. New York: Arno Press, 1975.

Harper's Weekly.

The Lawrence Journal. New Castle, Pennsylvania.

The Natchez Daily Courier. Natchez, Mississippi.

The Nation. New York.

The New Castle Courant. New Castle, Pennsylvania.

The New York Herald.

The New York Times.

The New York Tribune.

The Post and Courier. "The Civil War at Charleston," 21st ed. Compiled by Arthur M. Wilcox and Warren Ripley. Charleston, 2000.

The State. Columbia, South Carolina.

The Washington Times.

The Western Argus. Beaver, Pennsylvania.

OFFICIAL RECORDS, AND GOVERNMENT PUBLICATIONS

Ammen, Daniel. *The Navy in the Civil War*. Vol. 2: *The Atlantic Coast*. New York: Charles Scribner's Sons, 1883.

"Annual Report of the Adjutant General of Pennsylvania, transmitted to the Governor in Pursuance of Law, for the Year 1865." Harrisburg, PA: Singerly and Myers, 1866.

Barnes, Frank. *Fort Sumter National Monument, South Carolina*. Government Printing Office. National Park Service Historical Handbook Series, no. 12, 1962.

Bates, Samuel P., Jr. *History of Pennsylvania Volunteers, 1861-1865*. Vol. 3. Harrisburg, PA: B. Singerly, 1870.

Dyer, Frederick H., comp. *A Compendium of the War of the Rebellion*. 3 vols. New York: Thomas Yoseloff, 1959.

Lattimore, Ralston B. *Fort Pulaski National Monument, Georgia*. National Park Service Historical Handbook Series, no. 18, Government Printing Office. 1954.

McClellan (Ship). Logs of the McClellan and Atlantic, 1861-1864 (34/219), SCHS

"Military Service Records." NARA.

The National Covenant. City of Edinburgh Museums Pamphlet No. 5, Featherhall Press, n.d.

National Covenant of 1638: A List of Surviving Signed Copies." *Records of the Scottish Church History Society* 23.2 (1988): 255-299.

Northampton County Historical and Genealogical Society. *The Scotch-Irish of Northampton County, Pennsylvania*. Easton, Pa.: J. S. Correll, 1926.

Phisterer, Frederick, comp. *Campaigns of the Civil War*. Vol. 8: *Statistical Record of the Armies of the U. S.* New York: Thomas Yoseloff, 1963.

"Population Schedules of the Eighth Census of the United States: 1860. Beaver County, Pennsylvania." U. S. Department of Commerce. Bureau of the Census, NARA.

"Population Schedules of the Seventh Census of the United States: 1850. Beaver County, Pennsylvania." U. S. Department of Commerce. Bureau of the Census, NARA.

"Proceedings of the House, April. June and July Special Session, 1861," Maryland State Archives, 430:154-155.

Rawson, Edward K., George P. Colvocoresses, and Charles W. Stewart, comps. *Official Records of the Union and Confederate Navies in the War of the Rebellion, Series I.*, 1901.

Scott, Robert N. , Jr., comp. *The War of the Rebellion: A Compilation of the Official Records of the Union and Confederate Armies, Series I*. Washington, DC: Government Printing Office; reprint Harrisburg, PA: National Historical Society, 1985.

Society of Friends of the Kirk of the Greyfriars. *The Text of the National Covenant, First Read and Signed in Greyfriars Kirk, 28th February 1638*. Privately published, 1995.

Survivors' Association of the State of South Carolina. Survivors' Association of the State of South Carolina records, 1861-1878 (1122.00), SCHS

Tax lists of Washington County, Penna., 1784-85, 1793 (including present day Washington and Greene Counties and parts of Allegheny and Beaver Counties). Copied from the original records for the Washington Co. (Pa.) Chapter, Daughters of the American Revolution. Washington, Pa.: DAR, 1955.

SECONDARY WORKS

BOOKS, MONOGRAPHS, AND PERIODICALS

Andrews, J. Cutler. *The North Reports the Civil War*. Pittsburgh: University of Pittsburgh Press, 1955.

Ayers, Edward L. *In the Presence of Mine Enemies: The Civil War in the Heart of America, 1859 – 1863*. New York: W. W. Norton, 2003.

Bailyn, Bernard, and P. D. Morgan, eds. *Strangers Within the Realm: Cultural Margins of the First British Empire*. Chapel Hill, NC: University of North Carolina Press, 1991.

Baldock, Thomas Stanford. *Cromwell as a Soldier*. Edited by Walter H. James. Vol. 5. London: Kegan Paul, Trench, Trubner & Co., 1899.

Battles and Leaders of the Civil War. Edited by Robert Underwood Johnson and Clarence Clough Buel. New York: Thomas Yoseloff, Inc., 1956.

Bausman, Joseph Henderson. *History of Beaver County, Pennsylvania and Its Centennial Celebration*. 2 vols. New York: Knickerbocker Press, 1904. The full text is also available online at http://digital.library.pitt.edu/.

Bellah, Robert N. *The Broken Covenant: American Civil Religion in Time of Trial*. New York: The Seabury Press, 1975.

———. "Civil Religion in America." *Daedalus* 96 (Winter 1967): 1-21.

Bennett, Lerone, Jr. "Chronicles of Black Courage: African American Confederate sailor Robert Smalls." *Ebony*, November, 2001.

Beveridge, N. E. *Cups of Valor*. Harrisburg, PA: Stackpole Books, 1968.

Biographical Sketches: Beaver County, Pennsylvania. Beaver, PA: BCGS, 1977.

Black, George, comp. *The Surnames of Scotland*. Edinburgh: Berlinn, 1946.

Blethen, H. Tyler, and Curtis W. Wood, Jr., eds. *Ulster and North America: Transatlantic Perspectives on the Scotch-Irish*. Tuscaloosa, AL: University of Alabama Press, 1997.

Bolton, Charles Knowles. *Scotch-Irish Pioneers in Ulster and America*. Baltimore: Genealogical Pub. Co., 1972.

Bonzo, Gertrude. "Brief History of North Sewickley Presbyterian Church." Typescript, 1980, BCGS.

Bordewich, Fergus M. *Bound for Canaan: The Underground Railroad and the War for the Soul of America*. New York: Harper Collins, 2005.

Brennan, Patrick. *Secessionville: Assault on Charleston*. Campbell, CA: Savas Publishing Company, 1996.

Brinson, Claudia Smith. "Coosaw Holds Rich S.C. History." *The State*, 27 October, 2002.

Brockett, L. P., Mary C. Vaughn, et al. *Women's Work in the Civil War*. 1867. HCLA.

Brooks, Noah. *Washington D. C. in Lincoln's Time*. Edited by Herbert Mitgang. Chicago: Quadrangle Books, 1971.

Burton, E. Milby. *The Siege of Charleston, 1861-1865*. Columbia, SC: University of South Carolina Press, 1970.

Campbell, Thorbjorn. *Standing Witnesses: A Guide to the Scottish Covenanters and Their Memorials, with a Historical Introduction*. Edinburgh: Sultire Society, 1996.

Carnahan, J. Worth. *4000 Civil War Battles*. Fort Davis, TX: Frontier Book Co., 1975.

Commager, Henry Steele. *The Blue and the Gray*. New York: Fairfax Press, 1982.

Conrad, James Lee. *The Young Lions: Confederate Cadets at War*. Columbia: University of South Carolina Press, 1997.

Couper, William. *One Hundred Years at VMI*. Richmond: Garrett and Massie, 1939.

Cowan, Edward J. *Montrose: for Covenant and King*. Edinburgh: Cannongate, 1995.

Cullen, L. M. "Population Trends in Seventeenth-Century Ireland." *Economic and Social Review,* 6.2 (1975): 149-165.

Devine, T. M. "The Paradox of Scottish Emigration." *Scottish Emigration and Scottish Society*. Edinburgh: John Donald Publishers, 1992, 1-15.

Dunaway, Wayland F. *The Scotch-Irish of Colonial Pennsylvania*. Chapel Hill: University of North Carolina Press, 1944.

Durning, William, and Mary Durning. *The Scotch-Irish*. Edited by Margaret Harris. La Mesa, CA: The Irish Family Names Society, 1991.

Egle, William Henry. *Pennsylvania: Genealogies Chiefly Scotch-Irish and German*. Baltimore, Genealogical Pub. Co., 1969.

Eicher, David J. *The Longest Night: A Military History of the Civil War*. New York, Touchstone Books, 2001.

Eliade, Mircea. *Myth and Reality*. Translated by Willard R. Trask. New York: Harper & Row, 1963.

Faulkner, Harold Underwood. *American Political and Social History*, 7th ed. New York: Appleton-Century-Crofts, 1957.

Faust, Drew Gilpin. "The Civil War Soldier and the Art of Dying." *The Journal of Southern History* 67.1 (February 2001): 3-38.

Ford, Henry Jones. *The Scotch Irish in America*. Hamden, CN: Archon Books, 1966.

Fox, William F. *Regimental Losses in the American Civil War*. n.p., 1889.

Gavin, William G. *Campaigning with the Roundheads: The History of the Hundredth Pennsylvania Veteran Volunteer Infantry Regiment in the American Civil War 1861-1865*. Dayton: Morningside House, Inc., 1989.

Gragg, Rod. "A Bloody Half-Hour." *Civil War Times Illustrated* (February 1994), 46-57.

Gray, Malcolm. "The Course of Scottish Emigration, 1750-1914: Enduring Influences and Changing Circumstances." In *Scottish Emigration and Scottish Society*. Edinburgh: John Donald Publishers, 1992, 16-36.

Greeley, Andrew M. *The Denominational Society: A Sociological Approach to Religion in America*. Glenview, IL: Scott, Foresman, and Company, 1972.

Griffin, Patrick, *et al.* "Defining the Limits of Britishness: The 'New' British History and the Meaning of the Revolution Settlement in Ireland for Ulster's Presbyterians." *Journal of British Studies* 39.3 (2000): 263-287.

————. *The People with No Name: Ireland's Ulster Scots, America's Scots Irish, and the Creation of a British Atlantic World, 1689-1764*. Princeton: Princeton University Press, 2001.

Hanna, Charles A. *The Scotch-Irish or the Scot in North Britain, North Ireland, and North America*. 2 vols. Baltimore: Genealogical Printing Co., 1968.

Harrison, Andrew Joseph. *The South Carolina College Cadets, 1825-1862: A Company History*. Typescript. M. A. Thesis, University of South Carolina, 1994, SCL-USC.

Hazen, Aaron L., ed., *The 20th-Century History of New Castle and Lawrence County, Pennsylvania and Representative Citizens*. New Castle, PA, 1908.

Hill, Christopher. *God's Englishman: Oliver Cromwell and the English Revolution*. New York: Harper Torchbooks, 1970.

Himmelfarb, Gertrude. "Some Reflections on the New History." *The American Historical Review* 94 (June 1989): 661-670.

History of Lawrence County, Pennsylvania. L. H. Everts & Co., 1877.

"History of the Northeastern District of the County of Beaver," comp. Jeanne McMillan. Privately published.

Holland, Mary Gardner. *Our Army Nurses: Stories from Women in the Civil War.* Edited by Daniel John Hoisington. Roseville, MN: Edinborough Press, 2002.

Horwitz, Tony. *Confederates in the Attic: Dispatches from the Unfinished Civil War.* New York: Vintage Books, 1998.

Hull, Susan R. *Boy Soldiers of the Confederacy.* New York: Neale Publishing Co., 1905.

Irion, William E. *Beaver County Soldiers in the Civil War.* Apollo, PA: Closson Press, 2000.

Johnson, James E. *The Scots and Scotch-Irish in America.* Minneapolis: Lerner Publications Co., 1966.

Johnson's New Illustrated Family Atlas. New York: Johnson and Ward, 1864.

Jones, Samuel. *The Siege of Charleston and the Operations on the Atlantic Coast in the War Among the States.* New York: Neale, 1911.

Jones, Katherine M. *Port Royal Under Six Flags.* Indianapolis: Bobbs-Merrill, 1960.

Klett, Guy S. *The Scotch-Irish in Pennsylvania.* Gettysburg: Pennsylvania Historical Association, 1948.

Lake, Peter, and Michael C. Questier, eds. *Conformity and Orthodoxy in the English Church, circa. 1560-1660.* Woodbridge: Boydell, 2000.

Lawrence, R. DeT. "The Battle of Secessionville." *Confederate Veteran* (1922), 368-70.

Leasure, Joseph. "Exploits of Dr. Leasure and the Roundheads," *Washington Times*, June 19, 1993.

Leech, Margaret. *Reveille in Washington, 1860-1865.* New York: Harper and Brothers, 1941.

Leyburn, James G. *The Scotch-Irish: A Social History.* Chapel Hill: The University of North Carolina Press, 1962.

Linderman, Gerald F. *Embattled Courage: The Experience of Combat in the American Civil War.* New York, 1987.

Long, E. B. *The Civil War Day By Day: An Almanac, 1861-1865.* Garden City, NY: Doubleday and Co., 1971.

Lord, Francis A. *Civil War Collector's Encyclopedia: Arms, Uniforms and Equipment of the Union and Confederacy.* New York: Castle Books, 1965.

Lynch, Michael. *Scotland: A New History.* London: Pimlico, 1991.

McCauley, Thomas Babington. *The History of England from the Accession of James II.* 5 vols. Chicago: Belford, Clarke & Co., 1888.

McGregor, J. F., and B. Reay, eds. *Radical Religion in the English Revolution.* Oxford: Oxford University Press, 1984.

McKnight, William James. *My First Recollections of Brookville, Pennsylvania, 1840-1843: When My Feet Were Bare and My Cheeks Were Brown.* Philadelphia: J.B. Lippincott Company, 1905.

McPherson, Hector Copland. *The Covenanters Under Persecution: A Study of Their Religious and Ethical Thought.* Edinburgh: W. F. Henderson, 1923.

McPherson, James M. *Battle Cry of Freedom: The Civil War Era.* New York: Oxford University Press, 1988.

———. *For Cause and Comrades: Why Men Fought in the Civil War.* Oxford: Oxford University Press, 1997.

————. *What They Fought For: 1861-1865*. New York: Anchor Books, 1994.

Miller, Chandra. "A Perfect Institution Belonging to the Regiment: The Soldier's Letter and American Identity among Civil War Soldiers in Kansas," *Kansas History: A Journal of the Central Plains*, Vol. 22, No. 4 (Winter 1999 – 2000).

Miller, Randall M., Harry S. Stout, and Charles Reagan Wilson, eds. *Religion and the American Civil War*. Oxford: Oxford University Press, 1998.

Mitchell, Reid. *Civil War Soldiers: Their Expectations and Their Experiences*. New York: Viking Press, 1988.

————. *The Vacant Chair: The Northern Soldier Leaves Home*. Oxford: Oxford University Press, 1993.

Montgomery, Eric. *The Scotch-Irish in America's History*. Belfast: Ulster-Scot Historical Society, 1965.

Moore, Frank. *Women of the War: Their Heroism and Self-Sacrifice*. Hartford, CN: S. S. Scranton, 1866.

Nevins, Allan. *The War for the Union*. Vol. 1: *The Improvised War, 1861-1865*. New York: Charles Scribner's Sons, 1959.

Newton, Diana. *Papists, Protestants and Puritans: 1559-1714*. Cambridge: Cambridge University Press, 1998.

Nichols, Roy F. "1461-1861: The American Civil War in Perspective." *The Journal of Southern History* 16 (May 1950): 143-160.

Oliver Cromwell; or Cavaliers and Roundheads. London, 1841.

Parry, R. H., ed. *The English Civil War and After, 1642-1658*. Berkeley: University of California Press, 1970.

Perry, James M. *A Bohemian Brigade: The Civil War Correspondents, Mostly Rough, Sometimes Ready*. New York: John Wiley and Sons, Inc., 2000.

Phelps, W. Chris. *Charlestonians in War: The Charleston Battalion*. Gretna, LA: Pelican Publishing Company, 2004.

Queen, Matt. "The 100th Pennsylvania, Like Their Cromwellian Ancestors, Found Glory and Pain in a Civil War." *America's Civil War,* 3.10 (May 1990): 63-66.

Ram, Robert. *Cromwell's Soldier's Catechism*. 1644. Facsimile, edited by Walter Begley. London, 1900.

Randall, J. G. *The Civil War and Reconstruction*. Boston: D. C. Heath and Company, 1953.

Rose, Willie Lee. *Rehearsal for Reconstruction: The Port Royal Experiment*. New York: Bobbs-Merrill, 1964.

Rosen, Robert N. *Confederate Charleston: An Illustrated History of the City and the People During the Civil War*. Columbia, SC: University of South Carolina Press, 1994.

Schreadley, R. L. *Valor and Virtue: The Washington Light Infantry in Peace and in War*, privately published for the members. Spartanburg, SC: The Reprint Co., 1997.

Schriber, Carolyn P., ed. "A Scratch With the Rebels." *Civil War Times Illustrated*, February 1994.

Schultz, Jane E. *Women at the Front: Hospital Workers in Civil War America*. Chapel Hill: University of North Carolina Press, 2004.

Shackleton, Robert. *The Book of Washington*. Philadelphia: The Penn Publishing Co., 1922.

Simmons, Henry E. *A Concise Encyclopedia of the Civil War*. New York: A. S. Barnes and Co., 1965.

Steele, Alan J. *The National Covenant in Its Historical Setting*. Society of Friends of the Kirk of the Greyfriars, 1995.

Steiner, Paul E. *Disease in the Civil War: Natural Biological Warfare in 1861-1865*. Springfield, IL: Charles C. Thomas, 1968.

Stevens, Hazard. *The Life of General Isaac I. Stevens*. 2 vols. Boston: Houghton, Mifflin, and Co., 1900.

Stevens, William Oliver. *Washington the Cinderella City*. New York: Dodd, Mead, and Co., 1943.

Stone, Lawrence. *The Causes of the English Revolution: 1529-1642*. New York: Harper Torchbooks, 1972.

Switala, William J. *Underground Railroad in Pennsylvania*. Mechanicsburg, PA: Stackpole Books, 2001.

Thomson, Jack. *Charleston at War: the Photographic Record*. Gettysburg: Thomas Publications, 2000.

Voices of the Civil War. Alexandria, VA: Time-Life Books, n.d.

Walling, Henry F., and O. W. Gray. *Historical Topographical Atlas of the State of Pennsylvania*. Philadelphia: Stedman, Brown, and Lyon, 1872.

Walton, Denver L. "Savages and Settlers," *Milestones* (Autumn, 1996): 21-23.

Webb, James. *Born Fighting: How the Scots-Irish Shaped America*. New York: Broadway Books, 2004.

Welchley, Mark "Statistics of Beaver Co, as exhibited in the reports of the Deputy Marshals for the year 1840," *Beaver Argus*, March 3, 1841; reprinted in *Milestones* (Spring 1985): 10-12.

Wheeler, James Scott. *Cromwell in Ireland*. New York: St. Martin's Press, 1999.

Wiley, Bell. "Camp Newspapers of the Confederacy," *North Carolina Historical Review* 20 (1943): 327-335.

Wiley, Bell I. *The Common Soldier of the Civil War*. New York: Charles Scribner's Sons, 1973.

Wilson, Charles Readan. *Baptized in Blood: The Religion of the Lost Cause, 1865-1920*. Athens: The University of Georgia Press, 1980.

Yargates, James. "Steamboat Building in Beaver County," *Milestones* 7, No. 2 (Spring 1982).

INTERNET RESOURCES

100th Pennsylvania Veteran Volunteer Infantry Regiment, "The Roundheads". Available at http://members.aol.com/olecompe/Page1.html.

The Abraham Lincoln Papers at the Library of Congress, Series 1. General Correspondence. 1833-1916. Available at: http://memory.loc.gov/ammem/alhtml/alhome.html.

American Civil War Homepage. Available at http://sunsite.utk.edu/civil-war/warweb.html.

Beaver County [Pennsylvania] History Online. Available at http://www.bchistory.org.

Civil War @ Charleston. Available at http://www.awod.com/gallery/probono/cwchas/main.html.

The Collected Works of Abraham Lincoln. Available at http://www.hti.umich.edu/l/lincoln/.

Generals of the American Civil War. Available at http://www.generalsandbrevets.com/.

Harper's Weekly Original Civil War Newspapers. Available at http://www.sonofthesouth.net/lee-foundation/the-civil-war.htm.

Historic Pittsburgh Project. Available at http://digital.library.pitt.edu/.

Home of the American Civil War. Available at http://www.civilwarhome.com/.

Library of Congress, Prints and Photographs Online Catalogue. Available at http://www.loc.gov/rr/print/catalog.html.

Making of America [MOA]. Available at http://library5.library.cornell.edu/moa/.

Naval Historical Center. Available at http://www.history.navy.mil/.

South Carolina Civil War Maps. Available at http://www.sciway.net/hist/maps/mapscw.html.

Southern Presbyterian Review, Available at http://www.pcanet.org/history/periodicals/spr/.

U. S. Army Military History Institute [USAMHI]. Available at http://www.carlisle.army.mil/ahec/MHI.htm